FRANCE
1001 Sights

An Archaeological and Historical Guide

FRANCE
1001 Sights

An Archaeological and Historical Guide

James M. Anderson
and
M. Sheridan Lea

University of Calgary Press
Robert Hale • London

University of Calgary Press
2500 University Drive N.W.
Calgary, Alberta, Canada T2N 1N4

Robert Hale Limited
Clerkenwell House
Clerkenwell Green
London EC1R 0HT

National Library of Canada Cataloguing in Publication Data

Anderson, James M. (James Maxwell), 1933-
     France, 1000 sights

Includes bibliographical references and index.
ISBN 1-55238-042-4 (University of Calgary Press)
ISBN 0-7090-7092-6 (Robert Hale Limited)

1. France—Antiquities—Guidebooks. 2. Historic sites—France—
Guidebooks. 3. France—Guidebooks. I. Lea, M. Sheridan, 1932- II. Title.

DC16.A65 2001   914.404'839   C2001-911276-9

 We acknowledge the financial support of the Government of Canada through the
Book Publishing Industry Development Program (BPIDIP) for our publishing activities.

 The Canada Council for the Arts
Le Conseil des Arts du Canada

Printed and bound in Canada by AGMV Marquis.
Origination by Ford Graphics, Ringwood, Hampshire, U.K.

This book is printed on acid-free paper.

For Marie-Alice and Jean

Map 1. France

CONTENTS

Part I: HISTORICAL BACKGROUND

PART II: SITES AND SIGHTS

ACKNOWLEDGEMENTS

The authors gratefully acknowledge assistance given by:

Marie-Thérèse Andriot, La Maire de Faverolles
Sylvain Aubin, Drevant
Marie Bevalot and Pierre Petrequin (CNRS), Marigny
Dr. Jacques Blot, Président, Association Archéologique Basque (Herri Harriak)
Valerie Bourdel, Loupian
Sandrine Clauzier, Lyon
Gérard Dal Pra, Curator, Musée Archéoligique, Soyons
Thelma Dennis, Edmonton
Daniel Foucart, Marcilly-le-Hayer
Cathérine Geny-Dumont, Faverges
L'Abbé Giry, Nissan-les-Ensérune
Howard Greaves
Rosemary Härmä
Alain Jacques, Service Archéoligique, Arras
Lucien and Françoise Labedade, Anglet
Dr. Jean and Mme Marie-Alice Larroque, Anglet
Bruno Lebel, Directeur, Domaine de Samara
Daniele Lucet, S.I. Gennes
Manex Pagola, Musée Basque, Bayonne
René Marcel, Marcilly-le-Hayer
Perruchot de la Bussière, Izernore
Gérard Picquenot, Mairie de Valognes
Michel Queyrane, Gex
François Raynaud, Musée Archéologique, Soyons
Isabelle Renault, S.I. Bourges
Dr. Bernard Rochet
Marc Thuiller, Soissons (Terny-Sorny)
Liliane Tourneur, Saintes
Yvon Vidal, Luxeuil-les-Bains
Laurent Vignaud, Crazannes

The authors wish to express their gratitude to the University of Calgary Press and especially to Shirley Onn and John King. Also to Paul Killinger, Ford Graphics, Ringwood, England for the maps and diagrams 1, 2, 4 and 5 and for production of the book.

MAPS AND DIAGRAMS

MAPS

DIAGRAMS

INTRODUCTION

Vestiges of human habitation in France date back nearly a million years. A perspective on the progression of peoples and cultures that contributed to the formation of the country throughout most of its long history can only be obtained through artifacts and monuments unearthed at archaeological sites.

The purpose of this book is to assist the traveller, the visitor to France, or the non-travelling but curious individual, with the location and condition of archaeological sites, and to place these in a meaningful historical context. Many *sites,* a Roman city, for example, may have a number of specific *sights* such as an aqueduct, theatre, forum and baths. These are listed so that the reader may determine exactly what is to be seen. Some site plans are included here, but they are nearly always available at the locations in question or from the S.I. (*Syndicat d'Initiative*, or Office of Tourism) in the nearest town.

Most tourist books on France devote some space to the ancient monuments such as the megalithic alignments at Carnac or the Roman ruins at Nîmes. This guide also directs the traveler to hundreds of other lesser known, or "underdiscovered" sites, not found in the usual guidebooks.

Part I: "Historical Background" briefly describes the various epochs of human development that shared in the shaping of France from the earliest traces down to the Carolingian period in the tenth century A.D. when the formative years had nearly run their course.

Part II: "Sites and Sights" introduces the regions of the country and describes places of interest. The appropriate department is shown beside the name of the town or village where the site is situated, and locations are determined by reference to the region, the capital city, the department and the nearest town.

Looting and wanton destruction of ancient, irreplaceable sites has gone on for centuries and continues today in some unprotected quarters, but in recent years France has generally preserved its historical monuments rather well. Many are fenced and a small admission fee may be charged for upkeep. There are also archaeological parks where historical remains have been left in place and can be viewed along well marked trails. In some ways, the entire country can be thought of as one great museum as one travels through its history physically by road, or vicariously by the pages of this book.

New sites are constantly discovered while ongoing excavations continually bring to light new sights. At times, an excavation has been re-covered to protect it from the ravages of weather or from treasure seekers. Under such circumstances, no book on the subject can ever be a definitive statement of all the ancient treasures that France has to offer. Nevertheless, there is a great deal to see, enjoy, and contemplate while travelling the highways and byways of this prodigious land.

Preliterate and extinct societies can be defined only by physical remains. This necessarily leads to an incomplete picture, leaving other things such as spiritual values and social relationships in the realm of speculation. From the Romans onward, however, written documentation plays a large role in defining and explaining cultural features of the country.

GEOGRAPHY

The 547,026 sq. km of mainland France is roughly hexagonal in shape. It is bounded by Belgium and Luxembourg in the north, Germany across the Rhine River, Switzerland and Italy in the east, the Mediterranean and Spain in the south, the Atlantic Ocean in the west and the English Channel in the northwest. Only in the north is there no appreciable natural frontier.

The northern and central regions of the country are in the temperate zone while the south—at least the lower-lying land—enjoys a semitropical Mediterranean climate. Further variations of climate and vegetation correspond to the differences in elevation of mountain ranges.

Mountains

In the east stand the Alps with some of the loftiest peaks in Europe (including Mont Blanc), that form the frontier with Italy and Switzerland. In the southwest, the Pyrenees define the border with Spain.

The central Seine basin is surrounded by old mountain ranges: the Vosges to the east rising above the valley of the Rhine River, the Ardennes to the north (mainly in Belgium), the Armorican hills of Brittany to the west and the Massif Central, a mountainous plateau, that dominates the south-central region west of the Rhône River. These are much eroded hills of medium height. Younger mountains, the Jura, the Alps, and the Pyrenees are considerably higher. The remainder of the country is a patchwork of spacious river basins, fertile plains, ridges, hills, marshes and flat land.

Basins and Rivers

There are three primary river basins that have attracted people from the earliest times although settlements were separated by great tracts of forests and marsh. The basin of the Seine, with Paris in its centre, extends throughout the regions of Ile de France, Champagne, Lorraine, Bourgogne, Picardie, and eastern Normandie. To the southwest is the Aquitanian or Garonne Basin of limestone plateaux and fertile valleys, with Bordeaux and Toulouse the major cities. The third great basin is the Rhône-Saône depression opening into the Mediterranean in the south with Lyon and Marseille the principal centres.

Of the principal rivers, the Rhône flows southward into the Mediterranean while the Seine, Garonne, and Loire, all of which are fed by numerous tributaries, terminate in the Atlantic Ocean. The Loire is the longest, and enters the sea near Nantes. The Adour joins the Atlantic near Bayonne, the Somme and the Meuse flow into the North Sea and the Moselle into the Rhine.

Regions

Within its boundaries, the country contains twenty-one distinct regions, each with its own physical features, separate traditions and history. In three cases— Provence, Bretagne and southern Aquitaine—non-French languages are spoken side-by-side with French, that is, Provençal, Celtic and Basque. Many regions reflect earlier times when they were independent kingdoms, principalities or dukedoms, often at war with one another. They now contain departments formed for administrative purposes that are numbered, and often named after natural features such as mountains or rivers.

PART I
HISTORICAL BACKGROUND

1. Appearance of Humans in France

Homo habilis, an adroit tool user, emerged from the evolutionary hominid currents of East Africa some two million years ago and appears to have developed into man's true ancestor, Homo erectus. The latter expanded into the temperate zones of Asia and Europe, and human cultural traces that are evident in France recede through the ages to this common ancestor of Lower Paleolithic times. Remains take the form of primitive stone tools for chopping and scraping, hand-axes, and remnants of animal bones, that is, the leftovers of primitive human meals.

Lower Paleolithic Period

Paleolithic peoples were nomadic hunter-gatherers in constant search of a food supply and sought out caves and grottos for shelter from the elements.

Vallonnet cave near Menton, Alpes-Maritime, discovered in 1958, has yielded human-crafted flakes and pebble tools of the Lower Paleolithic dating back about 900,000 years. The Escale cave (Saint-Estève-Janson) in the Durance valley in southern France, discovered in 1960, contains evidence of the charcoal remains of fires that date perhaps as far back as 750,000 years. Recently, caves and grottos in the Massif Central have yielded further evidence of early humans.

The Acheulian is a Lower Paleolithic tool industry first identified at Saint Acheul along the Somme River. Earlier occurrences of Acheulian industry were in Africa some 1.7 million years ago. It eventually spread throughout Europe and was a predominant industry until about 200,000 years ago. This era is characterized by numerous varieties of oval, pointed, and cleaver-edged hand axes. Other sites in France have also yielded artifacts of the Acheulian industries, such as Terra Amata at Nice. This controversial site is reputed to be the oldest constructed shelter known in Europe in which timber poles embedded in the sandy beach were tilted inward to form an oval-shaped hut and perhaps covered with hides and leaves. Stones placed around the base of the poles helped support the structure. The interpretation of the site, placed at around 380,000 years ago, has been challenged by scholars who think too much has been read into the remains of floors surrounded by postholes and stones. Hominids of the time may not have been capable of such sophisticated dwellings.

The earliest physical remains include a human tooth found at Vergranne (Doubs), about half a million years old, and the human skull fragments of Tautavel found in the cave of the Caune de l'Arago in the eastern Pyrenees mountains. This prehistoric hunter roved the plains of Roussillon about 450,000 years ago. The cranium appears to forge an evolutionary but controversial link between Homo erectus, Neanderthals and modern humans.

The Massif Central is a rich area for early Paleolithic finds. The region was covered with lakes and lush vegetation, and animal life abounded. Volcanic activity promoted the preservation of perishable remains. The area of the Dordogne in southwestern France also had a particular attraction for prehistoric people even during the bitter cold times of severe glaciation. Millions of years ago, this area was covered by a warm sea that left a thick deposit of limestone from the tiny lime-containing marine organisms that lived in it. When the bottom was lifted and the sea disappeared, the exposed limestone plateau was eroded into a maze of bluffs, canyons, caves, and grottos. Shelter for primitive humans was easily accessible, as witnessed by the countless stone tools of early hunters found here.

During the period of the early Paleolithic, the north of the country was much less densely populated than the South. Sites there are rare, and human settlements do not appear in any number before the end of the Middle Paleolithic period.

Middle Paleolithic Period

The Middle Paleolithic is associated with Neanderthals, who appeared in Europe as short, stocky, large-headed individuals with a receding chin and pronounced brow ridges. Their habitats demonstrate striking differences from earlier periods, the remains of human skeletons, deliberate burials, more refined tools, and even a few stone and bone engravings being examples. In addition, a kind of bear-cult seems to have been practised, as shown by the careful layout of bear skulls in some of the caves. The subject, however, is controversial, as is the relationship of Homo Neanderthalensis to modern humans.

The culture associated with Neanderthals is known as the Mousterian, named after Le Moustier in the Dordogne, where quantities of stone implements have been excavated along with the skeleton of a Neanderthal man.

Cave dwelling Neanderthals made regular use of fire and stone flake tools. Fossilized remains dating from over 100,000-30,000 years ago have been found in France at La Chapelle-aux-Saints, near which the remains of an old Neanderthal man were discovered in a cave. A rock shelter at La Ferrassie yielded an adult male and the remains of several children, while a rock shelter at La Quina contained parts of several Neanderthal skeletons. From one site near Fontéchevade in southwestern France came skull fragments about 110,000 years old.

Sites associated with the Middle Paleolithic period are also found in the south of France, and at the cave of Hortus, where broken and charred human bones of some twenty individuals, mixed with other animal bones and food-refuse, suggest that some Neanderthals may have served as a meal for others.

If Neanderthals living in the area of present-day France had any inclination toward the symbolic or artistic, the evidence is sparse. In the cave of Pech de l'Azé in the South, a bone with a hole drilled through it may have been a sort of amulet. An ox rib from the same site bears scratches in groups of two on one side: these do not appear to be marks left from cutting away the flesh.

Upper Paleolithic Period

The Upper Paleolithic witnessed the advent of Homo sapiens (technically Homo sapiens sapiens), and the sophisticated development of cave and mobile art along with more precise tools. Sometimes, the term Cro-Magnon is used to designate the people of this period. These modern people became installed in Europe some 40,000 years ago and evidence in France—four adults and three children—was first found in the grotto Cro-Magnon near Les Eyzies-de-Tayac in 1868. Since then finds have multiplied. The controversy as to whether or not Homo sapiens was a direct ancestor of the preceding

Neanderthal type or a separate migratory people out of Africa, is still debated.

Cave dwellers of the Upper Paleolithic were different from all those who had gone before. Besides skill in painting, their craftsmanship in working stone, bone, antler, ivory and wood was superior to that of earlier peoples. Useful tools in the 100-plus tool-kit of Cro-Magnon included axes, scrapers, knives, perforators, spear points, stone saws, pounding slabs, needles, barbed harpoon tips, lances, and most importantly the burin or stone chisel, useful in the manufacture of other tools. For a firmer grasp, antler or bone handles were attached to stone tools. Similarly, objects were produced that appear to have had only symbolic and ceremonial value, such as the laurel leaf blade, too delicate for practical use, or the puzzling "bâton de commandement," a sometimes decorated reindeer antler perforated at one end. People of this period appear to have been the first to discover that flint struck against iron pyrites yielded sparks hot enough to set tinder afire.

The Périgord region of the Southwest, much of which falls within the Dordogne, contains numerous Paleolithic sites. The climate at the time was harsh, as the continent of Europe was in the grip of the last ice age, but limestone cave shelters offered protection from the cold, and seasonal migrations of animals provided food. Animal bones from the cave floor of Lascaux indicate that reindeer were the most heavily consumed of the various local quarry.

The greatest concentration of upper Paleolithic sites is found in the valley of the Vézère near the village of Les Eyzies. The region is famous for the caves and rock shelters, many of which contain rupestrian (or cave) art.

Cave Art

Cave art is the most spectacular achievement of the Upper Paleolithic cultures, the most prolific and magnificent examples of which occur in the Franco-Cantabrian region of Europe. More than one hundred decorated caves are known from this area, the majority located in France. The early art in France portrayed on the walls of caves and grottos was painted with vegetable and mineral dyes, such as ochre, and charcoal, sometimes mixed with blood. Others were incised or engraved in the stone. The earliest art forms date back over 30,000 years, to the Aurignacian period and continue through the Solutrean, depicting various kinds of animals. The climax of this artistic activity came in the Magdalenian period about 16,000 to 10,000 years ago, and many of the most important decorated caves are from this era, such as those at Les Combarelles, Niaux, and Font de Gaume. There are several Magdalenian bas-reliefs of animals such as those at Cap Blanc.

The magnificent cave paintings at Lascaux in the Dordogne may be a little earlier, but the evidence is still unclear. Radiocarbon dating of charcoal recovered from the cave floor shows occupation of about 17,000 years ago.

Homo sapiens of this epoch also sculpted realistic animal figures in horn and bone. The name "mobiliary" or portable art has been given to small figures ranging from a few centimetres to twenty or so, in length.

A recent, spectacular discovery was made in the region of Rhône-Alpes among the cliffs of the Ardèche near Vallon-Pont-d'Arc. Paintings of animals (some of which long ago disappeared from the area) portray bison, mammoths, panthers, lions, rhinoceros, hyenas, bear, an owl, horses, aurochs and deer, as well as symbolic signs and hands in positive and negative. They cover the walls of a 900 meter-long gallery and some are over 30,000 years old. There are more than 300 paintings and many engravings.

In spite of the closure of Lascaux, the most famous of all these sites, due to deterioration of the paintings, it is still possible to see many works of prehistoric art in other caves in the Pyrenees and in the valley of the Vézère. A good place to begin is the village of Les Eyzies-de-Tayac

2. Mesolithic Period

The Mesolithic Age (10,000-5000 B.C.) is characterized by the transition from the Paleolithic to the Neolithic period. People were food-gatherers like their ancestors but relatively few remains have yet been found in France other than in Languedoc and Provence. The period took place while the European continent was undergoing climatic changes as the ice sheets (Würm glaciation) covering large portions of the land   disappeared. This warming period began about 15,000 years ago and the low levels of the sea gradually rose, separating England from the continent by 6000 B.C. Animals that thrived on the cold weather of the late Paleolithic (reindeer, mammoth, woolly rhinoceros, giant elk and musk ox) are absent in the Mesolithic period in France, though some survived further north.

A change in environment seems to correspond to a shift from cave sites to open-air locations. The loss of cave art was replaced by artwork on bone and pebbles engraved or painted with simple geometric motifs, the earliest phase of which has been identified as Azilian (named after the cave site Mas d'Azil), and sometimes considered the last phase of the Paleolithic.

The Azilian culture was replaced by the Sauveterrian and then the Tardenoisian cultures. These people also polished their stone tools, and outcroppings of rock may be seen in various places with pronounced grooves, called in French *polissoirs*, in which the tools were rubbed to a smooth, polished surface. The efficiency of the flint industry increased dramatically over that of the Paleolithic, while the most important innovation was the advent of the bow and arrow.

Mesolithic people learned new methods of travel on skis, sleds and boats, and with the latter came new techniques in harvesting seafood, such as fishhooks made from bone or shell, fish spears, and fish traps. As seafood became a major component in people's diet, riverine, lake edge and seacoast habitation sites became more frequent. By the end of the period, settled communities were established and the dog became the first domesticated animal.

The period came to a close with the appearance of new cultural elements of the Neolithic

3. Neolithic Period

While hunting, fishing, and collecting sustained humankind through the Paleolithic and Mesolithic periods, a change occurred in which societies learned to collect naturally growing grains such as wheat and barley and to domesticate them, planting seeds, reaping the grain, and storing it for later use. Wild animals were still hunted and continued to form much of the diet, but some of these too were domesticated – beginning with sheep and goats. This practice of food production became fairly well established and represents the advent of a new period: the Neolithic (New Stone) Age.

According to one view, Neolithic currents reached France from the Middle East apparently by two routes: the first along the Mediterranean shores penetrating the south of France early in the sixth millennium B.C. The new society was characterized by pottery decorated by the use of the serrated edge of the cockle shell and known as Impressed Ware. Toward the end of the sixth millennium B.C., the coast of the western Mediterranean was dominated by this type of pottery, and remains have been found in rock shelters and caves on the Mediterranean coast such as at Cap Ragnon in the south of France and a cave on the Bay of Marseille displaying cockle-shell pottery, dated to about 6000 B.C.

In the fifth millennium B.C., other Neolithic peoples appeared in northeastern France, having arrived by a continental route up the Danube River and eventually penetrating into Alsace and Lorraine and then spreading out into the Paris Basin. Similarities in pottery and dwellings in the Danube Basin with those of northeastern France suggest this migratory route.

By the fourth millennium, local characteristics are in evidence among Neolithic peoples. Vases were decorated with meanders, chevrons or spirals, and they have been discovered in northeastern France and along the Seine and its tributaries. Neolithic agricultural villages were established in the Paris Basin by about 4600 B.C. and along the Rhône Valley about the same time.

Another view of developments in this period prefers a model in which domesticated plants and animals were introduced into France with minimal movement of people. The earliest farmers were simply the descendants of the Mesolithic population, importing new ideas and methods to sustain themselves.

From the fifth millennium B.C. onwards, Neolithic farmers developed a type of village in France and elsewhere consisting of an enclosure surrounded by one or several moats and sometimes palisades. Such sites vary from area to area. The moats are generally around 2 metres deep and about 6 metres wide. The oldest of these sites, so far discovered in France, is that of Menneville in the Aisne from the first half of the fifth millennium B.C., but most date back to the second half of the fifth or the beginnings of the fourth millennium B.C.

Developing perhaps in the Late Neolithic period and continuing into the Bronze Age are the Palafitte villages in which the dwellings were constructed on piles set in lakes. Such pile dwelling sites are found in the Alps. An important site in France is that of Lake Chalain in the Jura mountains. Another, Charavines, is still older, belonging to the Neolithic culture of the Saône-Rhône regions.

Neolithic peoples eventually settled in all four major river systems. One of the oldest known villages from this period is at Courthezon in the valley of the Rhône between Orange and Avignon. Huts discovered here each measure about 15 square metres and date back to about 4650 B.C.

An important Neolithic site is at Saint-Michel-du-Touch near Toulouse where some 300 buildings with baked clay floors have been identified. The site was occupied from about 4300 to 3300 B.C. There were both circular and rectangular structures. The base of the economy was mixed farming including a range of grains and domestic animals. Other sites include Carnac in Bretagne where the presence of numerous stone alignments, tombs and stone circles suggest a thriving population in Bretagne by the fourth millennium B.C. Just as the valley of the Vézère is the site *par excellence* for rupestrian art of the Old Stone Age, the fields around Carnac are the showcase of Neolithic stone monuments.

4. Megalithic Monuments

The stone structures referred to as megaliths (from Greek *mega* 'great,' and *lithos* 'stone') found throughout Western Europe and used as burial chambers, for sacred rites or for astrological observations are still preserved in great numbers and may constitute the oldest man-made monuments. Sometimes a single stone employed in their construction weighed several hundred tons and was quarried many kilometres from the building site. One method of moving the stones appears to have consisted of placing logs underneath and pulling them along with ropes, removing the logs from the back as the stone moved on and placing them again in the front. Hundreds of men were probably required to move the larger stones.

Menhirs

Megaliths often take the form of menhirs (from a single upright stone to alignments of great stones in rows or concentric configurations). The first megalithic monuments were probably the single, solitary menhirs, standing stones embedded in the soil to mark territorial boundaries or sacred ground. Some are clearly phallic symbols. They are generally undatable in any specific terms, but appear to go back to the early Neolithic period. Some of them were engraved with symbols such as stone axes which are representative of the early Neolithic. The general age of the decorated menhir of Kermarquer, for example, has been dated by this means. A few others have been uprooted and reused in the construction of dolmens whose artifacts and burials also date back to the Neolithic. Among menhirs, such as those pertaining to the alignments of Carnac in southern Bretagne, the enormous stone alignments, some stretching nearly a mile across the terrain, represent a colossal effort of Neolithic megalith builders. Here have been found a certain kind of crude ceramic which, along with the symbols engraved on some stones, places their origin near the end of the Neolithic period.

The tallest stone still standing (10 metres) is at Kerloas. In some cases, monuments have been converted to meet the demands of changing times: the 8.10 metre-tall menhir at Saint-Duzec in Bretagne, unadorned when it was erected in the third millennium B.C., was topped with a cross in the seventeenth century, and further Christian symbols, including a figure of the Virgin, were later added. Others in Bretagne have undergone similar remodeling.

Dolmens

It may be supposed that once the Neolithic farmers of Europe had settled into their new environment, cleared the land, and planted crops, they had time for ceremonial activities that earlier hunting and gathering peoples could ill afford.

One of these was tomb-building and paying more attention to the dead. While the villages themselves appear to have been constructed of perishable materials such as wood, mud and reeds, the megaliths were built to withstand eternity. There was once thousands more megaliths than there are today but many were destroyed to clear the land for farming or, obliterated by the church for religious purposes—to exorcise evil spirits. Others have naturally tumbled down from earth movement, wind and erosion. Stones have sometimes been broken up for use elsewhere.

The simplest dolmens consisted of a single chamber of standing stones roofed over by a large slab of stone or by corbeling. Here the bodies were interred. A more complex type was a passage grave or *dolmen à couloir* in which a narrow, low passage led to a generally circular chamber which itself may have had several smaller chambers leading off the main one.

Another type is called a gallery grave or *allée couverte*, a long tomb with no entrance corridor but where the entire structure constitutes the burial chamber. It may or may not have interior partitions. In all cases the entire structure was then covered over with earth to form a mound, some of which still remain to be excavated.

There are about 4500 dolmens spread out over some sixty French departments. Some of these, in Bretagne, appear to be the oldest. They range over a period of about 2500 years beginning with the earliest known passage graves at Barnenez of about 4500 B.C. One of the most majestic is that at Bagneux, near Saumur in the Pays de la Loire. Normally they were used for collective burials over generations and have on occasion yielded remains of more than one hundred bodies but the acidic soil of Bretagne has in most places generally destroyed all traces of bone. In many others that have not been looted, artifacts have been found such as knives or tools of flint and fragments of pottery, but generally there is little else in the way of funeral accoutrements. In some cases the stones of the graves have been inscribed, most often with signs of the ax, but also by triangles, meanders, zigzags and other patterns whose significance is unknown. The tombs may vary in size from small box-like structures to enormous gallery graves 20 metres long, such as the one at Bagneux. Other types of burial chambers also existed, including caves and chambers hewn from the living rock. Of the latter some of the finest examples are found about four kilometres northeast of Arles on private property. The cluster of rock-cut tombs dates to about 3500 B.C.

5. Age of Metals: Copper and Bronze

The first known objects in copper found in France are from the end of the fourth millennium B.C. and consist of small dagger blades and hammer-wrought jewelry found in the South. The earliest use of gold objects appeared about the same time. Such items may have been produced locally and independently of metallurgy already developed in the Near East where it was known long before, although the view is often expressed that, like the introduction of farming in the Neolithic, metallurgy reached Europe by way of migratory peoples via the Mediterranean and by the Danubian continental route.

By the third millennium B.C., metal objects such as axes and blades, imitating those made earlier of stone, became common. Some villages are known from the period such as La Conquette and Cambous in the Hérault where there are about forty oval houses, 12 metres long and 3 to 5 metres wide, built of drystone and clustered together. A turning point in the history of metallurgy occurred when copper alloyed with arsenic and later tin produced bronze, a harder and more durable metal than copper. This new technology arose in the Near East about 3000 B.C., and its origins in Europe are dated around 2000 B.C. In the search for tin, merchants and traders sailed as far as the western Mediterranean and through trade, personal contacts and indigenous skills, bronze metal-working came to France.

Industries in the first half of the second millennium B.C. flourished in only two regions in ancient France: in the Rhône Valley and in Bretagne where bronze artifacts have been found in long barrows. Elsewhere bronze objects first appeared in graves in the Middle Bronze period, about 1500 B.C. to 1200 B.C., for example those of the Haguenau forest. From this period hoards of bronze tools, especially axes, are known from all over France. A particular sword current among Late Bronze Age societies of western Europe was characterized by a broad slashing blade molded into a narrow tip for thrusting. It appears to have developed on the west coast from Bretagne to the Gironde after 1000 B.C.

6. Iron Age Peoples (Celts)

The Celts arrived in Europe from the East as part of a larger Indo-European period of expansion before 1000 B.C., and those that came to reside in present-day France were called Gauls by the Romans. They settled between the Rhine River and the Loire. A few dwelt between the Garonne and the Pyrenees but settlements here among the Aquitanians were sparse. In southern France the Ligurians, east of the Rhône and the later Iberians, west of the Rhône occupied much of the region.

Gauls

Mostly composed of Celtic peoples, the Gauls formed a loose confederation of tribes that lived in villages of thatch-roofed round huts amidst great dark forests prevalent at the time. They cleared some land for agriculture, worshipped natural divinities such as mountains, trees, springs and hollows, were skilled in producing iron weapons and celebrated the Festival of the Mistletoe under the guidance of their priests, the Druids. The major city of each tribe was often situated along, or at the confluence of rivers, for example, Lutèce (Paris) and Lugdunum (Lyon).

From the Paris Basin stretching well eastward the land was occupied by numerous communities, a patchwork of local tribes who were ethnically homogeneous with a common heritage known as the Western Hallstatt culture named after this primarily Iron Age site in Austria. The early period, from about 800 to 600 B.C., appears to exhibit a substantial degree of economic and social stability. While the ashes of a few individuals were interred with elaborate grave goods representing leadership and rank, the majority were interred with simple personal belongings consisting of pots with food offerings, horse-gear, and weapons. The Hallstatt culture comprised the earliest group that can be securely associated with the first Celtic-speaking peoples. It was based upon a mixed farming economy made more efficient by the use of iron implements.

From 600 to 450 B.C. after the founding of Massalia (Marseille), a transformation occurred. Contact with the Mediterranean world gave rise to the second great Celtic culture of La Tène, named after the Iron Age votive deposit found in the shallow water at the east end of Lake Neuchâtel in Switzerland. It was characterized by several Mediterranean features comprising weaponry, wine-drinking and personal ornamentation. New Celtic art styles grew out of this mixture of indigenous and imported elements.

Massaliot, Greek and Etruscan luxury goods begin to appear in quantity and the society reflects this accumulation of wealth in the hands of a few by a hierarchy of rich graves and a number of fortified hilltop towns, both of which display the rise of powerful aristocracies. It would seem that the Greek trading port created a demand for commodities from the North (furs, skins, honey, minerals, slaves, amber) in exchange for various luxury items (wine, bowls, jugs, small items of gold, ivory and other finished products).

Primary features of La Tène culture were decorated bronze jugs for the new fashion of wine drinking, fantastic animal designs, and blurring of the distinctions between naturalistic and abstract art continuing the Hallstatt tradition of geometric and abstract art but with new Mediterranean elements in the hands of Celtic craftsmen.

The oppida, or fortified settlements of the second and first centuries B.C., were true towns with stratified societies of wealthy chieftains, specialist craftsmen, workers in metal, glass and pottery, peasant farmers and no doubt slaves. This was the culture the Romans encountered when they moved the legions northward.

Greeks, Phoenicians and Carthaginians

Greeks first penetrated the western Mediterranean in the eighth century B.C. in search of raw materials, primarily metals, and established Massalia, present-day Marseille, in about 600 B.C. The site was wisely chosen as the main port of trade on the Gaulish Mediterranean coast providing easy access up the valley of the Rhône to the barbarian hinterland and to the headwaters of the Loire and the Atlantic seaboard. This was soon followed by the development of daughter colonies along the Mediterranean such as Nicaea (Nice). From Massalia, Greek and Etruscan goods from Italy traveled up the Rhône into native settlements such as Nages or Entremont which grew into fortified towns, and much trade continued onward into the valleys of the Seine and Rhine. Indicative of this trade is the grave site at Vix, where a local princess from the native oppidum on Mont Lassois was buried in the sixth century B.C. with a wealth of material of Massaliot, Etruscan, and Greek origins, a gold diadem probably from Spain, and an unusual bronze crater, that is, a large vessel from Taranto, 1.64 metres high and capable of containing some 1,100 litres.

Iberians

The earliest writing in ancient Gaul was introduced by the Greek colonists who founded Massalia. About the same time Iberian people crossed the Pyrenees and appeared in southern France. Their towns were not situated directly on the coasts, but were near enough to participate in the active coastal trade, and situated astride the land trade routes between Italy and Spain. The Greek colony at ancient Agathe (Agde) at the mouth of the Hérault river is thought to have been the major trading centre for the Iberian towns in southern France. The Iberians acquired the skill of writing derived from the Graeco-Phoenician script used throughout the Mediterranean. Iberian sites in southern France lie west of the Rhône River and can be identified by the inscriptional material in the Iberian language found among the ruins. Ensérune, is the best excavated and the type-site for Iberian presence in southwestern France during the Iron Age. The town was abandoned in the first half of the first century A.D.

Aquitanians and Basques

To the north of the present-day Basque region lies Aquitania in southwest France. The Aquitanians appear to have been descendants of stone age populations of the area. They lived in fortified villages and seem to have spoken a language akin to Basque. Aquitanian inscriptions written with the Latin alphabet are brief and consist of about 400 personal and 70 divine names with much similarity to Basque. There are about 100,000 speakers of Basque in France who were once much more widespread than today. As the Basque language has no proven affiliations with other language groups, and as positive migratory evidence of the people is lacking, an ethnic in situ development from Cro-Magnon is acceptable to many Basque scholars.

7. Roman and Gallo-Roman Period

Roman legions entered Gaul in 153 B.C. on behalf of their Greek allies in Marseille. They came in defense of coastal towns such as Nice from Celtic and Ligurian marauders and the incursions of Germanic tribes. In 125 B.C. the Romans conquered Provincia Gallia Narbonensis (Provence) and extended their control into Languedoc. By about 121 B.C. they controlled the Rhône River valley up to Vienne and along the Garonne River to Toulouse. Trading posts and military camps such as Narbonne, Nîmes, Arles and Aix soon developed into towns. In 58 B.C. Julius Caesar undertook campaigns that were to bring all of Gaul under Roman hegemony. The rivalry of the Gallic tribes greatly facilitated the conquest but not until the decisive defeat of Vercingetorix in 52 B.C. was Caesar's triumph complete.

Vercingetorix

Roman massacres and enslavement of Celtic people created much resentment and eventually revolt. Elected by the representatives of the Gallic tribes, Vercingetorix, from the Auvergne and Chief of the Auvergni, led a large-scale revolt against the legions of Caesar in 52 B.C. After suffering defeat, Vercingetorix withdrew to the earthwork stronghold or oppidum of Alesia. Caesar surrounded the area, building two contravallations, defensive lines against sorties by the besieged, and a circumvallation to protect his rear flank. The blockade forced Vercingetorix into surrender and he was later murdered in Rome after six years of captivity. The Gallic oppidum became a Gallo-Roman city which was abandoned by the inhabitants during the

Merovingian period and disappeared under a layer of earth. Excavations have revealed its true nature. Traces of Caesar's earthworks are obscure but the plan of the Gallo-Roman city is clearly visible.

Romanization

Gaul underwent cultural and linguistic Romanization and during Roman times the population is generally referred to as Gallo-Roman. The Pax Romana, the Roman Peace, spread over Gaul replacing intertribal wars and conflicts and the Celts thoroughly adopted Roman customs. The acquisition of Gaul opened up new commercial enterprises to the Roman Empire, supplied men for the Roman armies to protect the northern frontiers, and provided men of distinction who served in the Roman senate. Towns were founded and stone construction replaced the previous wooden buildings and dwellings, solidly built roads replaced the older dirt tracks, triumphal arches, circuses (only two known from the literature at Arles and Vienne), temples, and public buildings were erected along with theaters and amphitheatres, and public baths were established with their various hot, cold and temperate pools. Forests were cleared and villas constructed, and towns and necropoli laid out for the veterans of the wars and immigrants from Italy. From the first to the third centuries A.D. the country experienced an economic and cultural upsurge in agriculture, metal-working, textile production, and pottery-making. Industry and agriculture prospered, and the Latin language and law of the Romans unified the country.

Gaul remained a Roman province for over 500 years from the time of Caesar's conquest until the collapse of the empire in the late fifth century. At the confluence of the Rhône and Saône rivers Lyon became a great hub of commerce for the Western world connected by well-built roads and bridges.

Towns

Roman towns in France were sometimes constructed on the sites of existing Celtic towns and villages or built from scratch in new places where economic opportunities justified their existence. Some of the best sites available to the modern visitor are found at Glanum and Alesia, the latter where the Gauls made their last stand against the legions of Julius Caesar. There are also fine remains at Vaison-La-Romaine in the Vaucluse. The most important section of the Roman town was the forum around which urban life centred with its administration building, merchants' shops, temples and sometimes the market. The Roman towns were laid out in rectangular patterns and later surrounded by walls.

As early as the last few decades before Christ, indigenous towns were beginning to construct or rebuild their towns on the Roman model. In the reign of the emperor Augustus the major massive building took place, however. Most of the oppida from earlier times were abandoned but some remained to become country towns. The first two centuries of the first millenium were generally prosperous times but the third degenerated into economic instability and civil war, with barbarian incursions leaving towns and villages abandoned and in smoking ruins. Throughout the fourth century Marseille and Narbonne remained important cities while Vienne became a leading city, and Arles even more prominent since it was selected as the imperial residence.

Villas

The great Roman estates or villas were the backbone of the agricultural enterprises producing cereals, wine, olive oil, wool, or livestock. They were also centres of fishing industries on the coast.

Today they are sites of great interest with their various styles, drainage conduits, heating systems, baths, ponds and gardens and give an idea of the artistic inclination, cultural level and wealth of the owner. Those who could afford it decorated their villas with beautiful mosaic floors, the extent and richness of which indicates the prosperity of the owner. Some of the best villas may be seen at Andilly, Montcaret, Montmaurin and the large site with many mosaics near Montréal at Séviac.

Roads, Bridges and Aqueducts

The Roman engineers skillfully constructed roads of great durability in all parts of the empire. Rome laid down roads wherever its authority extended, initially in order to enhance troop movements. Each mile along the road was marked by a 2-metre circular pillar, a milestone. Measured from the gates of Rome, they were usually inscribed to the reigning emperor. Engineers tried to build the roads straight, flat, and level, digging tunnels and bridging valleys where required. There were often cisterns, resting stations, and garrisons at intervals along the route. The somewhat preserved Via Domitia ran from the Rhône River at Beaucaire through Languedoc-Roussillon to Le Perthus in the Pyrenees. Some of the many milestones along the route are still extant.

Some well-preserved bridges, further marvels of Roman engineering, may be seen throughout the country, for example Pont St.-Julien, near Apt. Aqueducts are among the most impressive remains of Roman engineering extant today, for instance the Pont du Gard a little northeast of Nîmes, spans the river Gardon in splendid grandeur.

Public Baths and Temples

Places for business undertakings, and social interchange as well as for hygiene, Roman baths were popular establishments throughout the empire and were often equipped with hot, tepid and cold water pools and changing rooms. They were frequently instituted in the vicinity of thermal hot springs. The baths fell into disuse and disrepair during the period of Germanic invasions. Good examples that survived the ravages of time many be seen at Metz, Peyrehorade and Sanxay. One of the largest of the bath complexes, and perhaps the last to be constructed in the south of the country, is situated at Arles.

To carry out the sacred duties required by the gods, the Romans built temples (unlike the Gauls whose animistic religious practices generally required only a clearing in the woods, a hilltop, or perhaps a stream or pond). The finest of these structures still extant, La Maison Carrée, is found at Nîmes. Another, the temple of Augustus and Livia at Vienne is well-preserved due to continuous usage as a church, a market place, and finally a museum (along with some restoration).

The Roman Heritage

Confirmation of the Roman presence can be seen everywhere in France. Besides palpable remains of buildings, engineering works and monuments,

Roman culture continues today not only in stone and concrete but in less tangible features such as language, Roman law and religion. The French language, albeit in highly changed form, is but a continuation of popular Latin, the lingua franca of the Roman Empire. Latin gradually replaced all the Gallic languages and dialects with the exception of Basque and Breton. The social, economic and political cohesion of the Roman Empire also promoted the spread of Christianity throughout Gaul.

8. Early Christian Monuments

Christianity, introduced into Southern Gaul near the end of the first century, spread slowly. In the third century the first saints and martyrs appeared. Saint-Denis (d. about 258), patron saint of France and first bishop of Paris, was one of these. The hilltop where his death took place, once sacred to the pagan god Mercury, became known as the Mount of the Martyrs, or Montmartre. In the fourth century Saint-Hilary (d. 367?), born in Poitiers of pagan parentage, was elected Bishop of Poitiers and immediately began a rigorous suppression of the Arian heresy widespread at the time. Saint-Martin (d. 397), Bishop of Tours, waged a holy war against paganism and established monasticism in Gaul. A defining moment for the Roman Catholic church occurred in about 497 when Clovis, leader of the Franks, chose Catholicism over Arianism, thus establishing the Franks as protectors of the Church of Rome. Throughout the period about the only important monumental construction was of churches and baptistries. Landowners frequently had a chapel built for those peasants who worked their land and for the artisans living on the estates. The chapel often became the parish church and the origin of the villages. These communities sometimes retained the name of the land owners, e.g., Flavigny "residence of Flavian."

Early and Medieval Christian monuments may be seen in many locations. The Merovingian church of Saint-Léger in the village of Alesia, dates back to 678-720. In the cathedral of Saint-Sauveur, Aix-en-Provence, is a fourth century Merovingian baptistry. In front of Notre Dame in Paris, excavations have revealed amidst a third-century Gallo-Roman complex the foundations of the sixth century Merovingian church of St.-Etienne. The St.-Oyand crypt of the sixth-to-eighth century in Grenoble was built on the site of a pagan burial ground. There are also Merovingian dwellings and a necropolis at Séviac as well as a Paleo-Christian chapel and baptistry. A Merovingian necropolis was installed at the villa of Andilly in the fifth century.

9. Germanic Invasions and the Early Middle Ages

Fertile and prosperous Gaul under Roman authority greatly attracted people from the dark forests east of the Rhine and Danube rivers, that then served as the frontier. The first clash between Romans and Germanic peoples in Gaul occurred in the second century B.C., when the Cimbri and Teutons were defeated in present-day Provence. In the first century B.C., further Germanic tribes on the move had attempted to settle in Gaul, only to be repelled by Julius Caesar. For the next hundred years, raids across the frontier resulted in the rise of strong-walled Gallo-Roman towns.

By the mid-second century A.D., Germanic pressures on the Roman frontiers intensified and by this time German mercenaries were beginning to be used by the Roman authorities to help stem the tide of their countrymen. Throughout the fourth century small groups of Germans began settling in Gaul with the permission of the Roman authorities. About 412 the Visigoths freely entered southern Gaul and formed the most important barbarian group in the south. Granted permissioin to settle Aquitaine, they occupied Toulouse and Carcassonne, and took Narbonne in 462. The Burgundians, meanwhile moving westward, occupied Vienne and the lower Rhône. This was the period of the main Germanic migrations and the demise of the Roman world. For the so-called barbarians it was no doubt a time of great adventure and bloody battles in which some tribes achieved glory and others disappeared, but for the settled peoples of the Roman Empire, it was a time of profound stress and uncertainty.

Brittany (Bretagne) and Burgundy (Bourgogne)

The two regions of Brittany and Burgundy reflect the deep ethnic and cultural divisions that were still in the process of formation in post-Roman France. Beginning in A.D. 449, the Celts were driven out of Britain by invading Germanic tribes, and many crossed the sea to the Roman province of Armorica in northwestern France and settled there, giving it its present name Bretagne (Brittany). They subsequently became known as Bretons. Their Celtic language, akin to that of Cornish and Welsh, persists today.

In 443 the Germanic Burgundians, after their defeat by the Huns on the Middle Rhine, invaded Gaul and established the first kingdom of Burgundy, which expanded until it included most of what is now southeastern France and part of present-day Switzerland. Lyon was occupied in 470. The Burgundians suffered a major defeat at the hands of the Franks at Autun in 432, and lost their independence to the Franks shortly thereafter.

10. Franks, Merovingians and Visigoths

The Franks, Germanic peoples, were established in Belgium as Roman allies since the middle of the fourth century. They advanced into Gaul from a solid base through a series of small steps. In this way, unlike most other tribes, they did not incur the wrath of the Romans and possible obliteration in pitched battles. Due to their long exposure as neighbours of the Romans, they were more civilized or perhaps Romanized than, say the Anglo-Saxon tribes who had little contact with Roman culture. Meanwhile, the Huns under Attila invaded Gaul in 451 and destroyed Metz but a combination of Roman, Frankish, Visigothic and Burgundian forces attacked and subsequently defeated them near Troyes.

In the last quarter of the fifth century, as imperial authority collapsed in the West, the Franks, under Clovis I, began the conquest of northern Gaul. He routed Syagrius, the last Roman governor of Gaul in 486.

The Visigoths were Arians in religion after their conversion by Ulfilas in the fourth century, and hence a threat to Roman Catholicism. In 507 they extended their territory across southern Gaul as far east as the Rhône River (they had taken Arles in the 470's) and as far north as the Loire. To stem this Arian threat Clovis, in cooperation with the church, invaded the Visigothic kingdom. The opposing armies met near Poitiers and the Visigoths were defeated and driven into Spain. Those who wished to remain had to accept baptism and convert to Catholicism. The Frankish military and the church became masters of the western European heartland. Clovis celebrated his success by establishing his capital at Paris. When he died in 511, the Frankish kingdom was divided between his four sons.

About 600, territorial expansion of the Franks under Merovingian kings came to an end. The noblemen, no longer having challenging wars to look forward to, began terrorizing the peasants. Anarchy and lawlessness prevailed through much of the realm. The clergy too became willing participants in debauchery, immorality and venality, their ranks swollen by semi-literate, greedy, and nepotistic aristocrats in search of power and prestige. In 639 Dagobert I, the last strong Merovingian monarch, died and was succeeded by a series of weak and incompetent kings.

According to Germanic custom, all the king's possessions, including the royal title, were divided among sons. Because of this practice, Merovingian France was beset by continual disunity and civil war. By dividing the land, the kings contributed to the disintegration of Gaul.

Due to the fact that the Franks occupied Roman territory, towns, villages, and institutions, and took up Roman ways, they constructed no monuments or architectural styles that were uniquely their own. Apart from items consisting of jewelry and weapons, their legacy is mostly one of spirit and genes infused into a Gallo-Roman substratum—one from which the Franks took their language, much of their culture, and their ideals.

11. Carolingians

The Merovingian dynasty was replaced by another, the Carolingian, whose greatest sovereign was Charlemagne (r. 768-814). In conjunction with the pope, he expanded his territory through conquest and was crowned Holy Roman Emperor in the year 800. Charlemagne established his seat of government at Aix-la-Chapelle (Aachen) and came to preside over a large territory that included France and much of Italy and Germany. The practice of dividing territories between sons upon the death of the monarch, however, caused the disintegration of the Carolingian Empire and France became a collection of independent feudal states under the control of dukes and counts and would not again be united for many centuries.

12. Norsemen and the Foundation of Normandy (Normandie)

Pagan Vikings from Scandinavia made their first appearance among the Franks about 840, sacking and burning towns and churches in search of anything valuable. They came in ships, and seaports, river towns, and nearby monasteries fell victim to these seafaring marauders. Rouen and Paris on the

Seine River, Nantes, Tours, Blois, and Orléans on the Loire, Bordeaux on the Garonne, and many other towns were pillaged and burned. Aided by the disunity and internal strife among the Frankish kings and nobility, the Vikings were able to attack and loot with little interference until a large company of Vikings was bought off and their leader, Rollo, made count of Rouen in 911. From the West Frankish king Charles III (the Simple), Rollo accepted the territory in the lower Seine Valley that became known as Normandy. In time the Vikings became less aggressive, were Christianized, and were integrated among the Franks, adopting the French language.

13. The Rise of France

Beneath the disorder and turbulence wrought by the barbarian hordes, a new set of social and economic patterns formed. Hybrid societies took shape as the Germanic peoples intermingled with and ruled over the Romanized populations. Germanic kings became the successors of the once mighty Roman Empire, and barbarian warriors of yesterday became great landowners and farmers. Functionaries trained in the Roman tradition maintained the machinery of state while the vast substrata of slaves and peasants generally remained unchanged.

Not until end of the fifteenth century, long after the great Carolingian barons fought among themselves for land, prestige and wealth, did France emerge from the divisions of its feudal past to become a national monarchy incorporating the territory stretching from the Pyrenees to the English Channel.

14. Conclusion

The land which was to make up France underwent great diversity in language, culture, customs and ethnic composition throughout its early history. United by the Romans after a drawn-out conquest (121-58 B.C.), Gallic towns often continued as Roman cities, later to become Medieval regional centres and capitals. After the expansion of the Franks or Merovingians over much of Gaul (conquering and displacing other Germanic tribes), the triumphant Carolingian kings, who succeeded them, expanded Francia (land of the Franks) to its maximum extent.

Continuity of settlement was facilitated by the adoption of regional centres as bishoprics by the Christian Church. While some disappeared and others arose, the ecclesiastical provinces had emerged by the tenth century to remain unchanged until the French Revolution.

15. Chronological Table

B.C.	Period	Culture*	Human type
1,000,000	Lower Paleolithic	Acheulian	Homo erectus
100,000 +	Middle Paleolithic	Mousterian	Neanderthal
40,000	Upper Paleolithic	Aurignacian (first cave art)	Homo sapiens
		Solutrean 20,000-15,000	(Cro-Magnon)
		Magdalenian 15,000-10,000	
10,000	Mesolithic	Azilian	
		Sauveterrian	
		Tardenoisian	
5000	Neolithic	Impressed Ware	Megalithic Structures
2000	Bronze	Early	
1500		Middle	
1200		Late	
1000	Iron		
900		Hallstatt (Celts)	
450		La Tène (Celts)	
50		Roman	
A.D.		Gallo-Roman	
400	Early Middle Ages	Germanic	
		Merovingian	
800	Middle Ages	Carolingian	
		Viking	

* Many of the periods have been subdivided into more cultural phases than those shown here. Considerable overlap occurred between cultural phases.

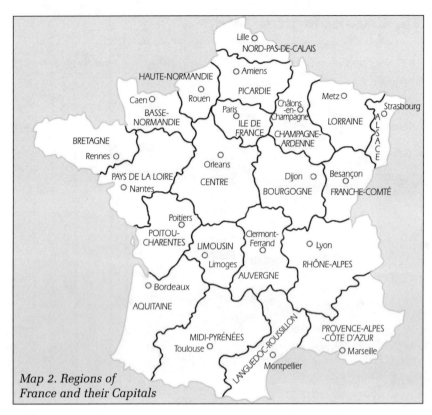

Map 2. Regions of
France and their Capitals

REGION	CAPITAL
Alsace	Strasbourg
Aquitaine	Bordeaux
Auvergne	Clermont-Ferrand
Bourgogne	Dijon
Bretagne	Rennes
Centre	Orleans
Champagne-Ardenne	Châlons-en-Champagne
Franche-Comté	Besançon
Ile de France	Paris
Languedoc-Roussillon	Montpellier
Limousin	Limoges
Lorraine	Metz
Midi-Pyrénées	Toulouse
Nord-Pas-de-Calais	Lille
Basse-Normandie	Caen
Haute-Normandie	Rouen
Pays de la Loire	Nantes
Picardie	Amiens
Poitou-Charentes	Poitiers
Provence-Alpes-Côte d'Azur	Marseille
Rhône-Alpes	Lyon

PART II
SITES & SIGHTS

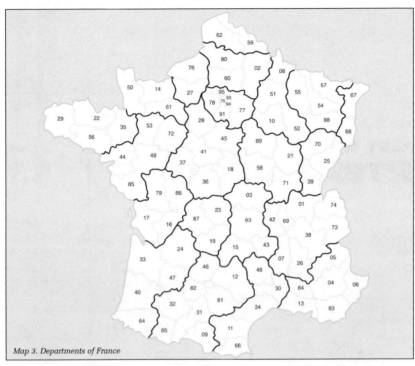

Map 3. Departments of France

01	Ain	32	Gers	65	Haute-Pyrénées
02	Aisne	33	Gironde	66	Pyrénées-Orientales
03	Allier	34	Hérault	67	Bas-Rhin
04	Alpes-de-Haute-	35	Ille-et-Vilaine	68	Haut-Rhin
	Provence	36	Indre	69	Rhone
05	Hautes-Alpes	37	Indre-et-Loire	70	Haute-Saône
06	Alpes-Maritimes	38	Isère	71	Saône-et-Loire
07	Ardèche	39	Jura	72	Sarthe
08	Ardennes	40	Landes	73	Savoie
09	Ariège	41	Loir-et-Cher	74	Haute-Savoie
10	Aube	42	Loire	75	Ville de Paris
11	Aude	43	Haute-Loire	76	Seine-Maritime
12	Aveyron	44	Loire-Atlantique	77	Seine-et-Marne
13	Bouches-de-Rhône	45	Loiret	78	Yvelines
14	Calvados	46	Lot	79	Deux-Sèvres
15	Cantal	47	Lot-et-Garonne	80	Somme
16	Charante	48	Lozère	81	Tarn
17	Charante-Maritime	49	Maine-et-Loire	82	Tarn-et-Garonne
18	Cher	50	Manche	83	Var
19	Corrèze	51	Marne	84	Vaucluse
20a	Corse-du-Sud	52	Haute-Marne	85	Vendée
20b	Haute-Corse	53	Mayenne	86	Vienne
21	Côte-d'Or	54	Meurthe-et-Moselle	87	Haute-Vienne
22	Côtes-du-Nord	55	Meuse	88	Vosges
23	Creuse	56	Morbihan	89	Yonne
24	Dordogne	57	Moselle	90	Territoire de Belfort
25	Doubs	58	Nièvre	91	Essonne
26	Drôme	59	Nord	92	Hauts-de-Seine
27	Eure	60	Oise	93	Seine-Saint-Denis
28	Eure-et-Loir	61	Orne	94	Val-de-Marne
29	Finistère	62	Pas-de-Calais	95	Val-d'Oise
30	Gard	63	Puy-de-Dôme		
31	Haute-Garonne	64	Pyrénées-Atlantiques		

Alsace (Strasbourg)

Bas-Rhin (67),
Haut-Rhin (68)

This historic frontier area of northeastern France is separated from Germany on the east by the Rhine River and from part of Lorraine in the west by the Vosges Mountains that climb to about 1400 metres at the highest point. Such cities as the modern Strasbourg began as Roman frontier forts in a no-man's land guarding the Rhine (whose banks have been occupied throughout the centuries by Celts, Germanic invaders who were expelled back across the Rhine by Julius Caesar and, in the fourth and fifth centuries Alamans, Vandals and Huns who successively devastated the region). The Merovingians became the dominant power in the sixth century, to be followed by the Carolingians. After the breakup of Charlemagne's empire in the ninth century, the region became the object of disputes between French and Germanic rulers, passing from the control of one to the other.

Avolsheim Bas-Rhin

Sights:

The village preserves a pre-Romanesque ninth-century baptistry in the form of a cloverleaf. 500 m SE is a church reputed to be the oldest in Alsace.

Location:

W of Strasbourg some 24 km on D 45.

Kembs Haut-Rhin

Sight:

Vestiges of a cement Roman bridge are found where the Grand Canal merges with the Rhine River, demolishing the theory that along the Rhine, Romans always constructed their bridges of wood, so that they could be burned in case of invasion.

Location:

S of Strasbourg. Take the D 56, 8 km SE from Habsheim in the SE outskirts of Mulhouse.

Marmoutier Bas-Rhin

Sights:

Under the Abbey church the archaeological crypt contains an altar from the church of 724, showing traces of destruction by fire (827) of the monastery, once a place of pilgrimage. Here also are remains of the vaulting and painted murals, an eighth-century limestone sarcophagus, later anthropomorphic sarcophagi and the tomb of the founder, St.-Léobard.

Traces of a Gallo-Roman temple suggest a transition from pagan to Christian beliefs.

Location:

NW of Strasbourg on the N 4 approx. 33 km. Site in town.

Niederbronn-les-Bains Bas-Rhin

Alsace: Oberbronn (Niederbronn-les-Bains). Roman Temple

Sights:

A spa town since earliest times with one spring reputedly Celtic, the other Roman. There is an ongoing excavation in town on the rue des Romains which includes a (reconstructed) hypocaust and praeforium, an entrance-way, and drains, all from the first century B.C. to the fifth century A.D.

Across the street is a cistern and drains and possibly a Roman house. In the house of the Curé are some excavations of a Roman marketplace.

At the Château de Wasenbourg stands a temple dedicated to

Mercury. The site includes two Roman inscriptions, and three columns, one broken and supporting an inscribed lintel.

Location:

N of Strasbourg and NW of Haguenau approx. 20 km on the N 62. For the temple go from Niederbronn to Oberbronn 2.8 km (from S.I.) then turn right on rue de la Wasenbourg. After 900 m turn left at T-junction. Continue on poor road 300 m then take left path (which says no entry) 300 m to Maison Forestère. Walk past house and take left path following signs for La Wasenbourg. At fork go left, continue to crossroads and signs pointing right. Walk 300-400 m and take the narrow path up to the left. A brisk 20-minute walk, mostly uphill.

Ste-Odile Bas-Rhin

Sights:

The prehistoric Iron Age Mur Païen (Heathens' Wall) is composed of large roughly hewn blocks of stone. It is over 10 km long and in some places 2 m thick and 3 m high. The stones were originally bonded together with oak dowels. The best preserved section is the N end near the ruins of the castle of Dreystein. Trails in the forest are well marked in a beautiful setting.

To be seen are the wall, a Roman road in two parts, Grottes des Druides (a jumble of large stones), necropoli (tumuli, some Merovingian), and the Medieval Route of the Galois.

Location:

SW of Strasbourg on the N 422 about 21 km, turn W to Obernai and continue W 4 km to Ottrott and then 11 km more to Ste.-Odile. The wall can be reached from

Alsace: Ste.-Odile. Mur Païen

Obernai (15 km on D 426) or from Barr (S of Obernai 6.5 km), ca. 8 km. The roads are marked to Mont Ste.-Odile.

Saverne Bas-Rhin

Sights:

The parish church beside the museum displays Gallo-Roman and Frankish remains in the garden. There are five anthropomorphic-style coffins, one with a cover, and various Gallo-Roman stones from pillars, bases, etc.

Location:

NW of Strasbourg 37 km on d 41.

Strasbourg Bas-Rhin

Sights:

Eglise St.-Pierre-le-Jeune, now protestant. Three churches were constructed on this same site. From the church of the seventh century remains only a vault with five funerary niches.

Location:

Strasbourg is the capital of the region of Alsace and is in the NE of France by the German border. The church is in town.

Other sights in the area include OTTMARSHEIM. The octagonal church is said to be a unique example of Carolingian architecture in Alsace. S of Strasbourg and NE of Mulhouse 4 km on D 39, it is on the edge of the forest of la Haith in the Rhine Plain.

Aquitaine (Bordeaux)
Dordogne (24), Gironde (33), Landes (40), Lot-et-Garonne (47), Pyrénées Atlantiques (64)

The region is well endowed with prehistoric caves and grottos, predominantly in the Valley of the Vézère. The Aquitainians, a people perhaps akin to the Basque, occupied the southern part of the area in pre-Roman times. The name from Latin *Aquitania* for SW France, was first used by Julius Caesar. Under the Romans, the province of Aquitania was created by Caesar, and extended almost as far north as the Loire River. After 500 years of Roman rule, Aquitaine fell to the Visigoths in the fifth century and then to the Franks when they defeated the Visigoths in 507. In the seventh century Gascony, the area south of the Garonne, was separated from Aquitaine and was ruled by semi-independent dukes, but about 725 the region was raided by the Muslim conquerors of Spain, and the dukes were forced to seek the protection of the Frankish ruler Charles Martel, who defeated the Muslims. The last duke of Aquitaine was William X (1099-1137). His daughter, Eleanor of Aquitaine, married the heir to the English throne in 1152. The area became an English possession and remained so until the fifteenth century when it was annexed by France at the end of the Hundred Years' War.

The capital of the region is Bordeaux situated on the Garonne River. Once called Burdigala, it was founded in the third century by a Celtic tribe. In 56 B.C. it was seized by the Romans who occupied the town and carried out further development building aqueducts, temples and an amphitheatre. After the barbarian invasions in 276 the town was fortified with walls.

Barsac Gironde
Sight:
Well preserved section of Gallo-Roman road nearby.
Location:
SE of Bordeaux approx. 35 km on N 113. At Barsac turn into street opposite the church and continue straight on. Pass the Hôtel de Ville and a green square on the left, turn left then first right and over train tracks. Go for 1.5 km on D 118 and shortly after Hallet continue in direction of Le Basque and Illats until you pass Château Caillou (R) and Château Guiteronde du Hayot (L). 200 m after this, take the dirt road left, pass a small farmhouse (R) and you are at the eastern end of the Roman road. The woods mark the western end of it. Ask for *route romaine guiteronde*.

Bordeaux Gironde
Sights:
On the far side of rue Fondaudège, the Palais Gallien provides the only remains of ancient Burdigala, consisting of some ruins of the third-century Roman amphitheatre which once accommodated 15,000 spectators. Sections of walls constructed of bands of stone and brick, several arches, and the entrance are visible.

The church of St.-Seurin contains in its eleventh-century crypt Roman columns and sarcophagi of the sixth and seventh centuries. Check with S.I. for visiting times, also for the excavated Paleo-Christian cemetery in the Place des Martyrs-de-la-Résistance.
Location:
Bordeaux is the capital of the region and lies SW of Paris on the Garonne river, near the coast.

Bourg Gironde
Sights:
Nearby Grottes de Pair-non-Pair contain engravings of mammoth, bison, ibex, and horses from the Aurignacian period (a flint culture of the Upper Paleolithic displaying the first cave art). Of particular interest is one of a horse known as l'Agnus Dei.
Location:
N of Bordeaux 5 km on E 606 to St.-André, then NW on D 669. The caves are 6 km E of Bourg.

Brantôme Dordogne
Sights:
Dolmen of Pierre Levée, mounted on an artificial brick base, with a large capstone. The Grotte de Villars contains prehistoric paintings of manganese oxide which date back about 17,000 years. Particularly good examples of ibex, horses and bison covered by a film of calcite which gives them a blue colour.
Location:
Brantôme is slightly NE of Bordeaux and N of Perigueux some 27 km on D 939. Pierre Levée is 1 km E on D 78 toward Thiviers, in the courtyard of Relais

de Dolmen. Another dolmen is SW of the town some 10 km on D 78 to Bourdeilles, 5.5 km on D 106 to St.-Vivien, then just N on D 93. For Villars, go N of Brantôme on D 675, 6 km, and just before Bouriaux go right (E) on D 82, 7 km, then left (N) on D 3 through Villars. Signposted.

Le Bugue Dordogne
Sight:
Cave of Bara-Bahau has on the ceiling drawings from the Magdalenian period made in the soft rock with sharpened flints and with fingertips. The finger drawings are of horses, a large bull, bison, bear, aurochs and deer. There are also bear-claw marks from Mousterian times.

Location:
E of Bordeaux and W of Les Eyzies approx. 11 km on D 706/D 703.

Dax Landes
Sights:
Roman Aquae Tarbellicae. Some remains of the fourth-century Roman wall along the Promenade des Remparts near the S.I., but it was largely demolished in the nineteenth century. Originally the wall was 1465 m long with four towers and four gates.

Beside the Musée de Borda and with entry via the museum, is an archaeological crypt containing foundations of a second-century Roman temple.

Inside the church of St.-Vincent-de-Xaintes there is a tenth-century monogram above the door; in the chancel is a Gallo-Roman mosaic, said to have been discovered under the foundations of an earlier church here.

Location:
S of Bordeaux and NE of Bayonne 49 km on N 10.

Les Eyzies-de-Tayac Dordogne
Sights:
The Valley of the Vézère comprises numerous limestone bluffs where prehistoric humans inhabited grottos and caves and left many wall paintings. To visit the large number of sites in this valley it is wise to go first to Les Eyzies (or to Montignac) where the S.I. will provide maps and information.

The paleolithic shelters of Vignaud and Pataud are in town by the museum, but only Pataud (with its own museum) has visible remains of occupation. An ibex from the Solutrean period is engraved in bas relief.

W of Les Eyzies and situated in the vale of Gorge d'Enfer on the right

Aquitaine: Les Eyzies.
Roque St.-Christophe

bank of the Vézère River is the Abri du Poisson with a metre-long engraved salmon or trout, the first known representation of a fish.

St.-Cirq, Grotte du Sorcier, contains many fine engravings, especially a male figure with a face. It is about 5 km SW of Les Eyzies on the N side of the river.

The Grotte de Font-de-Gaume, about 20 m above the valley floor, consists of a passage with a series of chambers, and numerous depictions of animals in black and ochre include bison, goats, mammoth, and reindeer, all from the Magdalenian period. Steep climb up pathway.

The narrow tunnel in the Grotte des Combarelles is decorated with more than 300 animal drawings from the Magdalenian period (the final Paleolithic culture of France).

In the Grotte de Bernifal are hands in negative, engravings and paintings of mammoth, bison, and horses, among others from the Magdalenian. It is located a few km beyond Combarelles.

The Abri du Cap-Blanc is a rock shelter containing animals in high relief including deer-heads and bison and a frieze of sculptured horses and other animals.

Just before Abri du Cap-Blanc, in a side valley on the left, the cave of La Grèze contains incised bisons.

At Roque-St.-Christophe, 9 km NE, the cliffs and hollows have been extensively excavated revealing occupation by troglodytes especially in the Middle Ages when it was used as a fortress. Across the river is an important site, Le Moustier, which lent its name to the Mousterian period.

Within easy reach of Les Eyzies are the Grotte du Grand Roc, Cro-Magnon (where the remains of a 30,000-year old Cro-Magnon skeleton was found), and several other prehistoric sites, but check with the S.I. to see which ones may be visited.

Gisement de la Madeleine has a troglodyte village which may have been first occupied in the tenth century.

Near Castel-Merle there are several shelters including l'Abri Reverdit which

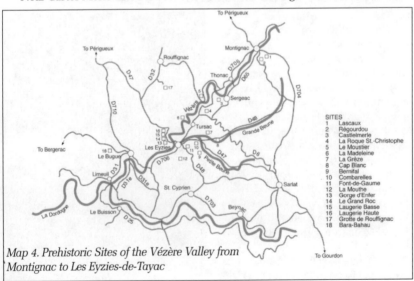

Map 4. Prehistoric Sites of the Vézère Valley from Montignac to Les Eyzies-de-Tayac

SITES
1 Lascaux
2 Régourdou
3 Castelmerle
4 La Roque St.-Christophe
5 Le Moustier
6 La Madeleine
7 La Grèze
8 Cap Blanc
9 Bernifal
10 Combarelles
11 Font-de-Gaume
12 La Mouthe
13 Gorge d'Enfer
14 Le Grand Roc
15 Laugerie Basse
16 Laugerie Haute
17 Grotte de Rouffignac
18 Bara-Bahau

has sculptures from the Magdalenian, and some strange symbols of an earlier period.

See also entries for Le Bugue, Montignac, Rouffignac.

There are many other cave and shelter sites in the region and it is advisable to check with the S.I. to see which ones are open to the public.

Location:
Les Eyzies is E of Bordeaux and S of Périgueux 37 km on D 710, then E 11 km on D 703/D 706. Good maps are available from the S.I.

Isturitz Pyrénées-Atlantiques
Sights:
Three prehistoric caves—Isturitz, Oxocelhaya and Erberua (the first two connected by a recent man-made passageway and the latter not open to the public at present). Here are some engravings and paintings but mostly they are caves of natural beauty. Guided visit of 45 minutes (14 degrees inside).

Location:
S of Bordeaux and SE of Bayonne. Go 14 km on D 932 to Cambo-les-Bains, then take the D 10 through Hasparren and ca. 11 km from here to St.-Esteban. Turn left at sign: *Grottes 3 km.* Well signposted.

Limeuil Dordogne
Sights:
Located here are two caves from Magdalenian times with about 100 engravings of reindeer and horses.

Location:
E of Bordeaux and S of Périgueux. SW of Les Eyzies 11 km on D 706/D 703 to Le Bugue, then S about 5 km on D 31.

Montcaret Gironde
Sights:
The Romanesque church stands in the midst of excavated foundations of a Gallo-Roman villa. In its choir are two Corinthian capitals from the sixth and seventh centuries. It is thought that there was originally a pre-Romanesque church here which suffered damage from Saracen attacks in the eighth century and from the Vikings in the ninth century.

The peristyle villa is of Graeco-Roman design. In the trefoil-shaped dining room are mosaics and frescos of the third and fourth centuries with designs of flowers, animals and geometric forms. There are several graves around the floor of this room

Aquitaine: Montcaret

with skeletal remains, and many others of both Merovingian and Carolingian type in the excavation as the site was used as a church and burial ground after the sixth century. There is also a large fourth-century Roman bath and hypocausts with sculptural and architectural remains.

In the courtyard by the church, the Christian mosaics were made by monks in the eighth century but they are considered a poor imitation of the Roman original. Museum *in situ.*

Location:
Montcaret is E of Bordeaux some 50 km. It is W of Bergerac approx. 35 km on D 936. Church and excavation are signposted in the village.

Montignac Dordogne
Sights:
Located at the head of the prehistoric valley of the Vézère. The famous site of the Grotte de Lascaux, discovered in 1940, is 2 km from the town.

The cave itself is closed to the public since its paintings were showing signs of deterioration, but there is a replica, Lascaux II, containing faithful reproductions of the paintings, located 200 m from the original site.

Location:
NW of Bordeaux and E of Périgueux. Go W of Brive N 89-E 70, 27 km, then S, 9 km on D 704.

Pays Basque Pyrénées Atlantiques
Sights and Locations:
The Pays Basque encompasses the western Pyrenees both in Spain and France, and is replete with ancient human vestiges. A few examples are given here but precise directions should be obtained locally since most monuments, like pin pricks in a vast mountainous terrain, require a hike, and are difficult to find. Most are in poor condition.

Near the commune of Itxassou is situated the Col de Méatse with numerous prehistoric stone monuments, including several cromlechs. Itxassou is S of Bordeaux and SE of Bayonne and is reached by taking the D 932 to Espellette, then the D 918, 3.5 km SE.

Near the commune of Bidarray may be seen the Monolith of Artzamendi, 4.2 m long and weighing about four tons. It appears to be a fallen menhir or one that was never erected. Another, the Monolith of Baigura, is of similar size and also appears as if it was never set up vertically in the manner of a menhir. Bidarray is about 12 km S of Itxassou on the D 918.

In the commune of Lecumberri S of Bordeaux and SE of St.-Jean-Pied-de-Port on D 18, is the Necropolis of Apatesaro consisting of a number of cromlechs of about four to five metres in diameter and containing crematorial burial sites.

The Dolmen de Gaxteenia with three standing stones and triangular capstone (on private property but visible) is located in the commune of Mendive SE of St.-Jean-Pied-de-Port 6.5 km on D 18.

Dolmen de Buluntza, about 15 m in diameter, in the commune of Ahaxe, stands in a field to the W of the Col de Buluntza at an altitude of 672 m. It has three large stones and an enormous fractured capstone. A little SE of St.-Jean-Pied-de-Port off the D 18/D 20.

In the commune of Ascain in the shadow of the La Rhune (Larrun) mountain are the Cromlechs of Gorostiarra (nine circles fairly well preserved). The Menhir de Gaztenbakarre 2.3 m high and triangular in shape is in the commune of Sare about 6 km south of Ascain on the D 4. Walk up to Trois Fontaines and the menhir can be seen in the valley to the W, 150 m lower down. To reach Ascain take the D 918, 6 km S of St.-Jean-de-Luz.

For the cromlechs, walk on E to the edge of the woods, cross the river at the old dam, and ascend straight up toward the rocks on the left. (2½-3 hours). Not a difficult walk.

Near Olhette 4.5 km W of Ascain on the D 4 is a fairly well-preserved stretch of Medieval road along the gorge of the river Insola.

The Roman trophy of Urkulu dates from the end of the first century B.C. There were only four built: one in Romania (now destroyed), and two more in France – at Le Perthus and La Turbie (see entries). Built of calcite, it originally had a conical roof of stone covered with earth and grass. The trophy was mounted on top and consisted of bronze arms (lances) of the defeated. (The Romans were already using iron weapons by this time.)

While the tower is actually situated in Spain, access is only possible through France. It is some 120 m in diameter at the base and nearly 4 m high (originally probably 4.50 m).

Located S of St.-Jean-Pied-de-Port approx. 48 km SE on the Spanish border. Take the D 301, then D 428, 31 km and the tower can be seen on the left on top of the mountain. Walk up. It can also be reached via Arnéguy, 16.5 km from here, on a very winding road.

Périgueux Dordogne
Sights:

Gallo-Roman Vesone still displays substantial remains today, even though it was used as a quarry by Medieval builders. In the city park is an enceinte which contains a few fragments of the first-century elliptical amphitheatre which reputedly had a capacity for 20,000 spectators.

The Tour de Vesone, a round tower some 24 m high with an internal diameter of 17 m, was the cella of a second-century Gallo-Roman temple dedicated to Vessuna, tutelary god of the Roman city. It had a colonnade and stairway with pillars on each side. Located at the end of rue Romaine (S).

The twelfth-century Château Barrière, a fortified house with a keep, together with the Maison Romane, is built over the foundations of the fourth-century Roman wall. The wall was constructed

Aquitaine: Périgueux. Tour de Vésone

during the earliest barbarian invasions with materials taken from Roman monuments.

The Porte Normande, which lies at the N end of the Château Barrière, is part of the protective wall made from very large stones taken in desperate times from temples, public buildings and tombs. Its name comes from the role it played during an attack by Vikings.

Under cover are excavations of the first-century Gallo-Roman Villa Pompeia. Part of a wall from the third century is visible but the Porte de Mars, in a private garden, cannot be seen. The cathedral of St.-Front contains a number of Merovingian sarcophagi.

Location:
Périgueux is E of Bordeaux about 190 km on N 89-E 70. The S.I. will give out a map showing where the Gallo-Roman enceinte is located.

Peyrehorade Landes

Sights:
Sorde-l'Abbaye. The former Benedictine abbey church is built over a fourth-century Gallo-Roman villa. An excavation outside shows the well, atrium and foundations, and also substantial remains of the baths inside including caldarium, tepidarium and frigidarium. The latter had a mosaic floor, part of which is still visible. The mosaics exhibited came from the outside excavations. There are also three Visigothic graves, still containing skeletal remains, along with a roof section with tiles and an apoditarium for massages beside the pool.

Nearby, at Cagnotte, the Romanesque church contains a marble fifth-century sarcophagus and another seventh-ninth century tomb hollowed out of the trunk of a beech tree.

Location:
Peyrehorade is S of Bordeaux and E of Bayonne. Sorde l'Abbaye is SE of the town 4 km on D 29. Cagnotte is 7 km NE on D 29 on a winding road.

Plassac Gironde

Sight:
Near the church excavations have revealed three successive Gallo-Roman villas built between the first and fifth centuries. Whereas the first two were built in Roman style, the third was decorated with polychrome mosaics in Aquitanian style. Museum in situ.

Location:
N of Bordeaux and 3.5 km S of Blaye on D 669. Site is under the church in town.

Rocamadour Dordogne

Sight:
Grotte des Merveilles. Apart from its natural beauty, this small cave has paintings dating back to the Solutrean period. Represented are horses, a cat, the outline of a deer and outlines of hands.

Location:
E of Bordeaux and S of Brive. Take the N 20-E 09 out of Brive to Cressensac,

17 km, then the N 140 for 29 km to where the D 673 crosses it. Turn W on this road for 4 km.

Rouffignac Dordogne

Sight:

Grotte de Rouffignac, also known as La Grotte aux Cent Mammouths, with some 250 paintings or engravings of prehistoric animals dating from the mid or late Magdalenian period. Included are mammoth, rhinoceros, horses, ibex and bison. The galleries are several km underground and reached by a small train. Expect about an hour for the visit.

Location:

E of Bordeaux and NW of Les Eyzies. Take the D 47 NW to Manaurie and continue another 7 km to where the D 32 forks, right, toward Rouffignac. Signposted.

St.-Emilion Gironde

Sights:

In the Place du Marché stands the Eglise Monolithe, hewn out of a single, solid block of rock by Benedictine monks in the eighth century. Later it was used as an ancient burial ground with tombs chiselled in the rock.

In nearby St.-Sulpice de Faleyrens, standing in a vineyard, is a large 5 m-high menhir, Pierrefitte, said to mark the old river harbour of St.-Emilion. Signposted in town.

Near Lussac, slightly N of St.-Emilion on the D 122, then N on CD 21 toward Petit Palais, is the Megalithe de Picampeau, a large stone with hollowed-out bowl, a trough leading from it, perhaps sacrificial. It is attributed to the Druids.

Location:

E of Bordeaux 25 km to Libourne on N 89-D 70, then SE 8 km on D 670 and St.-Emilion lies just to the N, 3 km. For the menhir, leave town in the direction of Libourne. After 1.7 km on D 19, the menhir is on the left beside the sign. At Lussac, from the sign *megalithe* in the village, go 300 m following road, and at fork go right, up a path, 500 m to the woods. The stone is in a clearing to the left with an explanatory sign.

Aquitaine: St.-Sulpice (St.-Emilion). Pierrefitte

Val d'Ossau Pyrénées Atlantiques
Sights:
There are several sights along this valley which lies between Pau and the Spanish frontier. Arudy advertises a Roman bridge but in fact there are only some foundations underneath a modern bridge, crossed as you leave the town on the way to Buzy and Oléron.

Bilheres has several cromlechs nearby but they are mostly overgrown and only one is in fair condition. Excellent hike up there, however, and magnificent views over the Val d'Ossau.

Buzy has a dolmen with eight standing stones situated on the edge of town. The capstone is in the shape of a turtle shell but the entrance passage is filled in. Coming from Arudy on D 90, the dolmen is in a picnic area on the right, immediately after the turn-off toward Bescat. Signposted.

Location:
S of Bordeaux. Leave Pau on D 934 going S. Arudy is ca. 23 km. Buzy is NW of Arudy on D 920, and Bilheres is approx. 30 km S of Pau on D 934. To find the cromlechs, go to Bielle, then take the road to Bilheres, 3 km W. Go through town, pass church and follow signs for Le Bénou. Continue past a small chapel on the right. 300 m after this turn right up road marked with no entry sign (from the church in the village to turnoff past chapel is ca. 2.2 km). Walk up path, through gate taking the left fork up the hill when it divides. As the road swings to the right, there is a wide grass swathe to the left going uphill between the bushes and trees. The cromlechs are on top of this hill, on the left, the best one being the last in the group. About a twenty-minute walk from the gate.

Villeneuve-sur-Lot Lot-et-Garonne
Sight:
In Villeneuve, next to the fire station and across from the prison, is an excavation of a Gallo-Roman site. The Archaeological Society building is opposite, next to the church, where foundations of buildings and an extensive water channel system are to be seen. There is an exposition in the afternoons of July and August.

Location:
SE of Bordeaux on A 62-E 72 to Agen, then N, about 29 km on N 21. Site can be found by turning off the N 21 at sign: *EYSSES*.

Other sites in the area include: AIRE-SUR-L'ADOUR. The former bishop's palace, now the Hôtel de Ville, contains part of a Gallo-Roman pavement. SE of Bordeaux and N of Pau 50 km on N 134. ANDERNOS-LES-BAINS. Beside the church of St.-Eloi are vestiges of a fourth-century Gallo-Roman basilica. SW of Bordeaux in the Bay of Arcachon, Andernos lies on the D 3 beside the water. BAZAS. Traces of a seventh-century oppidum have been revealed by recent excavations. SE of Bordeaux on A 62, 26 km to Langon, then S on D 932, 12 km. HASPARREN. Found in the church in 1665 and now embedded in the wall under glass outside on the right side facing the church is a fourth-century inscription relating to the origin of the province of Novempopulania. S of Bordeaux and SE of Bayonne 14 km on D 932 through Cambo-les-Bains, then E 10 km on D 22 to Hasparren. **MAS-D'AIRE**. The church of Ste.-Quitterie has in its crypt a fifth-century Merovingian sarcophagus. SE of Bordeaux and N of Pau about 50 km on N 134. **MOULIS-EN-MÉDOC**. Excavations here brought to light vestiges of a fourth-fifth century cult site along with several Merovingian sarcophagi. NW of Bordeaux on D 1, 21 km to Castelnau-de-Médoc, then N, 2 km further on D 5. **RIBÉRAC**. The nearby Château de la Rigale has a Gallo-Roman tower. NE of Bordeaux and 14 km E of Ribérac on D 710. **SARBARZAN**. Some vestiges of the Gallo-Roman villa of Brion. NW of Bordeaux on N 15 approx. 50 km to St.-Gaux, then E on D 4 about 4 km.

Auvergne (Clermont Ferrand)
Alliers (03), Cantal (15), Haute-Loire (43), Puy-de-Dôme (63)

The Auvergne is a land characterized by a chain of approximately two hundred volcanic mountains running north to south, with deep gorges and rolling pasture land. It forms the core of the Massif Central, a rugged and geologically diverse area. The most well-known peak is the Puy de Dôme, west and a little north of Clermont-Ferrand. Celtic tribes associated the summit with the residence of the god Lug, and in the Middle Ages it was thought to be the home of witches.

Here are some of the oldest human settlements in France, dating back to the lower Paleolithic. Some fifty dolmens and twenty or more menhirs attest to Neolithic communities in the region. During the Bronze Age, the adjacent Rhône Valley became the major tin and amber trade route. Of the Celts who then came to the area, the Averni, who gave their name to it, produced the famous leader Vercingetorix (victim of Roman expansion). With the fall of the Roman Empire the Visigoths came to control the region on the right bank of the Rhône while the Burgundians ruled the left bank. After the battle of Vouillé and the defeat of the Visigoths, the province passed into the hands of the Franks, and the Auvergne later became subject to the Carolingian kingdom of Aquitaine. In 1095 Pope Urban II preached the first crusade from Clermont-Ferrand, which is today the major city of the region.

Clermont-Ferrand Puy-de-Dôme
Sights:
The cathedral of Notre Dame de l'Assomption incorporates an altar made up from a sixth-century sarcophagus. A fourth-century tomb is found in the crypt which pertained to an earlier church.

3.5 km W of the city lies Royat where, along with two Merovingian tombs N of the Casino and gardens, are vestiges of Gallo-Roman baths including a water conduit and steps (rebuilt) of sculptured stones. A restored pool has arches covered with mosaics along with marble walls.

S of the city on N 89-E 70, about 7 km is the dolmen de Samson with standing stones and capstone. A three-hour hike in the Gorges de Ceyrat for those who like to walk.

Further W of Clermont is the 1416-m Puy de Dôme, the highest summit in this extinct volcanic chain. On top are vestiges of the square based cella of a temple to Mercury which can be reached on foot from Ceyssat Pass on a winding Roman road. It was up this road that wagons pulled by eight horses in tandem conveyed the building materials to the site of the enormous temple. A television transmitter now occupies the site.

Location:
Clermont-Ferrand is located S of Paris and W of Lyon about 176 km on A 72-E 70. For Royat, go S on N 89 and turn right at the end of the village of Beaumont. One block down hill past the S.I., the baths are on the right. For the dolmen, start out on the same road as for Royat, going beyond Beaumont to the end of the village of Ceyrat. The road curves sharply to the left and on the right (W) is a bus stop and information map in a large parking area, right on the curve. A half-covered sign points to the dolmen and the Gorges de Ceyrat. Walk up path, about twenty minutes on a gentle incline, to dolmen. Puy de Dôme is signposted in the city.

Néris-les-Bains Alliers
Sights:
The Gallic town of Nerios became Romanized (Aquae Nerii) in the first century, probably due to its thermal waters. It was also the military centre of the Eighth Augustan Legion.

In the centre of town, right behind the swimming pool, next to the S.I. are two rectangular restored Roman pools and one round one. They all have benches, and are currently used. In the modern thermal centre, less than 300 m S, there are remains of a peristyle with a number of inscribed Roman stones, Corinthian columns, and an inscribed tablet.

Also near the S.I., just across the boulevard, is the Parc des Arènes with remains of an amphitheatre. The outline is obvious but there are only bits of wall left. Trees have been planted around the perimeter and a children's playground occupies the centre.

The parish church, in the Place de la République, contains masonry possibly from the sixth century. Beside the church, excavations have revealed a Merovingian and Carolingian necropolis. The earliest tombs are from the sixth century when Néris was evangelized by St. Patrocle. The last phase of the necropolis (ninth-tenth centuries) is marked by sarcophagi with a cephalic (head-shaped) cavity. In the eleventh century it was abandoned and

a fortified château established on the site. The necropolis itself occupied the entire square and most of the tombs were made of stone blocks extracted from the Gallo-Roman town.

Location:
NW of Clermont-Ferrand, Néris is 8 km S of Montlucon on N 144.

Auvergne: Néris-les-Bains. Roman Pools

St.-Etienne-des-Champs Puy-de-Dôme
Sight:
Dolmen de la Pierre des Fées (or Pierre Fade) in good condition, with five standing stones and capstone.

Location:
From Clermont take D 941 ca 51 km W to le Cheval Blanc. Turn left (S) on D 82 and continue about 5 km to turn-off, left to St.-Etienne. Just before the village, turn right toward Chez Geille. Dolmen is signposted throughout but the wooden signs are small and can easily be missed. Turn right by farm and take right fork approx. 1100 m down track to dolmen. This entails driving to the end of the path and then walking over grass to path directly ahead, leading to bottom of hill roughly 400 m. At fork go straight ahead on very narrow track (ignore path to the left). Dolmen is about 3 m on right.

Other sights in the area include: **BRIOUDE.** Scene of pilgrimages, the Basilica of St.-Julien was built between the eleventh and twelfth centuries. Here is the tomb of the fourth-century martyr. S of Clermont about 64 km on N 102. **MAURIAC.** The Monastère St.-Pierre has some Gallo-Roman vestiges as well as part of the foundations of a ninth-century church. SW of Clermont on N 89-E 70 to where it joins the D 922 just S of Rochefort-Montagne. Then some 70 km SW on D 922. **LE MONT-DORE.** Under the Roman baths are remains of pools used by the Gauls. SW of Clermont on E 70-N 89, 21 km, then SW on D 983, 28 km. **LE PUY-EN-VELAY.** N of the town, the chapel of St.-Michel d'Aiguilhex, perched on a high volcanic pinnacle, has well-preserved frescos from the tenth century. The town lies S of Clermont-Ferrand ca. 113 km on the N 9-E 11/N 102. (Also SW of Lyon on the A 47/N 88 ca. 136 km). **THIERS.** In the church of St.-Genès are fragmentary mosaics from a sixth-century church. E of Clermont some 38 km on A 72-E 70.

Bourgogne (Dijon)
Côte d'Or (21), Nièvre (58),
Saône-et-Loire (71), Yonne (89)

The northern section of the region consists of ancient limestone plateaux dissected by the Yonne River, while the southern part contains the fertile plain of the river Saône. A particular type of flint tool discovered at Solutré gave rise to the Upper Paleolithic cultural designation—Solutrean. The area has long been a crossroads between the Paris basin and the Saône, and between the Mediterranean and northern peoples. One of the most powerful Celtic tribes in Gaul, the Aedui, established their fortified camp at Bribracte in the second century B.C., and here Vercingetorix was appointed chief of the Gallic tribes in revolt. With the breakup of the Roman empire, Germanic Burgundians, originally from the shores of the Baltic, settled in the Saône plain and gave their name to the region. About 534, the Franks seized the area and were in turn replaced by Carolingian rule under Charlemagne. Throughout the Middle Ages, Bourgogne (Burgundy) was subject to numerous partitions and reunifications.

The major city and historic capital is Dijon.

Alise-Ste.-Reine Côte d'Or

Sights:

Excavations of the Gallo-Roman city of Alesia on Mont Auxois have uncovered foundations of houses, remains of shops, a guild house for bronze workers, a heating system, temple, streets and Gallic huts. The first-century theatre is visible by the outlines of the cavea and orchestra. It was about 80 m in diameter and probably sat about 5000 spectators. There are also ruins of a seventh-century Merovingian church surrounded by a cemetery.

On the summit of Mont Auxois is a huge modern statue of Vercingetorix, who resisted Caesar's decisive siege in 52 B.C. The outline of the old earthen ramparts and trenches are still visible.

In the village, the Merovingian church of Saint-Léger dates back to 678-720. It was burned by Vikings and about half was rebuilt in the ninth-tenth centuries. It has the layout of an early Christian basilica including a nave with a flat, wooden ceiling, an oven-vaulted apse, and a sacristy. The pulpit has a Gallo-Roman stele inset. The southern wall is Merovingian while the opposite is of Carolingian vintage. Museum in situ.

Location:

Alise-Ste.-Reine is NW of Dijon. Take the D 905 to Vanarey-les-Laumes, just S of Montbard. Turn right (E) on D 103. Alternatively, go SE from Auxerre on Autoroute A 6, 70 km to Semur turnoff. Then NE from Semur on D 954 about 16 km. Well signposted.

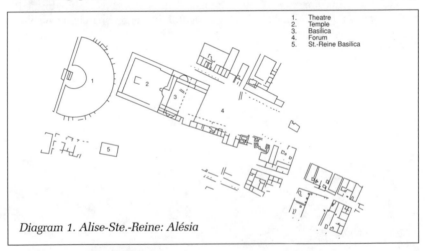

1. Theatre
2. Temple
3. Basilica
4. Forum
5. St.-Reine Basilica

Diagram 1. Alise-Ste.-Reine: Alésia

Arcy-sur-Cure Yonne

Sight:

Les Grottes d'Arcy (half-hour walk from the Grande Grotte) display prehistoric wall paintings of horses, mammoth, hyena, ibex, and hand prints. At time of writing, visits needed to be arranged in advance. Check with S.I. See also entry for St.-Moré.

Location:

NW of Dijon and SE of Auxerre. Arcy can be reached by Autoroute A 6, ca.

26 km S of Auxerre. The caves are just to the W of town.

Autun Saône-et-Loire
Sights:

The Roman city of Augustodunum was founded in the first century B.C. by order of Emperor Augustus, in honour of the Aedui Gallic tribe who abandoned their mountain bastion of Bibracte (see Mont Beuvray), and flocked to the town, which at that time was second only to Lyon. The local inhabitants, early converts to Christianity, founded a vast city surrounded by about 7 km of walls.

The ramparts retain a Gallo-Roman base, and two of the original main double-arched town gates still survive:

Bourgogne: Autun. Pierre de Couhard

the Port d'Andre, 14.5 m high and 20 m wide and the Port d'Arroux, 17 m high and 19 m wide, both with two main arches for chariots and wagons, and flanked by smaller openings for pedestrians. The upper gallery of the latter is supported by Corinthian pilasters dating from the time of Constantine.

From the N side of the river Arroux, a path leads NW to the Temple of Janus which consists of two walls of a square tower, 24 m high.

There are only slight remains today of one of the largest theatres of the Roman empire, constructed in the first century. Recently a second theatre, with elements of amphitheatral design, has been discovered .

Near the village of Couhard, 1 km from the Porte de Breuil, is the first-century Pierre de Couhard, a partly ruined pyramid of Roman masonry, 33 m high. It was probably a tomb, since it was originally placed in a large burial ground. Only the interior stone filling now remains.

Location:

SW of Dijon, 48 km W of Beaune and 112 km E of Nevers, Autun is at the crossroads of the N 81, D 973, D 978 and N 80. Couhard is SE of town and well signposted.

Auxerre Yonne
Sights:

Gallo Roman Autessiodurum. The ninth-century pre-Romanesque crypt of St.-Germaine, remodelled in the eleventh century, consists of a nave and two aisles with barrel vaulting dating from Carolingian times. In the inner crypt are frescos dating from about 850 in shades of red depicting the martyrdom of St.-Stephen, the adoration of the Magi, and two bishops. They are reputedly some of the earliest extant in France. Also to be seen are the tomb of St.-Germanus, two Merovingian tombs, and four Gallo-Roman columns.

Location:

Auxerre is NW of Dijon and NW of Beaune on the A 6-D 15. Sites in town.

Champallement Nièvre
Sights:
On the road to Saint-Révérien, in the forest of Compierre, lie the remains of a Gallo-Roman village. Permanently open to visitors, the site presents an octagonal temple of Gallic tradition, and bordered by small shops and workshops. Further on is a butcher's house and at the edge of the village, a theatre.
Location:
W of Dijon and S of Auxerre 43 km on N 151 to Clamecy, then SW on D 34, 32 km.

Châtillon-sur-Seine Côte-d'Or
Sights:
The church of St.-Vorles has a very small crypt from the ninth century.

While museums are generally not listed, an exception has been made since the one here houses the Vix Treasure along with its Gallo-Roman collections. The Treasure was discovered in 1953 in a collapsed barrow on Mont Lassois above the village of Vix, some 7 km NW of Châtillon. It consisted of a royal tomb containing the skeleton of a princess of about 500 B.C., buried with her jewellery, a chariot, and a huge, decorated bronze vase that was probably the work of a Greek artist. The vase (with a large lid) is 1.64 m high, holds 1100 litres, and weighs 208.6 kg.
Location:
NW of Dijon 84 km on the N 71.

Couches Saône-et-Loire
Sights:
The megalithic group of Epoigny includes menhirs dating from the end of the Neolithic. Five have been re-erected and one is lying down. They have been regrouped at the crossroads of D 115 and C.V. 4. The largest of these measures 7.35 m.

Bourgogne: Couches. Epoigny

Other menhirs in the region are:

Le Menhir de Saint-Micaud, 6.35 m high with engravings of a horned serpent on one side. It is the only one left from an ensemble of three, known as the Pierres aux Fées. SW of Dijon and SW of Chalon-sur-Saône, then SW on D 977, 4.5 km to La Galoche and S on D 28 about 6 km to St.-Micaud. Menhir on the left side of the road.

Le Menhir de Massy in the village of Les Ublaies beside the route D 980 is only 2.50 m high and located near a hill. It is 10 km N of Cluny.

Le Menhir de la Chapelle-sous-Brancion is 4.50 high, and known as Pierre Levée. There is a cross on the top, and druid ceremonies are still practised at each summer solstice. It is also engraved.

Location:

SW of Dijon and W of Chalon. Couches is approx. 28 km NW of Chalon-sur-Saône. Leave Couches toward Autun on D 978. From the campground, on edge of town, go 2.1 km, then turn left and the Epoigny menhirs are 800 m farther on.

Cry-sur-Armancon Yonne

Sight:

Sixth-century Merovingian sarcophagus in a very small, ancient crypt at the Eglise de S.-Julian.

Location:

NW of Dijon and NW of Montbard ca. 15 km on D 905 then turn right (E) on the D 228 to Cry. See owner of pink house beside the bridge for entry into crypt.

Curtil-sous-Burnand Saône-et-Loire

Sights:

At nearby Munot, a Merovingian cemetery with more than 400 sixth-seventh century tombs has been excavated. Today there are only seven tombs in place and most of these are broken. Only one is in reasonable condition.

Location:

SW of Dijon and due west of Tournus. Taking the D 981 N of Cheny, go W at St.-Gengoux-le-National. From here follow the D 84 toward Curtil. After 5 km, a road goes left to Munot. Pass straight through village 1.2 km. Cemetery at top of hill, 400 m. Signposted.

Escolives-Sainte-Camille Yonne

Sights:

The ruins of Scoliva consist of a rather extensive thermae from the third and fourth century, with a number of structures in its complex. On the W end are several rectangular and circular pools with depths of less than a metre. Each side of the courtyard opens onto rooms heated by hypocausts. There was a frigidarium, caldarium and sudatorium (sauna). Latrines have been uncovered, as well as what appears to be a small palaestra.

This is an ongoing excavation, and burial areas nearby indicate that there were settlements here preceding the Romans. However, the Gallo-Roman period seems to have been most important, with its substructure of baths, remains of an arcaded monument, mural paintings and sculptures—all from the first-third centuries. Merovingian sarcophagi from a fifth to eighth century necropolis of some 324 tombs are under excavation. Museum *in situ*.

Location:

NW of Dijon and 10 km S of Auxerre on N 6, signposted on highway. It is 200 m off the N 6 on the right.

Flavigny-sur-Ozerain Côte d'Or

Sights:

At the Abbaye de Flavigny, Ste.-Reina crypt contains a large, two-tiered Carolingian apse with finely carved decorated columns and capitals, and vaulted chambers. The eighth-century church displays standing remains from that period as well as later additions. The lower part, built in 758, contains the tomb of Ste.-Reina who was buried here in 864 after her martyrdom at Alise-Ste.-Reine.

Location:

Flavigny is NW of Dijon. Go S of Alise-Ste.-Reine (see entry) on D 905 and turn right (E) on D 9 to Flavigny. Crypt signposted in village. Ring the bell of the Anis factory for assistance.

Fontenay-près-Vézelay Yonne

Sights:

In the forest of Vézelay of Ferrières, at Le Crot au Port, was an important Gallo-Roman metallurgical centre. Some remains of the iron-smelting excavations remain, but there is not much left to see except for vestiges of hypocausts, forges, and parts of a villa. Ca. 120 m beyond, on the right as you pass the sign, are foundations of a small, (4 x 4 m) temple to Mercury. Several pathways are marked by signs indicating Roman roads, but no stones remain. Pleasant walk through forest.

Location:

NW of Dijon and SE of Auxerre to Vézelay. Free access from the route Vézelay-Clamecy. Signposted a few km out of Vézelay on D 951 just after sign on left (S) for forest of Chauffours-Ferrières, *Les Ferrières-Centre Sidérurgique Gallo-Romain*. Follow road in and there is a sharp turn right and another left where a forestry road goes straight on, signposted. Walk in about 400 m to site. From the D 951 to the forestry road is 1.6 km. From Vézelay to turn-in is 5 km.

Malain Côte d'Or

Sights:

Mediolanum. first-third century Gallo-Roman town with well-preserved ruins of temples, street, bronze-work shop, sanctuary, hypocausts, columns and porticos. The site was destroyed in the third century.

Location:

25 km W of Dijon on the A 38, exit at Pont-de-Pany. Take the D 33, 3 km to Malain. Site (under cover) lies outside the town on D 104 road to Ancey, 600 m past cemetery.

Mont Beuvray Saône-et-Loire

Sights:

On the summit are excavations showing foundations of Gallic houses in the first-century fortified camp of Bibracte. Here, in 53 B.C. Vercingetorix was elected chief of the Gauls. The site is currently under restoration. The defences, known as the Beuvray Trench, were 5 km long.

Location:

SW of Dijon. Going W of Autun, take the N 81, 16 km then turn right (NW) for 7 km on D 61. Mont Beuvray is 8 km W of St.-Léger-sous-Beuvray. Access is gained to the site via a one-way loop from the D 3.

Mont Dardon Saône-et-Loire

Sights:

The area was occupied from the Late Bronze Age to the fourteenth century. Some evidence of Celic defenses, Roman villas, a late ninth-century Christian chapel and Medieval fortifications. The summit is surrounded by a rampart, traces of which are still visible.

Location:

SW of Dijon. SW of Autun 11 km on N 81 then 28 km on D 994 to Toulon-sur-Arroux. Mont Dardon is W of Toulon 7 km on D 42, then 7 km on D 225, near the village of Uxeau.

Quarré-les-Tombes Yonne

Sights:

Around the village church are rows of Medieval limestone sarcophagi, the remains of a large necropolis of over 1000 tombs dating from the seventh-tenth centuries. 10 km E is the Abbaye Ste.-Marie-de-la-Pierre-qui-Vire in the woods. To the right of the abbey is a dolmen surmounted by a statue of the Virgin Mary.

Location:

NW of Dijon, SE of Auxerre and S of Avallon 19 km on D 10.

St.-Moré Yonne

Sights:

The Gallo-Roman camp of Cora on the Via Agrippa lies between St.-Moré and Arcy-sur-Cure. To be seen are the towers and wall of the ancient camp, a quarry preserved since Merovingian times, and sarcophagi from the Middle Ages. See also entry for Arcy-sur-Cure.

Location:

NW of Dijon and SE of Auxerre on N 6, 36 km to Voutenay. The ruins are to the W of the highway. In St.-Moré, just N of Voutenay on N 6, go to Bar Camp de Cora, and they will provide a map showing how to reach the site by car or on foot. By car go 1300 m from the bar to parking spot on left and walk in 500 m. There is a small museum in St.-Moré.

Ternant Côte d'Or

Sights:

Two dolmens: one has an extremely large capstone and chamber, recently reinforced with bricks and cement. The other is a small, intact dolmen with many standing stones and capstone.

Location:

SW of Dijon off the Paris Motorway A 38. Go W of Dijon 20 km to Pont-de-Pany and take the D 35, signposted for Urcy. Follow it approx. 15 km to Ternant. From here go W on D 104B. Dolmens signposted on right about 2.5 km from village and before the hamlet of Rolle (just past km stone #3), are located right behind the sign—one to the right and the other to the left.

Tournus Saône-et-Loire
Sights:
Extensive re-use of stones and columns from Roman, Merovingian and Carolingian times can be seen in the abbey church of St.-Philibert which presents the rare instance of three separate churches superimposed.
Location:
Tournus lies S of Dijon, S of Chalon-sur-Saône and N of Macon 27 km on A 6-E 15 Motorway. Sites are in town.

Vézelay Yonne
Sights:
St.-Père-sous-Vézelay. At Fontaines-Salées, saltwater springs have been in use since the sixth millennium B.C. Excavations have revealed prehistoric water catchments, a field of burial urns from around 900 B.C., and the remains of first-century Gallo-Roman baths with apodyterium, caldarium, tepidarium and hypo-caust. Two circular pools provided hot water

Bourgogne: Vézelay. Fontaines-Salées

treatments.The baths were built on a Gallic sanctuary and the whole site, used for medicinal purposes and the production of salt, is in a large area dedicated to the gods of the springs. Museum in the village. Signposted. A remarkable site.

In the Eglise Notre-Dame is a Carolingian baptismal font.
Location:
NW of Dijon and SE of Auxerre on N 6/D 951. The site is 2 km from St.-Père which is 2 km S of Vézelay.

Other sights in the area include: ARLEUF. Recently discovered rural theatre of Les Bardiaux. SW of Dijon. From Autun go NW on D 978 ca. 27 km. BEAUNE. SW are two dolmens. SE of Paris on E 15-A 6 and 39 km SW of Dijon. The dolmens are on high ground opposite the church and are found by taking the D 973 SW 16 km to Château de la Rochepot. The signposted Archeodrome near the motorway, is an open-air museum showing human settlement in Bourgogne from earliest times to the end of the Gallo-Roman period. BLANOT. At the priory, near the church, are three Merovingian graves which formed part of a sixth-seventh century necropolis, of which twenty-two sepulchres were excavated. S of Dijon and SW of Tournus, 10 km NE of Cluny. **BREUGNON.** On the edge of the forest to the left of the N 15, 6 km S of Clamecy, is the menhir Pierre Fiche. W of Dijon and S of Auxerre 43 km on N 151. **DIJON.** The E end of the rotunda in the crypt of the cathedral of St.-Bénignus leads into a sixth-century chapel which may have been a sanctuary. Remains of the tomb of St.-Benignus. **PONTAUBERT.** The bridge, which gives the village its name, was built in the ninth century by Aubert (or Albert), Count of Avallon. W of Dijon and E of Auxerre 45 km on A 6-E 15, then W, 7 km on N 6. Pontaubert is 4 km SW of Avallon on D 957. **SAULIEU.** In the church of St.-Andoche is the fifth-century sarcophagus of St.-Andocius. It is decorated with pagan and Christian symbols. There are also some Gallo-Roman tombs. W of Dijon, NW of Beaune, SE of Auxerre, Saulieu is 41 km N of Autun on D 980. **SEINE (SOURCE).** Excavations close by have brought to light remains of a Gallo-Roman temple. Finds indicate that the river source was worshipped during the Roman era. NW of Dijon 35.5 km on N 71, then W, 2 km. The site is about 10 km NW of St.-Seine l'Abbaye.

Bretagne (Rennes)
Côtes-du-Nord (22), Finistère (29),
Ille-et-Vilaine (35), Morbihan (56)

The Bretagne (Brittany) peninsula forms a distinctive geographical entity with a rugged, 1200-km coastline, jutting out 240 km into the Atlantic Ocean. It was once a land of towering mountains but is now worn away by erosion. In ancient times the region formed part of Armorica, the centre of a confederation of Celtic tribes. The Romans under Julius Caesar conquered the area in 56 B.C. In the fifth and sixth centuries A.D., after the withdrawal of the Romans, many Britons (Celtic people of Britain), in flight from Germanic invaders of their homeland, crossed the sea and took refuge in the NW portion of the peninsula. They gave the region its present name and gradually converted the pagan Armorican Celts to Christianity. During the seventh and eighth centuries a number of petty principalities developed in Bretagne, becoming subject to Charlemagne early in the ninth century; but the Bretons revolted against his grandson, Charles the Bald, and won independence. In the latter part of the tenth century the Bretons acknowledged the rule of the dukes of Normandy.

Within this area the largest concentration of megalithic structures in Europe lies near Carnac, with nearly six km of stone alignments. Also within a short radius of the town is a profusion of other megaliths including the largest stone ever set up (over 12 m high), the Grand Menhir of Brisé at Locmariaquer, now toppled and broken.

Because there is such an abundance of sites in Bretagne, only some have been selected to be covered in this guide but a list of others (not described) is at the end of this section. Local S.I.'s are very helpful and provide maps and information.

Arzon Morbihan

Sights:

Beyond the Butte de Tumiac is a partially restored late Neolithic grave site known as the Tumulus de Tumiac of La Butte de César. Legend has it that Caesar watched the naval battle against the Veneti from here.

The Tumulus du Petit-Mont is a passage grave, and the Dolmen de Grah-Niohl (also known as Pierre Men Guen) is a fine dolmen with a unique transept. A lamp is needed to see the engravings.

Location:

SW of Rennes and off the D 780 on the opposite side of the strait from Locmariaquer. Tumiac is 16 km SW of Vannes, 8 km W of Sarzeau. Taking the D 780 W of Sarzeau, the tumulus is on the right of the road, easily seen. Petit-Mont is found by going on D 780, 9.5 km W of Sarzeau, then left (S) for 1 km, leaving the marina of the Port du Crouesty to the right. Continue straight ahead to the summit of the hill of Petit-Mont. (Signposted.)

For Grah-Niohl, take the road WNW of Sarzeau for 9.5 km, then, from the church at Arzon go N in the direction of Bernon. Go right on the first road (rue du Presbytère) and almost immediately, on the left, the dead end road of Graniol. The dolmen is 300 m further on, on the left (W) of the road.

Auray Morbihan

Sight:

Dolmen of Kirivin-Brigitte with an enormous capstone resting on large support stones.

Location:

SW of Rennes and W of Vannes. Go 3.5 km SW of Auray on D 768, then take the left turn toward Crach and after roughly 250 m go right for 200 m more; the dolmen is on the right in a field.

Bégard Côtes-du-Nord

Sights:

Along the D 767 from Guingcamp heading toward Lannion stands the 10-m high Kergueuzennec menhir (one of the tallest in Bretagne), and the Pédernec menhir, 8.50 m high.

Location:

NW of Rennes and N of Guingcamp. For Kergueuzennec take the D 15 NE of Bégard toward Brélidy and after passing the hamlet of l'Enseigne, turn right. The menhir is 1.5 km on the left. For Pédernec go S of Bégard on D 15 and after 2.5 km, take the second road to the left and walk ca. 600 m to the menhir.

Belle-Ile Morbihan

Sights:

There are two menhirs, Jean et Jeanne Runelo, beside the D 25 on the W side of the road 300 m apart. Legend has it that these two lovers were turned to stone because the Druids disapproved of their plans to marry. A fairy supposedly releases them from time to time.

Location:
SW of Rennes and 46 km SW of Quiberon, Belle-Ile is the largest of the Breton islands. Bicycles and cars can be rented at the boat dock on the island.

Bono Morbihan
Sight:
The restored Dolmen du Rocher, a passage grave with a corridor of 11.50 m and lying amidst pine trees, is enclosed in an oval tumulus 28 x 21 m, 4 m high. Several of the stones have engravings including ones that resemble a serpent, a U-shaped design and other geometrical forms.
Location:
SW of Rennes and W of Vannes. Leaving Auray, go S on to the D 101 for 4 km toward Bono. 150 m after crossing the bridge, turn right and after 250 m go on foot a further 100 m to the woods on the right of the road.

Brennilis Finistère
Sight:
V-shaped Dolmen Ty-ar-Boudiged (the House of the Fairies) is enclosed in a large, oval mound of which only the northern part is still preserved. It has a narrow entry, a corridor, and an enlarged area with three huge capstones. The tomb seems to represent a transitional type between the earlier passage grave and the later rectangular gallery grave. It is well preserved.
Location:
W of Rennes in the centre of Finistère, 25 km S of Morlaix. Go N of Brennilis on D 36 and turn right at Bellevue. The dolmen is 200 m to the right of the road.

Brignonan-Plage Finistère
Sight:
Men Marz is an 8 m-high menhir surmounted by a small cross. 2 m away is another large menhir, lying down.
Location:
NW of Rennes and N of Brest on D 788/D 770 (30 km), the town lies on the coast. Walk from Brignogan following signs for: *Phare-Menhir*. Menhir is found to the left of the road beside a chapel.

Camaret Finistère
Sights:
Nearby are the Alignments de Lagatjar consisting of 143 menhirs overturned by an earthquake and set up again in 1928. The longest line consists of forty-two stones.
Location:
W of Rennes and SW of Brest in the Crozon Peninsula. The alignment is just W of Camaret. Go from Crozon on D 8, W, but don't enter the town of Camaret. Instead, turn right at the junction of the D 8a, and the stones are to the left.

Carnac Morbihan

Sights:

This is the most famous megalithic area for its thousands of standing stone menhirs. Some stand alone, others are in parallel lines or alignments. Still others are in circles or cromlechs. There are also dolmens, barrows and passage graves.

Examples of alignments are the Kerzerho group along the Erdeven-Plouharnel Road D 781. They begin 1 km S of Erdeven and are divided into three distinct groups between the two hamlets of Kerlescan and Ménoc, but they may have once been part of the same alignment. The Kerlescan group consists of 555 small standing stones and a cromlech of thirty-nine stones. The Kermario group has 1029 standing stones in ten rows. At the S end is a dolmen. The Ménec alignments nearer Carnac include 1099 standing stones in eleven lines. There is also a semicircle of seventy standing stones partly hidden by the houses.

The large tumulus of St.-Michel is 125 m long and 60 m wide and has several chambers. On top is a chapel with a small cross dedicated to the saint. The dolmen of Beaumer has four standing stones and capstone. It is located at the entrance to Camping Dolmen.

The Tumulus of Kercado is a passage grave with a circular capstone surrounded by a circle of menhirs. There are engravings on some stones of an axe with handle and other symbols. It is on private land but can be visited.

Mané-Kerioned is another fine passage grave with engravings.

The sheer number of megaliths in this area makes it impossible to list them all here and the traveller is advised to visit the local S.I. to procure maps.

Location:

Carnac is SW of Rennes and SE of Brest. Take the N 165-E 60, 176 km from Brest to Auray, then SW, 14 km to Carnac on the D 768/D 781.

Bretagne: Carnac. Mané-Kerioned

Colpo Morbihan

Sights:

Larcuste. There are only two cairns (known as Min-Goh-Ru) left here now. The one to the N, Colpo I, has two small dolmens with anterooms, one of which has a large capstone. Colpo II, to the S, has one transeptual dolmen with six small chambers on both sides of the central corridor, 9.70 m long. It has been dated to around 4400 B.C. with a second usage around 3450-2650 B.C. Although pillaged at some time, pottery and carbonized wood has been found in and around the site.

Location:

SW of Rennes and N of Vannes 18 km on D 767 to Colpo. Then SE 1.5 km on a small road to Larcuste. Dolmens are slightly to the N of the village, on a hill.

Commana Finistère
Sight:
Impressive (restored) large gallery grave of Mougau-Bihan, 14 m long and 1.5 m wide has eighteen standing stones and five capstones. The tomb on the inside is decorated with engravings of daggers and with two pairs of superimposed breasts in relief on the second southern standing stone after the entrance.
Location:
W of Rennes. Take the D 785 20 km S of Morlaix then go 5 km W on D 764 to Commana. At the crossroads, turn left (S) and the dolmen is 1 km on the right, just after the village of Mougau-Bihan.

Corseul Côtes-du-Nord
Sights:
Near here stands a ruined octagonal tower of Roman stonework which may represent the Fanum Martis (Temple of Mars). In Corseul in the wall to the right of the church, there is a Roman cippus dedicated to Silicia by her son Januarius.
Location:
NW of Rennes. Leave Dinan to the SW on N 176. Turn right (NW) on D 794 and the tower is on the left after some 4.5 km. Corseul is 2 km beyond on the same road.

Bretagne: Dol de Bretagne. Champ-Dolent

Dol de Bretagne Ille-et-Vilaine
Sight:
At the Champ-Dolent is the impressive menhir, 9.50 m high. It is said to mark the site of a legendary battle in the Field of Pain which ended with a stone falling from heaven (or in some accounts rising from the ground) to separate two warring brothers. It is one of the largest menhirs in Bretagne.
Location:
Dol is N of Rennes, NE of Dinan 35 km on N 176-E 401. Mont Dol is 3 km N and the Pierre du Champ-Dolent lies 2 km to the S. Leave Dol on N 795 and turn left onto the (signposted) road to the menhir.

Essé Ille-et-Vilaine
Sight:
Roche aux Fées (about 3000 B.C.) is an extremely fine megalithic chamber tomb 19.50 m in length and consisting of 42 stones, some of which weigh around 40 tons and were transported over 4 km. A large entrance leads into a corridor which in turn goes into a divided room with a high ceiling. This 'Rock of the Fairies' may not

have been a funerary monument even though it looks like a gallery grave, since nothing to indicate this has been found, nor was it covered over. Young couples come here on the night of a full moon and walk around it in opposite directions counting the stones. According to legend if their tallies coincide, all is well. If not, it may be best to call off the romance!

Location:
Essé is SE of Rennes approx. 28 km. The Roche aux Fées is located 2.5 km SSE of Essé. Take the D 41 SE of Rennes about 20 km. Do not enter Janzé but take the route to the left, just after the town, signposted *Essé*. From here go S on D 341 and the monument is 2.8 km on the right.

La Forêt-Fouesnant Finistère
Sights:
Dolmens at the Cairn de Kerleven. Part of this tumulus was destroyed by the extension of the campground, but two passage graves remain.

Location:
SW of Rennes, on a campground between the beach of Kerleven and the estuary of l'Anse St.-Laurent. Go 15 km SE of Quimper and from La Forêt-Fouesnant a further 3 km to Kerleven. The site is 30 m from the sea.

Fougères Ille-et-Vilaine
Sights:
In the Forêt de Fougères are remains of several megalithic monuments including two damaged dolmens and an alignment.

Location:
Fougères is NE of Rennes 42 km on N 12. The forest is on the D 177 some 8 km N.

Gâvres Morbihan
Sight:
A good example of an angled dolmen is that of Goërem. It has engravings on both sides of the corridor. At the end of the nine-metre passage, a doorway, blocked by a large movable granite stone, leads into a 17-metre-long room at a right angle to the corridor and which is divided into compartments. There are more engravings here. Carbonized wood found in the last compartment has been dated to the end of the fourth millennium B.C. The tomb was used until about 2400 B.C.

Location:
SW of Rennes and 45 km W of Vannes. It is 7.5 km E of Plouhinec in the presqu'île of Gâvres.

Huelgoat Finistère
Sights:
Iron Age Camp d'Artus. The 'camp' was once a Celtic village, later used by the Romans. There are only slight traces of houses and ramparts. Menhir of Kerampeulven.

Location:

W of Rennes, S of Morlaix about 34 km on D 785/D 764. The camp is somewhat complicated to find as it entails about 45 minutes' walk. The S.I. will give details but go out the D 14 and turn right after reaching the top of hill (500 m) onto unpaved road. Drive 200 m to large open space and walk from here. It is signposted.

For the menhir, go 1 km out of town on D 14 toward Morlaix. The menhir is signposted left (W). Follow signs roughly 400 m from turnoff.

Ile Gavr'Inis Morbihan

Sights:

(Island of the Goats.) Late neolithic drystone tumulus, approached by a gallery with exceptional engravings including concentric hoops, chevrons, U-shaped signs, hooks and serpents. It is 50 m in diameter and 8 m high with a long gallery of 11.80 m. There are twenty-three inscribed supports holding up nine capstones. The profuse decorations with spirals, intersecting multiple semicircles and whorled patterns have made this site famous. Flashlight is advised.

Location:

SW of Rennes and SW of Vannes. From Vannes go SW on D 101 continuing on D 316 to Larmor-Baden. The Ile Gavr'Inis, at the mouth of the Gulf of Morbihan, can be reached by boat (15 minutes) from Larmor-Baden. The number of visitors is restricted, so check with S.I. before going.

Laniscat Côtes-du-Nord

Sights:

The shale necropolis of Liscuis consists of three passage graves. Liscuis I, the oldest, is 12 m long and V-shaped with a narrow entrance. An angled slab separates it from the main chamber. There are three capstones. Liscuis II and III are classic gallery graves: Liscuis II is 15 m long with a chamber and anteroom separated by a notched slab. It has been dated to 2500 to 2200 B.C. Liscuis III, 500 m to the S, also a passage grave, is 13 m in length. All three had paved flooring.

Location:

W of Rennes some 134 km to Gouarec. Leave here on D 76, NE 3 km. Turn right (SE) and take the road to Restirou, and after 1.5 km go right.

200 m beyond is a sign: *sentier piétonnier, interdit à tous véhicules* (footpath, forbidden to all vehicles). Follow this 400 m to a small crest and a sign for the dolmens which are a further 100 m.

Lanmeur Finistère

Sights:

Modern church built over sixth-century St.-Mélard crypt. This is one of the oldest religious structures in Bretagne. To visit, ask at the presbytery behind the apse. There is also a menhir nearby.

Location:

NW of Rennes and NE of Morlaix. For the menhir take D 78 and turn left after

2.8 km. After 800 m, turn left again at crossroads and it is 100 m on the right, on private property. Not much to see!

Lannion Côtes-du-Nord

Sights:

The Christianized menhir of St.-Duzec is 8.10 m-high, surmounted by a cross placed there in the seventeenth century. The sculptures on its S face include a cockerel, the Virgin beside a sun and a moon, instruments of the Passion, and a large crucifix. The menhir is 9 km NW of Lannion on the D 21, close to Penvern, and signposted.

Prajou-Menhir is a long, engraved gallery grave with transversal slab. Located 10 km NW of Lannion. From Trébeurden where the D 21 meets D 788, go 500 m toward Ile Grande. Park on left (W) of road, walk about 20 m more and there is the sign Prat-ar Mino-Hir. Walk through field 50 m.

Gallery grave of Pleumeur-Bodou. Continue up the road to Ile Grande about 750 m to where the rue Roi Arthur turns off left. 150 m further on, turn left on to the rue du Dolmen. There is a dolmen 250 m on, on the left of the road, covered by two long slabs of granite.

Dolmen of Kergüntuil. At Trégastel, 10 km NW of Lannion, there is another dolmen with an enormous capstone measuring 5 x 2.50 m. A modern wall helps support it. Leave Lannion on the D 788 and after 2 km take the D 11, left. When the road goes off to Trégastel, stay on D 11 and after 1 km turn right (N) by the farm, Kergüntuil. The dolmen is on the right, 150 m.

At Tréguier the Chapelle St.-Gonéry has a ninth-tenth cent-ury tower. E of Lannion some 18 km on D 786 and the chapel is 7 km on D 8.

Also near here is Kerbors, Men-ar-Romped gallery grave. It is 7.50 m long, with thick granite stones supporting three huge capstones. From Trég-astel go 6 km on D 20 to

Bretagne: Lannion. Prajou-Menhir

Kerbors and leave here on a local road NW of the church. Continue 1.5 km to l'Ile à Poule and take the path 300 m on the NE bank of the estuary. The tomb is on the N side in a small field.

Location:

Lannion is NW of Rennes and NW of Saint-Brieuc near the coast.

Locmariaquer Morbihan

Sights:

In this area are some remarkable megaliths. One of them is the largest known monolith, Mané-Er-Grah or Men Er-Hroëch, a fallen menhir split into four sections with the whole measuring over 20 m and weighing 350 tons. It is near the cemetery just before entering town.

50 m behind this is the Table des Marchands, a long, half-buried dolmen inside which are some engravings that seem to represent an axe, ears of corn and the sun.

Another dolmen, Mané-Lud, has supports decorated with stylized motifs. The large tumulus measures 107 x 54 m and is nearly 6 m high. At the western end of the mound there is a passage grave that has several engraved stones. The corridor is 5 m long. At the east end is a convex arc of six small menhirs. Mané-Lud is N of Locmariaquer 800 m on the D 781, on the left.

Location:
Locmariaquer faces the Gulf of Morbihan and is SW of Rennes and SE of Brest, 13 km E of Carnac on D 781.

Plestin-les-Grèves Côtes-du-Nord
Sight:
A small excavation of the first-century Gallo-Roman Thermes du Hogolo currently under restoration includes the frigidarium and caldarium.
Location:
NW of Rennes and SW of Lannion 18 km on D 786. The site is on the E side of the Plestin peninsula on the border of Côtes-du-Nord and Finistère.

Plouaret Côtes-du-Nord
Sights:
Next to the church is a reputedly Roman sculpture of a horseman trampling a dragon.

N of the town is the eighteenth-century Chapelle des Sept-Saints, with a dolmen forming the crypt.
Location:
NW of Rennes and S of Lannion 20 km on D 11. The Sept-Saints is ca. 6 km NE on D 74.

Ploudalmézeau Finistère
Sight:
L'Ile Carn consists of three dolmens sealed in a round cairn that was damaged in World War II. They each have fairly well conserved anterooms.
Location
NW of Rennes. From Ploudalmézeau go N, the small island is just off the coast, accessible only at low tide. Extreme N of Finistère.

Plouezoch Finistère
Sights:
The 6700-year-old Cairn of Barnenez is a large, restored tumulus consisting of two adjoined stone structures, of which one contains five dolmens and the other six dolmens, i.e., there are about eleven passage graves in two cairns. Several of these are engraved. Legend has it that in earlier times it was the House

of Fairies. The site is one of the principle attractions in Bretagne, but not all the chambers are visitable.

Location:

NW of Rennes Plouezoch is N of Morlaix 8 km on D 76. From here continue on the same road 3 km more and then take the road left toward Saint-Goulven and Barnenez. The site is to the left, at the entrance to the village.

Quiberon Morbihan

Sights:

There are several megaliths in the area including the following:

Dolmen of Roh-An-Aod consists of a passage grave with a large circular chamber and two capstones. Located near St.-Pierre Quiberon. Leave the D 768 going toward Portivy, and the dolmen is in the small hamlet of Roch.

Pors-Guen (Port-Blanc). Damaged passage graves, important because skeletons were found here. Take the D 186 out of St.-Pierre Quiberon and after 500 m turn right toward Portivy. Follow signs for Pors-Guen; 250 m E of a house called *Observatoire*, beside the cliffs, are the vestiges of the two small dolmens.

At St.-Pierre is the Moulin alignment which has five ranges of menhirs covering a distance of nearly 60 m. At the western end, a small path leads 120 m to the remains of the Cromlech of Kerbourgnec.

Conguel. Behind the SNCF vacation colony is the large menhir of Goulvarch, while at the entrance to this colony, 100 m to the S, is the small dolmen of Conguel, but it is hardly visible. There are several other menhirs in town including one facing the Town Hall, and one near Place Hoche. The nearby chapel of St.-Clément has Merovingian tombs.

Just NW of Quiberon, by Kervihan, the Kroh-collé was a Neolithic camp of 3000 B.C. and today there are four arches of vertical small stones left. At Le Manémur to the W, there is a dolmen and two menhirs that have been re-erected. There are also several menhirs along the coast. A gallery grave with a small menhir is located at the point of La Guérite.

Location:

Quiberon is SW of Rennes and 11 km SW of Auray on D 768. S.I. provides good maps of the area.

St.-Brieux Côtes-du-Nord

Sights:

The Camp de Péran, a Carolingian fortress oval in shape, measures some 160 m in diameter. Not a great deal to see today except part of the earthworks.

La Roche Camio is a gallery grave. The interior rectangular chamber measures 15.50 m x 1.30 m, reached by a low, narrow passage. Seven headstones remain in place above the chamber.

Champ Grosset at Quessoy is another gallery grave which is damaged, but similar to La Roche Camio in that both have lateral entries.

Location:

St.-Brieux is on the coast, NW of Rennes. For the Camp de Péran, go SW of St.-Brieux on D 700 some 4 km. The D 27 runs S from St.-Brieux to Plédran, and ca. 2 km before this town turn W on road marked for Ploufragan. Go up road 1.2 km and turn left at sign *Camp*. Follow road through village to site, 1 km.

For Roche Camio, ca. 1.5 km N of Plédran turn E off D 27 at sign: *Ville Folle, Roche Camio*. Follow signs and at T-junction go left 500 m to water treatment centre on left. Follow path into left of water centre ca. 150 m and the gallery grave is in a clump of oak trees to the left of the larger group of trees. From turn-off to water centre is 1.8 km.

Champ Grosset is located 11 km SW of St. Brieux between St.-Carreuc and Quessoy. 1 km before Quessoy turn left (S) for 1.5 km; the dolmen lies on the W edge of a small wood 50 m away.

St.-Guénolé Finistère

Sights:

There are several monuments between Pont l'Abbé and St.-Guénolé. The Musée Préhistorique de Saint-Guénolé houses collections from the Gallo-Roman period and the reconstructed burial sites of Saint-Urnel and Roz-en-Tre-Men. Surrounding the building are some Iron Age steles, menhirs and a reconstructed dolmen of Run-Aour (brought from Plomeur).

The 3000-year-old dolmen at Point de la Torche on the coast has a 15-m corridor with a chamber on each side (in shape of a cross).

There is also a reputed 4000-year-old shell midden from the Mesolithic, but erosion has erased much of this site.

Location:

On the extreme southern end of the Bretagne peninsula, the site is SW of Rennes and SW of Quimper some 34 km on D 785.

St.-Just Ille-et-Vilaine

Sights:

The following are just a few of the many megaliths to be seen in this area. The S.I. will give details of more but there are well marked walking routes pointing out the sites, amongst which are the following:

Alignments de Moulin run for about 400 m and consist of three groups of menhirs in line. Found by leaving St.-Just on D 65 and turning right after 600 m. Continue a further 250 m and the menhirs are on the left.

Another alignment, Demoiselles, is a small one of just thirty-two large stones on the side of a hill off the D 65 but closer to St.-Just. Go a little N of the Moulin group to the first curve in the road. Pass the farm, and 1 km farther on, take the path to the left marked *Point de vue*. After 200 m, turn left. Signposted.

The Demoiselles Roche Piqués alignment on the Lande de Moulin consists of 30 menhirs located to the left of the road just before entering Langon, SE of St.-Just on D 59, then E on D 56.

In Langon itself, is the Chapelle St.-Agathe, housed in a small single-naved Gallo-Roman building. It contains frescos depicting Venus surrounded by fish, thought to have come from the baths of a Roman villa. In the sixth-seventh century, the building was converted into a Christian chapel, originally named Eglise St.-Venus. Two Merovingian sarcophagi are in the church. Close by, on the road from Langon toward Brain-s-Vilaine is a small stretch of Gallo-Roman road beside the river. Signposted.

Château Bû is an oval-shaped tumulus with three menhirs delimiting the structure. Nearby are the dolmens of Tréal and Le Four Sarrazin, passage graves with lateral entrances.

Location:
St.-Just is S of Rennes and NE of Redon approx. 20 km on D 177.

Sarzeau Morbihan
Sights:
Several sites worth seeing in this area include:

Le Net, a long gallery grave 5.5 km from Sarzeau, found by taking the D 780 W. Just after the junction with D 198, the dolmen and a small menhir, covered in brambles, are seen to the left.

Tumiac and Grah-Niohl (see entry for Arzon).

The Menhir de Larguéven, 3.5 km W, Menhir de Corporh 3 km E, and the Dolmen de Lannek Er Men 3.5 km NW.

The fine Menhir de Kermaillard-le-Net, known as 'Scalehir' or 'La Motte de Beurre' (Lump of Butter) is 5 m high and nearly 8 m in circumference. Engraved. Travel 5.5 km past Sarzeau then turn right and pass the village of Kermaillard. Go right again (N) in the direction of Logeo. After the first house, turn right on to a local road; the menhir is on the left.

Location:
Sarzeau is SW of Rennes and S of Vannes on D 780.

There are hundreds of other megalithic monuments in the region of Bretagne and the S.I. in any given town will supply information as to their location. A general list of sites here is given below:

CÔTES DU NORD

Bégard	Pédernec, Kergueuzennec (menhirs)
Cleguerec	Bod-er-Mohed (gallery grave)
Dinan	Roman
Guingamp	10-11th c crypt
Ile Grande	Ile Grande (gallery grave)
Laniscat	Liscuis I, II, III (dolmens, gallery graves)
Louarget	Pergal (menhirs)
Mur de Bretagne	Coët-Correc (angled dolmen)
Penvern	Saint-Duzec (menhir)
Pledran	La Roche-Camio (gallery grave)
Plenée-Jugon	Saint-Mirel (menhirs)
Plesidy	Caillouan (menhir)
Pleslin	Champ des Roches (alignments)
Plevenon	Aiguille de Gargantua (menhir)
Ploeuc-sur-Lie	Bayo (menhir)
Plouaret	Roman, Sept-Saints (chapel on dolmen)
Ploubazlanec	Le Mélus (gallery grave)
Ploufragen	La Couette (gallery grave)
Quesoy	Champ Grosset (gallery grave)
Le Quillo	Notre-Dame-de-Lorette (gallery grave)
Quintin	Plaine-Haute (menhirs)

Rostreuen	Glomel (menhir)
St.-Brieuc	Iron Age fort, (gallery grave)
St.-Michelo-en-Goève	menhir
Saint-Quay-Perros	Crech Quillé (angled dolmen)
Saint-Samson-sur-Rance	La Tremblais (gallery grave)
Trébeurden	Prajou-Menhir (gallery grave)
Trégastel	Kergüntuil (dolmen), (angled dolmen)
Trégon	Ville-Génouhan (gallery grave)
Tréguier	9-10th c tower, Kerbors (Men-ar-Romped) (gallery grave)
Yvias	Tossen-ar-Run (passage grave)

FINISTERE

Beuzec-cap-Sizun	Kerbannalec (gallery grave)
Brennilis	Ty-ar-Boudiged (V-shaped dolmen)
Brignogan-Plage	Men-Marz, Kervezvel, Kervizouarn (menhirs), Diévet (allée couverte) (ruined)
Camaret-sur-Mer	alignments
Commana	Mougau-Bihan (gallery grave)
Daoulas	Rungleo (menhir)
Dirinon	9th-c tomb (?)
La Forêt-Fouesnant	Kerleven (passage graves)
Huelgoat	Iron Age camp, menhir, logan stone
Landéda	Ile Guennoc (3 large cairns, passage graves)
Lanmeur	6th-c crypt, menhir
Léhan	Léchiagat (menhir)
Melgven	Coat-Menez-Guen(Coat-Luzuen), Saint-Antoine, Cadol, Kerambrunou (gallery graves)
Moëlan-sur-Mer	Kerandrèze, Kermeur-Bihan (gallery graves)
Morgat	Rostudel (dolmen), Ty-ar-Churé (alignments)
Penmarch	menhir
Plobannalec	Quélarn (3 passage graves)
Plomeur	Beg-an-Dorchenn, Lestriguiou (passage graves), Kerfland (alignment), Lanvénaël (menhir)
Plouarzel	Kerloas (Kervéatoux) (menhir)
Ploudalmézeau	Ile Carn (passage graves-3 sepulchres)
Plouescat	Kernic (gallery grave), Saint-Eden (menhir)
Plouézoch	Barnenez (passage grave)
Plourin	Kergadiou (menhir)
Plovan	Crugou (dolmen à couloir)
Plozévet	Plozévet Cemetery (menhir)
Pont Aven	Kerangosquer (menhir)
Pont l'Abbé	Centre megalithique includes Le Guirec, Kerdalae, Kerégard Vraz, Kernévez, Pen Loic
Porspoder	Kerenneur (Kerhouézel), Saint-Gonvarch (menhirs)
Poullan-sur-Mer	Lesconil (gallery grave)
Saint-Goazec	Castel-Ruffel (gallery grave)
Saint-Guénolé	museum, Run-Aour (dolmen), mezolithic shell middens

Saint-Po-de-Léon	Kerivin (passage grave)
Treffiagat	Le Ruen (menhir), V de Run (sepulchre)
Tregunc	Kerangallan (menhir)

ILLE ET VILAINE

Bazouges-la-Pérouse	La Pierre de Lande-Ros (menhir)
Dol de Bretagne	prehistoric remains, Champ-Dolent (menhir)
Ernée	La Contrie (gallery graves)
Essé	La Roche aux Fées (Angevin dolmen)
Foujères	centre megalithique, La Pierre du Trésor, La Pierre Courcoulée (ruined dolmens), Rocher-Jacquot (ruined gallery grave), Le Cordon des Druides (alignment)
Langon	Les Demoiselles (alignments)
Médréac	Lampouy (alignments), La Roche Carrée, Le menhir du Chênot (menhirs)
Paimpont	alignments, gallery graves, etc.
St.-Just	megalithic centre, Alignements du Moulin, Les Demoiselles (alignments), Château-Bû (tumulus), Le Four Sarrazin (sepulchre), tumulus, Tertre de la Croix-Saint-Pierre (cromlech), Tréal (passage grave)
Saint-Suliac	Dent de Gargantua (menhir)
Trédion	gallery grave
Tressé	La Maison des Feins (gallery grave)

MORBIHAN

Arzon	Tumiac (carnacéen-type mound), Grah-Niohl, Petit Mont(passage graves), Cromlech de Grah-Niohl (cromlech), menhirs
Auray	Kerivin-Brigitte (dolmen), Roman bridge of Rozo
Belle-Ile	Jean et Jeanne Runelo (menhirs)
Belz	menhirs
Bono	Le Rocher (passage grave)
Campénéac	alignments (destroyed)
La Chapelle-Caro	La Maison trouvée (angevin dolmen)
Colpo	Larcuste (passage graves), tumuli, menhir, gallery graves
Cournon	Les Tablettes (angevin dolmen)
Crach	Luffang, Parc Guren I et II (passage graves)
Elven	Jean et Jeanne Babouin (menhirs)
Er Lannic	menhirs (private)
Erdeven	Kerzerho, Kerascouet (alignments), Ty-er-Mané (dolmen vestiges), menhirs, Mané-Bras (dolmens), Mané-Grah Les Sept-Saints (passage graves)
La Gacilly	Les Roches-Piquées (menhirs), megalithic centre.
Gâvres	Goërem (angled dolmen)
Golfe du Morbihan	megalithic centre, Kergonan (cromlech), Kerno, Roh Vras, Pen-Hap, Pen-Nioul, Nioul, (dolmens), Brouel (alignment)

Ile aux Moines	cromlech, dolmens, aligments
Ile d'Arz	menhirs, dolmen
Ile Gavr'Inis	tumulus, menhirs
Ile Longue	Ile Longue (passage grave)
Kerlegad	Mané Roch (menhir)
Larmor-Baden	Gavrinis (passage grave)
Locmariaquer	Megalithique centre, Table des Marchands, Kercadoret, Saint-Pierre Lopérec, Kerveresse, Mané Rutual (passage graves), Le Grand Menhir Brisé (menhir), Er Grah, Kerlud (tumuli), Les Pierres- Plates (passage grave), Mané-er-Hroeck, Mané-Lud (carnacéen-type mound)
Locoal-Mendon	Centre megalithique, Pierre des Moines, the stele of Prostion from the Iron Age, Christianized stones Wegil Brehed and Goured Brehed, Mané-er-Hloh, Mané-Bras(remains of dolmens), Locqueltas (passage grave)
Malestroit	Saint-Guyomard, Pierre Droite, Menhir des Bois (menhirs), Sournan (ruined dolmen)
Mehand	tumulus
Moustoir-ac	Kermarquer (Mein-Bras) (menhir)
Plaudren	Men-Goarec (gallery graves), Kerallan (ruined dolmen à couloir), La Quenouille de Gargantua (menhir)
Ploemeur	Cruguellic, (passage grave), Courégan, Point du Talut, Kerbenès (menhirs
Plouharnel	tumulus, alignments, Cosquer (Men-er-Roh), Crucuno Rondossec (passage grave), Sainte-Barbe, Vieux-Moulin (alignments) Crucuny (cromlech du Champ de la Croix), Quadrilatère de Crucuno
Ploërmel	menhirs
Plouhinec	Kerzine (alignments)
Pontivy	La Houssaye (menhir)
Quiberon	Conguel (dolmen à couloir), alignments, Goulvarch (menhir)
Saint-Gildas-de-Rhuys	Le Net (gallery grave)
Saint-Jean-Brévelay	Megalithic centre , Le Menhir du Colého, Le Menhir de Kerdramel, Lann Douar, Goh, Menguen- Lanvaux (menhirs), Kerhern Bodunan, Kerjagu, Kerallan (dolmens)
St.-Pierre-Quiberon	Moulin de Saint-Pierre-Quiberon (alignments), Pors-Guen (Port-Blanc) , Le Roch (Roh-An-Aod) (passage graves), stone circle
Sarzeau	Centre Megalithique, Kermaillard, Larguévan, Corporh (menhirs), Lannek er Men (dolmen)
Trédion	Kerfily (La Loge aux Loups) (gallery grave)La
Trinité-sur-Mer	Kermarquer, Kervilor (Mané- Bras) (passage grave)

CARNAC

Kermario	Megalithic ensemble , Lann Mané Kermario (passage grave), alignments, Manio I (tertre tumulaire)
Klud-er-Yer	passage grave
Kercado	passage grave
Kerderff	menhir
Kériaval	passage grave (nearby are ruins of 4 alignments)
Kelescan	Megalithic ensemble , Cromlech Ouest, Tertre tumulaire, Cromlech Nord, Alignments, passage grave
Le Lizo	passage grave
Manê-Kerioned	passage graves
Le Manio	menhir (Manio III ?)
Ménec	ensemble megalithique, Cromlech Ouest, Les Alignments, Cromlech oriental
Le Moustoir	carnacéen-type mound
Petit Ménec	alignments
St.-Michel	carnacéen-type mound

Centre (Orléans)

Cher (18), Eure-et-Loir (28), Indre (36), Indre-et-Loire (37), Loiret (45), Loir-et-Cher (41)

Watered by the Loir, Indre and Eure rivers, this region was once heavily forested but now only scattered woods remain—the result of agricultural deforestation beginning in pre-Roman times around villages and hamlets and their accompanying farms and homesteads. Most archaeological sites are known today only through aerial photography. Place names, however, offer evidence of Celtic origins, for example Châteaudun (Celtic *-dun* "hill, fort") was once a fortified hilltop village above the Loir. Dispersed megalithic structures reveal the presence of other ancient cultures.

Argenton-sur-Creuse Indre

Sights:

In the suburb of St.-Marcel is the on-going excavation of Gallo-Roman Argentomagus. Visible is a sanctuary with two temples, the house of Quinto Sergius Macrinus, a grotto or nymphaeum (the largest currently visible in France), a Roman bridge (originally 110 m with five supports—it collapsed in the floods of the sixteenth century). To the W on a sloping hill facing S and the river is the first-century theatre (which is actually two successively imposed theatres), under restoration. Its diameter was about 60 m and the excavated orchestra, 18 m. It appears to have accommodated about 2500 patrons.

Farther S is the town of La Souterraine, built on the site of a Gallo-Roman Villa Sosterranea. The Church of Notre-Dame-de-l'Assomption has a crypt which leads to what are probably relics of the cella of a Gallo-Roman temple containing classical columns and a well.

Location:

S of Orléans on the river Creuse approx. 100 km E of Poitiers and 30 km SW of Chateauroux on N 20. Signposted.

For La Souterraine take the A 20/N 20 S ca. 20 km to Les 5 Routes, and from here continue on S, 23 km to the town.

Beaugency Loiret

Sights:

The dolmens Pierre du Vert Galand and Pierre Tournant (only a large capstone), lie in a field by some recent graves and a monument from the Franco-Prussian War.

Location:

21 km SW of Orléans on N 152 to Tavers, just SW of Beaugency. From the edge of the village travel 1.4 km to the sign (right): *Dolmens*.

Blois Loir-et-Cher

Sights:

The cathedral of St.-Louis has the tenth-century crypt of St.-Solenne. Dolmens and menhirs are in the vicinity.

Location:

Blois is SW of Orléans approx. 50 km on A 10-E 05-E 60. One of the dolmens is some 7 km NW of Blois beside the D 957. It has three large capstones and seven standing stones, all very weathered. Just W of the turnoff (right) to Siany, go left on the Chemin du Dolmen. It is visible from the D 957.

After the dolmen, go E off the D 954, 3.5 km to Averdon and from there after 600 m take the road to Villiers. Pass road going toward Marolles and take the next right, *Chemin de la Grande Pierre*. Follow it ca. 1.2 km and there is a small menhir on the right, very weatherbeaten.

Return to Villiers and take the road to Marolles. The Grande Pierre is signposted in the village. Drive down unpaved road to end of the wall on the right. A plan of the Reserve Naturelle de la Vallée de la Grande Pierre et de Vitain is here. There have been many finds, in this area, of flint tools, utensils, and pottery attesting to a fairly intense occupation from the Neolithic onward. A good hour's walk through the reserve.

Bourges Cher
Sights:
The fourth-century Gallo-Roman ramparts are visible in various parts of the city, notably near the cathedral. They date from the same era as those of Tours and Orléans, and were originally 3-m thick with some fifty towers extending over 25 hectares. Gallo-Roman foundations are also visible at the Château of Jacques Coeur, on the west side.

There is reputedly a Gallo-Roman well in town, beside the main bridge, but S.I. permission is needed to visit it.

One of the crypts in the cathedral of St.-Etienne is a Carolingian vestige of the ninth-century church.

A Roman road, the Levée de César, is said to run parallel to the N 151 going S to St. Florent-sur-Cher 20 km SW on N 151 where there are remains of a Roman bridge. There are also said to be Roman roads to the NE on the Chemin de Turley (the old road to Sancerre) and to the SE, the Chemin de Blet. None of these roads is now visible however.

Location:
Bourges is 104 km S of Orléans on the A 71-E 09.

Bruyère-Allichamps Cher
Sights:
Bruyère is the centre of France, indicated by an inscribed third-century Roman boundary stone set in the middle of the village at the crossroads of the N 144 and the D 92.

Several fourth-century sarcophagi and part of a Roman road lie alongside the Prieuré d'Allichamps, built on the site of a Gallo-Roman villa. Inside are more tombs, separated by the church wall.

Location:
S of Orléans, go S of Bourges on the A 17-E 11 to exit #8 for St.-Amand-Montrond. From here take the N 144, 8 km NW to Bruyère-Allichamps. The priory can be found by following the signs to the campground and then continuing 1 km beyond on the same road.

Cinq-Mars-La-Pile Indre-et-Loire
Sight:
Second-century Gallo-Roman tower, or pile, a mausoleum (although the function of these towers is much disputed), 30 m high surmounted by four small pyramids. It lies a little E of the town.

Location:
SW of Orléans and 14 km SW of Tours on N 15-E 60.

Drevant Cher
Sights:
At Roman Derventum, founded in the first century, are the partially reconstructed remains of a Roman theatre-amphitheatre with an almost circular cavea. This was built on an earlier Celtic sanctuary. Visible are some columns and enclosures for wild beasts and a wall, 3 m high, built to protect the

spectators. The original seating capacity is estimated at 2500. In the fifth and sixth centuries, the Merovingians used it as a fort after it had been pillaged by the Visigoths. The forum and baths were watered by two aqueducts coming mainly from Fontaine de Meslon. The baths have been excavated but were re-covered and lie under the local school.

The wooden temple or fanum constructed by the Celts was later rebuilt by Romans in stone. Slight remains of lodgings for high-class citizens who visited the sanctuary are also to be seen. The forum, which is 200 m from the theatre, was surrounded by galleries containing merchants' stalls.

Location:
S of Orléans, go S of Bourges 44 km on the A 17-E 11 to exit #8. Drevant is less than 3 km SE of Saint Amand-Montrond on the D 97, signposted for Montluçon.

Germigny-des-Près
Loiret
Sights:
A squat little Byzantine church (restored in the nineteenth century) was built in 806 by Theodulfus, Bishop of Orléans and friend of Charlemagne. It contains a ninth-century mosaic in the E apse, the Oratoire Carolingian, consisting of 130,000 cubes of coloured glass depicting the Arc of the Covenant surrounded by angels, the only known work of the school of Ravenna in France. It also contains horseshoe arches, a development of the Visigoths.

Centre: Germigny-des-Près

Location:
SE of Orléans some 32 km on the N 60-E 60/D 952. The town is about 5 km NW of Saint-Benoît-sur-Loire.

Graçay Indre
Sights:
Dolmen with four standing stones and a large capstone. The passage has disappeared and the chamber is fairly filled in with dirt. Three of the support stones are askew. There is a seat beside it for those wishing to relax and contemplate at this pleasant spot.

Location:
S of Orléans and SW of Vierzon 15 km on the D 63. 7 km NW on the D 922, turn left at sign for Bagneux. Turn left again, just before bridge over the river and there is a sign *Bué, le dolmen.* The dolmen is visible in the woods, on the right, after 1 km. Signposted.

Langeais Indre-et-Loire
Sights:
The château, originally a stronghold of Foulques Nerra, Count of Anjou (known as the Black Falcon), shows the ruins of the keep of ca. 984, one of the oldest extant in France. It surmounts the ridge separating the Loire from the valley of the Roumer.

The church of St.-Jean Baptiste has a tenth-century crypt.
Location:
SW of Orléans and W of Tours 24 km on the N 52-E 60.

Mettray Indre-et-Loire
Sight:
Nearby is the spectacular dolmen Grotte aux Fées with three enormous capstones of 40-60 tons and large standing stones. It is 10 m long and 3 m high.
Location:
SW of Orléans and N of Tours some 6 km on N 138-E 502, then NE to Mettray on D 76. Go through town toward St.-Antoine-de-Rocher; the dolmen is ca. 1 km, signposted right, with a large information sign.

Moulins-Sur-Céphons Indre
Sights:
Iron Age Gallic village excavated in Levroux and subsequently reconstructed here to depict a fortified gate, house, workshops, and a granary along with objects of every day living. There is also a motte beside the Mairie.

Close by lies a dolmen with two large capstones, one supported by three standing stones, the other capstone has collapsed into the recess among four standing stones.
Location:
S of Orléans and NW of Châteauroux approx. 21 km on D 956 to Levroux then 6 km NW on the D 8. For the dolmen, take the D 23 SW of Moulins and go 1.5 km. A sign, *La Pierre*, is on the left. Turn in by farm and follow signs 300 m. The dolmen is on the left.

Orléans Loiret
Sights:
The cathedral of Ste.-Croix has foundations of three previous buildings which may be seen in the crypt. Further E is the Lycée St.-Euverte, built over the tenth-eleventh century crypt of St.-Avit, to the right of which is the former bishop's palace with vestiges of fourth-century Gallo-Roman walls in the garden.

In the suburbs on N 152, 5 km SW along the river, is La Chapelle-St.-Mesmim, with a Merovingian grotto. To gain entry, ask at the Mairie for a key.
Location:
Orléans is S of Paris about 121 km on the A 10-E 05.

Paulnay Indre

Sights:

Excavations here have revealed the remnants of a seventh-century church and a Merovingian necropolis.

Location:

SW of Orléans and NW of Châteauroux 25 km on N 143 to Buzançais, then 19 km SW on the D 926 to Mézières and another 6 km NW on the D 925 to Paulnay.

St.-Maure-de-Touraine Indres-et-Loire

Sights:

S of town, off the RN 10, are two megaliths: the menhir La Pierre Percée has a hole in it and is one of the tallest in the region. It is said that human victims were sacrificed, and their heads cut off and passed through the hole. This is also known as the Menhir des Arabes and popular tradition says there was a Moorish (Saracen) cemetery here. Nearby is the Dolmen des Bommiers, a heavily-weathered tomb with a large capstone supported by three standing stones.

Location:

St.-Maure-de-Touraine is located SW of Orléans and S of Tours 31 km on the N 10. For the menhir, head S of town on RN 10. After 3.5 km, turn right (W) at sign (opposite restaurant La Pierre Percée) and continue 700 m to menhir. For the dolmen, keep on the same small road past the first menhir, and just before the road passes under the motorway, turn right, going back toward Ste.-Maure to a village where the road splits. Go left here. Just beyond the houses is a sign (right): *Dolmen des Bommiers*, at the end of the path, to the left of a farm.

Sceaux de Gâtinais Loiret

Sight:

Ville Antique d'Aquis Segeste. Remains of a large Gallo-Roman town including a courtyard bordered by a colonnaded gallery, and vestiges of a pool which received water from a sacred source, hence the name *aquae* "water," *segeta* (name of a divinity). At the end of the courtyard was a temple.

Location:

E of Orléans and SW of Château Landon. From Orléans take the N 60-E 60, E ca. 47 km to Landon. From here go N on D 118, 9 km to Corbeilles, then follow signs to Sceaux and continue to next village of La Rivière. The site is signposted throughout and easy to find. To enter, permission is needed from the local Mairie; however it is clearly visible through the fence.

Suèvres Loir-et-Cher

Sights:

The earliest part of the church of St.-Christophe is seventh century with Merovingian motifs.

The eleventh-century church of St.-Lubin was built with materials from a pagan temple, and on a sacred site, the Roman Cosmis Lucan having also built a temple here dedicated to Apollo. One of the extant marble columns comes from the Roman temple and has acanthus leaves on the capital. In the sacristy are two engraved Roman stones and one said to be of Druid origin, which are visible in the enclosure beside the church. To see St.-Lubin, go to the S.I. or ask at the house beside the church.

Location:
SW of Orléans and NE of Blois ca. 12 km on the N 152.

Centre: Thésée-la-Romaine

Thésée-la-Romaine
Loir-et-Cher
Sights:
Ancient Tasciaca. Ruins of this vast second-century Gallo-Roman monument which was a stage on the Roman road from Bourges to Tours, are at Les Mazelles. To be seen are large walls which are fairly intact, a room 40 x 14.70 m, pottery workshops and ovens, vestiges of a sanctuary. This may once have served as an administrative, judicial and commercial establishment.

Location:
SW of Orléans and S of Blois, Thésée is reached by taking the D 764, 34 km to Montrichard, then the D 176 E ca. 10 km. Signposted.

Centre: Azay-le-Rideau. St.-Symphorien

Tours Indre-et-Loire
Sights:
Behind the cathedral are some Gallo-Roman vestiges, and the archbishop's palace is partly built onto the Gallo-Roman wall. Remains can also be seen at #11 Rue Blanqui or on application at #4 Rue des Ursulins where there is a defensive tower known as Petit Cupidon, and its gate. In Place St.-Pierre-le-Puellier, amidst the gardens, excavations have revealed a first-century Gallo-Roman public building, as well as a late Medieval necropolis.

At nearby Larçay are reputed remains of a Gallo-Roman fort and there are some vestiges of a Roman aqueduct signposted from Luynes which is ca. 10 km W of Tours on the N 152.

Location:
Tours is on the A 10-E 05 SW of Orléans. Larçay is 4 km E on the N 76-E 604.

Other sights in the area include **Azay-le-Rideau**. The façade of the Church of St.-Symphorien incorporates reliefs which are reputedly from the fifth and sixth centuries. SW of Orléans and 23 km S of Tours on the D 751. **Briare**. At the Château Pont-Chevron, there are second-century Gallo-Roman mosaics. SE of Orléans 20 km on the N 60-E 60 to Châteauneuf then ca. 48 km on the D 952 to Briare. The site is N of Briare some 7 km on the N 7, then E ca. 2 km on D 122. **Chartres**. In the crypt of St.-Lubin which is entered on the S side of the cathedral, the base of a circular column backs onto a clearly visible Gallo-Roman wall. In the Chapelle St.-Martin is the sixth-century tomb of St.-Calétric. Chartres is NW of Orléans and SW of Paris. **Châteauroux**. The Church of St.-Etienne at Déols has a Gallo-Roman crypt with the tomb of St.-Ludre, a third-century sarcophagus, and one of his father Leocade, the senator and founder of Déols. Déols is a suburb of Châteauroux which lies S of Orléans. **Landes-le-Gaulois**. Dolmen de Bouges. SW of Orléans and NW of Blois on the D 68. The dolmen is located just NE of Landes on the D 26 to the left of the road. **Levroux**. Excavations in process reveal traces of a Gallo-Roman theatre and several villas. S of Orléans and NW of Châteauroux 21 km on D 956. **Tripleville**. Various megalithic monuments include the Menhirs de la Nivardière. Near Ouzouer-le-Marché is a 3.5 m sculptured menhir. W of Orléans ca 23 km on the N 157 to Ouzouer, then N, 6 km on D 25. The monument is found on the right (E) on entering the village.

Champagne-Ardenne

(Châlons-en-Champagne, previously Châlons-sur-Marne) Ardennes (08), Aube (10), Marne (51), Haute-Marne (52)

Since early times, the region has been a gateway to France, a continuation of the great plains of Asia and Central Europe. It lies on the crossroads from east to west between Lorraine and the Ile de France, bounded on the north by Belgium and on the south by Bourgogne. The name derives from Latin *compania* meaning an expanse of open country. This region has seen many brutal invasions and battles from Attila the Hun to Hitler. The last invaders were German Panzer divisions in 1940.

Tools of Paleolithic times in the valley of the Marne and Neolithic dolmens, menhirs and polissoirs along the edge of the the forest are clear reminders of early humans.

The people of the Urnfield Culture passed this way, as did the Celts; the Romans constructed towns such as Reims and also villas in the area but they were often destroyed by the barbarian invaders. Impressive monuments to the Gallo-Roman period still remain, however, such as the Porte de Mars of Reims.

Andilly Haute-Marne
Sights:

Excavation of first-century Gallo-Roman villa with two separate sections organized around a peristyle courtyard includes hot, cold and tepid baths, the luxury residence of the owner, fishpond, servants' quarters, and artisanal workshops along with a separate agricultural quarter. Abandoned in the fourth century, it was taken over by Merovingians who had a necropolis here in the fifth century. Good site.

Champagne-Ardenne: Andilly.
Gallo-Roman Villa

Location:

SE of Châlons and N of Dijon 54 km on N 74 to Langres. From here take the D 74 NE, 8 km and after crossing the Reservoir de Charmes go E on the D 3 ca. 10 km to Andilly. Signposted.

La Cheppe Marne
Sight:

So-called Attila's Camp. Signposted in La Cheppe and on RD 394. A Gallic fortified encampment or oppidum of first century, B.C. An important site for the Gallic tribe known as the Catalauni and one of the best preserved in NE Gaul. It stands on the right bank of the river Noblette, a tributary of the Vesle. According to legend, this was the site of the Champs Catalauniques battle against the Huns in 451. The interior measures 22 hectares, the rampart is 4.2-5 m high, depth of the moat is 8-10 m and the circumference is 1785 m.

Location:

NE of Châlons 12 km on RD 977, then E on RD 994 ca. 4 km to La Cheppe. Signposted just before and also in the village. Field is now used for farming and football.

Faverolles Haute-Marne
Sights:

Remains of a grand Gallo-Roman mausoleum discovered in 1980. Unfortunately the structure, which is composed of large blocks of stone, served as a quarry in the Middle Ages, but enough remains to estimate its height in three levels at over 20 m. The square base is about 8 m per side. The site is currently being prepared for visitors and there are plans to rebuild the mausoleum. There is also part of a Roman road nearby. Finds from the mausoleum are in the atelier in town.

Location:

SE of Châlons and N of Dijon 54 km on the N 74 to Langres. Then N on N 19 and after 9 km turn left (W) onto the D 254, 7.4 km to Villiers. Go left again on D 143 ca. 5.7 km to Faverolles. The site is signposted. Excavation is 1.7 km on the route to Mongessey. Turn right onto the path by the sign and go ca. 300 m. Roman road is signposted by the site. Path can be muddy.

Isle-Aumont Aube
Sight:
On the hillock was once a thriving Merovingian and Carolingian monastery, one of the first in Gaul. Around it was a cemetery containing some 600 sarcophagi. The monastery appears to be have been destroyed in the ninth century by the Vikings. The twelfth-century church, Eglise-St.-Pierre, was constructed on top of a succession of buildings from the fifth to the ninth century. Along the aisles and walls are sarcophagi from the Merovingian cemetery excavated here, but now covered over. A piece of a sarcophagus embedded in a wall has the inscription *CHALDUALDAS*, the name of a Germanic chief. Pilgrims to Santiago de Compostela stayed at the abbey and there are shells (their symbol) carved into the wall. A complete Merovingian sarcophagus lies under the floor of the church, and can be seen by removal of stones (with permission).
Location:
S of Châlons and just S of Troyes on the N 71 approx. 5 km and after crossing the motorway E 511, turn right (SW) on the D 66 to Isle-Aumont.

Langres Haute Marne
Sights:
A first-second century Gallo-Roman town gate (walled up) was one of the four earlier entrances to Langres, serving as a watch tower in the Middle Ages. Remains of the 4 km, third-century ramparts which surround this old fortified town are still visible.
Location:
SE of Châlons and N of Dijon 63 km on the N 74.

Marcilly-le-Hayer Aube
Sights:
This is an area rich in sights:

Dolmen de Vamprin, with three standing stones and capstone but no corridor, is located behind the campground. Go along wheatfield and turn right.

For the Dolmen des Blancs Fossés continue past the Dolmen de Vamprin 700 m (on left).

To find the Dolmen de Bercenay, go W of Marcilly toward Bercenay, at 1.5 km dolmen is on the right.

Merovingian stone coffins lie outside the church in the village.

Other sites in the vicinity of Marcilly are: the Menhir de la Pierre au Coq and a polissoir beside it with seven grooves for polishing flint tools. Go to Trancault, 5.5 km beyond Bercenay on the D 374. Continue 1.4 km beyond the village on the D 374; just beyond the silo on the left are the remains.

At St.-Maurice-aux-Riches-Hommes is the Dolmen de Lancy with a menhir beside it. From Trancault go 3 km on the D 19, then take the D 25 toward Thorigny. 2.8 km from the edge of town is a small sign on the left: *Dolmen 700 m*. Go down small, rutted path 300 m to T-junction of forestry road. Walk straight across and up path in forest ca. 400 m to dolmen and menhir in a clearing on the left. Two standing stones and capstone. The menhir is crude and unelaborated (like most in this region).

Continuing, take the D 110 forestry road (at T-junction) to the right to La Chaume, and on the way to La Charmée, just before km stone #5, opposite the forest building offices on the right, is a path, left, leading to the Polissoir de Lancy.

1.9 km further down the D 110 is a small sign, left: *Les 3 Polissoirs de la Pierre-à-l'eau.* Take a 600 m-walk down the forestry road, then turn and go right, into the woods. Three polissoirs lie close together (30-40 m apart). There are many others in the forest, but a large number have been lost with the building of the autoroute.

Location:
Marcilly is SW of Châlons and W of Troyes. Go 28 km on the N 60-E 11 to Villemaur-s-Vanne, then right (N) 15 km on the D 374. All sights above have been directed from here and most are signposted.

Reims Marne
Sights:
An important city in Roman Gaul. Here Clovis was baptized by St.-Rémy in 496 and many kings of France were subsequently crowned here. In old Reims are a number of Gallo-Roman remains.

In the Place du Forum (site of the Roman forum) there is a vaulted second-third century cryptoporticus. To visit, apply to the adjacent Musée Le Vergeur. (This is one of only four known cryptoportici in France, the others being at Arles, Bavay, and Narbonne.)

Champagne-Ardenne: Reims. Porte Mars. (Courtesy Bryan Pryce)

The Roman triumphal arch, the Porte Mars, erected in about 200, was the largest arch in the Roman Empire. It marks the N entrance to the city. Carvings on it include the months of the year, and under the side arches are Jupiter and Leda, and Romulus and Remus suckled by the wolf.

Enclosed in the central doorway of the Basilica of St.-Rémi are some Gallo-Roman columns.

Currently there are excavations beside the cathedral revealing fourth-century Roman public baths, a fifth-century baptistry and a ninth-century church and cloister. There are plans to make these available to the public.

In many of the Champagne caves (and included in their tours) are the remains of Gallo-Roman quarries with several km of galleries.

Location:
Reims is NW of Châlons 34 km on the A 4-E 50.

St.-Quentin-le-Verger Marne
Sight:
Well cared-for dolmen of four upright stones and capstone. No corridor.

Location:

SW of Châlons and S of Sezanne on the RD 373 to 2.5 km S of Queudes. Turn right (W) and follow signs for St.-Quentin-le-Verger. From here take the D 350 W toward Fontaine-Denis 1.8 km. Dolmen is on the left opposite milestone #8 on the right.

Other sights in the area include: **BOURBONNE-LES-BAINS**. On the right bank of the river Borne, in the Parc du casino, are Gallo-Roman remains. SE of Châlons and S of Neufchâteau. Take the A 31-E 21 S toward Dijon and exit at #8, Montigny-le-roi. Follow the D 417 E ca. 19 km to the town. **CONGY**. Remains of a menhir, one large standing stone easily seen from the road. Another is reputed to be to the E of the D 9 between Aulnay-aux-Planches and Fère-Champenoise. Congy is SW of Châlons. Folow RD 33 40 km to Etoges, then go left (SW) 3.5 km on D 343. The menhir is ca. 70 m off the road. To reach Aulnay, go SW of Châlons on RD 33, 29 km to Bergeres-les-Vertus, then left (S) on D 9. **MOUZON**. Gallo-Roman sanctuary of Flavier. Slight remains of three rectangular foundations of three temples dating from 50 B.C. to A.D. 350. NE of Châlons and E of Charleville-Mézières. It is 7 km SW of Carignan (near the Belgian border). From Mouzon take the road E toward Stenay and go 4 km. Signposted at entry to forest. Little to see. **LA SAULSOTTE**. Menhir de la Pierre Aiguë. Triangular-shaped weatherbeaten stone ca. 2 m high. SW of Châlons and SW of Sezanne ca. 30 km on RD 51 to La Saulsotte. Turn right into village and pass through on road to Resson 1.5 km. The menhir is signposted here. At T-junction go right up hill on badly rutted farm track. From sign in village to menhir is 800 m. Not the usual menhir shape!

Franche-Comté (Besançon)
Doubs (25), Jura (39), Haute-Saône (70), Ter. de Belfort (90)

This frontier region extending along the Jura Mountains and bordering Switzerland has yielded artifacts from the Paleolithic and Neolithic periods but not until Roman times did the area begin to prosper as indicated by trade items of Mediterranean provenance. Vestiges of Roman imperial architecture in the region are relatively rare but there are some remains in the capital, Besançon, an important site in Gallo-Roman times. The area was severely overrun by barbarian tribes in later centuries. The region is still little-known archaeologically.

Besançon Doubs
Sights:

Near the cathedral in the Grande Rue, is the 10-m high, second-century Porte Noire. Well-preserved with abundant sculptures, it has a double row of columns. In the Place Archéologique nearby are what were originally thought to be the remains (now being questioned) of an ancient theatre and cistern and eight re-erected Corinthian columns marking the site of a reservoir.

Close to the far end of the Pont de Battant are the remains of a Roman bridge, originally with five arches.

Franche-Comté: Besançon. Porte Noire

Les Arènes. There are a few vestiges of a first-century building in the courtyard of the Lycée Condé at 3, Place Marulaz and on the rue Marulaz.

Location:
Besançon is located SE of Paris, E of Dijon and NE of Beaune 101 km on the A 36-E 60.

Jonvelle Haute-Saône
Sight:

A second-century Gallo-Roman villa was discovered here in 1968 but there is little to see of the excavation. Inside, under cover, are the hypocaust and baths (hot, cold and tepid) and there is a fine mosaic on the floor of the tepidarium, depicting fish and flowers.

Location:
SE of Châlons, E of Chaumont and S of Neufchâteau. Going S on the A 31-E 21 motorway, take exit #8 at Montigny-le-Roi following the D 417 E ca. 35 km to the town. Signposted on D 417 and in town. The site is 1.6 km from town on the D 417.

Mandeure Doubs
Sight:

Roman theatre of Epamantadurum, built at the end of the first century, with a seating capacity of about 14,000. Abandoned at the end of the second century, it was a ruin by the fourth. Blocks of stone were removed and re-used to build a defensive castrum beside the Doubs river. The theatre has been partially excavated and partially restored. It appears to have had four tiers of arcades bordered by galleries accessible from internal corridors.

Location:
NE of Besançon 80 km, and about 13 km W of the Swiss border, just 8 km S of Montbéliard. The site stands on both banks of the Doubs River. Signposted in town.

Marigny Jura
Sight:

At Lac de Chelain there are excavations currently not open to the public. There are, however, reconstructions of two dwellings on pilings from the Neolithic period of 4000-2000 B.C. and an exposition in the village where a conducted tour of the reconstructed site may be arranged. It is thought to have been a village of ten-fifteen houses, each with room for six-eight people.

Location:

S of Besançon ca. 59 km on N 83 to Poligny, then SE, 12 km on N 5 to Montrond. From there go S, 11 km on D 23 to Pont de Navoy and continue S, 10 km more on D 27 to Marigny. The reconstructed site is signposted.

Villards-d'Héria Jura
Sight:

Here, remnants of temples, thermal establishments with two pools, sacred fountains, and the Pont des Arches (remains of an aqueduct) are all that exist today of a Gallo-Roman town known as Ville d'Antre.

Location:

S of Besançon and SE of Lons-le-Saunier 20 km on the D 52 to Orgelet, then 21 km SE on D 470. It is in the Parc du Haut Jura. The excavation is signposted in the upper part of the village.

Other sights in the area include: ANNEGRAY. Sarcophagi, carved in the solid rock. N of Besançon and 18 km E of Luxeuil-les-Bains. Take D 6 NE to Faucogney-et-la-Mer, then S on D 73 ca. 2 km to Annegray. LUXEUIL-LES-BAINS. There are slight remnants of Roman baths at the Etablissement de Luxe, beside the pool. They can be seen through glass windows from the outside. N of Bescançon, W of Mulhouse, and N of Vesoul 28 km on the N 57-E 23.

Ile de France (Paris)

Essonne (91), Hauts-de-Seine 92), Seine-et-Marne (77), Seine-St.-Denis (93), Val-de-Marne (94), Val-d'Oise (95), Ville de Paris (75), Yvelines (78)

The region represents the heartland of France and the central crossroads of the country. It is drained by the rivers Seine and Marne, and contains Paris, the capital of France. The first inhabitants appeared some 400,000 years ago and hunted elephants and perhaps hippos on what was then a vast savanna, later transformed into forest land as the climate changed. Their camps have been discovered along the Seine and its tributaries. In the fifth millennium B.C., the animal skin tents of their predecessors gave way to wooden buildings of Neolithic farmers, and individual burials were replaced by collective tombs of the family or clan. Celts of the Hallstatt period moved into the area about 900 B.C. and in the fourth century B.C., another wave of Celts of La Tène culture settled in the region, taking up residence in Lutèce (Paris) where they remained until the Roman conquest.

The Romans converted the village into a town with the usual Roman monuments: theatre, amphitheatre, baths and so on. Christianity reached the area around the middle of the third century A.D., when Bishop Denis came and established a church. In the third century also, the Germanic invasions began. Not until the tenth century did the name Ile de France come into usage.

Bonnières-sur-Seine Yvelines
Sight:
Neolithic multiple grave housed in the Centre Louis Jouvet on the main street in town. The grave, discovered in 1950, contains numerous bones in situ. Interesting site.
Location:
W of Paris on the E 05-A 13. Take exit for Bonnières, which is 10 km E of Vernon on the N 15. Ask to see the grave.

Jouarre Seine-et-Marne
Sights:
Behind the parish church is the Musée Briard built over two Merovingian crypts. That of St.-Paul has two rows of three Gallo-Roman columns. There is also a Merovingian wall with a mosaic of geometric design near the entrance. The second crypt of St.-Ebrégésile, with Merovingian capitals, is just beyond, constructed between the walls. It contains the tomb of a local bishop and others.
Location:
E of Paris 33 km on N 3, then S, 3 km on D 402.

Paris Ville de Paris
Sights:
Under Notre Dame, excavations have revealed third-century Gallo-Roman rooms with hypocaust, columns, and tiles, and the foundations of the sixth-century Merovingian church of St.-Etienne. Explanatory signs give details of each sector of the remains. To visit these, go to Crypte Archéologique in the Place du Parvis-Notre Dame on the S side of the Hôtel Dieu.

N of the Sorbonne, by the Hôtel de Cluny at the intersection of the Blvd St.-Michel and the Blvd St.-Germaine, the Musée de Cluny extends into the ruins of the Gallo-Roman baths (facing Blvd. St.-Michel), including a vaulted frigidarium 15 m high. In addition there is the Autel des Nautes, a monument dedicated by boatmen to Jupiter. Remains of an amphitheatre, Les Arènes de Lutèce (49 rue Monge) are situated at the intersection of the rue Monge and rue des Arènes. The structure underwent several changes between the first and third century. Restored in 1917-18, it is now used as a soccer field, for *boules* (bowls) and for dramatic and musical festivals. It is located near the metro station.

In the church of St.-Pierre-de-Montmartre, beside Sacre Coeur, are two columns, possibly from the Roman temple to Mercury originally on this site.
Location:
All sites found in town.

St.-Martin-du-Tertre Val de Oise
Sights:
The gallery grave Pierre Turquaise has two large and one smaller capstone still in place. Two others are lying askew. The passageway is pretty much intact.

There is a second grave nearby under excavation and reputedly a third at l'Isle d'Adam.

Ile de France: La Roche Guyon.
Tenth-century Keep

Location:

Go N of Paris on the N 1 to Moisselles (ca. 7 km), then take D 909 NE approx. 5 km, turning left on the D 85 to St.-Martin. The dolmen, signposted, is in the forest of Carnelle, slightly S of the village. From the edge of the village go 3 km and turn left down a forestry road with a sign saying, *Parking*. From parking lot pass by auto barrier and walk about 2 km on the paved road (signposted: *R.F. de Francoville*). Follow this road until you reach another barrier and a map of the forest on your left. The Pierre Turquaise is just behind in a fenced area. A pleasant walk.

Other sights in the area include :

ETAMPES. Notre Dame du Fort, beneath the NE chapel is a Merovingian crypt. S of Paris on the N 20 and 44 km W of Fontainebleau on the D 837. LA ROCHE GUYON. Château of the La Rochefoucauld family. The keep was built in the tenth century by Baron Guy. NW of Paris 28 km on N 190 (or take Exit 11 off the E 05-A 13). Then turn N for ca. 9 km on the D 147 to Vertheuil and go W on the D 913 6 km. ST.-ARNOULT. Church with a crypt from the sixth century. W of Paris on the D 988 toward Chartres. ST.-DENIS. In the crypt of the basilica are remnants of a Carolingian wall and necropolis with several sarcophagi including the sixth-century tomb of Princess Arégonde, the wife of the Merovingian, Clothar I.

Languedoc-Roussillon (Montpellier)

Aude (11), Gard (30), Hérault (34), Lozère (48), Pyrénées-Orientales (66)

With its gentle Mediterranean climate, the region extends along the southern coast from the Rhône River to the Pyrenean mountains, its capital at Montpellier. From the area come the oldest human remains (Tautavel of 400,000 years ago) yet found in France. Numerous bones and artifacts from the Middle Paleolithic attest to the presence of Neanderthal man, and later cave art and more sophisticated tools signal the advent of Homo sapiens in the region. Celts, Iberians, Greeks and Phoenicians all left traces of their cultures: the Greeks founded a colony at present-day Marseille in the seventh century B.C., and traded along the coast and inland with the indigenous tribes. Other Greek sites along the coast were at Port-Vendres, Saint-Giles, the ancient Agathe, now Agde, and Citium, now Sète. Iberian tribes inhabited the area in pre-Roman times and have left inscriptions in some places. Extant Roman architecture at Nîmes and the Pont du Gard, nearby, is the finest found anywhere in the country.

Many dolmens and oppida are listed in the brochures on Hérault but most are on private property, or difficult to find. Frequently there is nothing left to be seen at the site. (The authors spent many fruitless days chasing down such sites listed in these tourist books.)

Beaucaire Gard

Sights:

On La Redoute, a hill on the N side of town where the castle is situated, there are Gallo-Roman excavations along with a small museum in situ. On the S side of this hill are seven semi-circular buttresses 3-4 m high. It is thought that they may have supported part of a temple.

Beaucaire advertises the best-preserved stretch of Roman road, along with four groups of military stones. Near the Marronniers cemetery, at the Rouanesse crossroad are two milestones on the edge of the Jardin d'Ugernum. A large double tomb marks the spot.

Further on, 5 km on the D 38 toward Bellegarde, is the Mas Gallo-Romain des Tourelles, a former Gallo-Roman villa with workshops and a pottery kiln for making amphora, and a reconstructed, operational wine cellar. From here you can walk to the Via Domitia and see three milestones (known as Caesar's Columns) in situ.

In the area is the Abbaye de St.-Roman, where excavations have revealed the troglodyte abbey dating from the fifth century. Carved into the limestone are arches, an Abbot's seat, monks' cells, and rock-cut tombs. A splendid view complements the visit.

The museum here displays the reconstructed remains of a mausoleum, along with some of its decorative sculpture.

Location:

Beaucaire is NE of Montpellier and E of Nîmes 24 km on the D 999. The milestones near the Villa des Tourelles can be a little difficult to find. The abbey is reached by heading NW of Beaucaire on the D 999 and at the sign, turning off onto a small uphill road. After reaching the parking lot for the abbey, continue on foot for approximately half an hour. Signposted.

Languedoc-Roussillon:
Béziers. Ensérune

Béziers Hérault

Sights:

Near the Musée du Biterrois in Place St.-Jacques are slight vestiges of a Roman arena currently being excavated, However it looks as if it will be a long time before it is open to the public as there are still houses built right into the seating area. In the crypt of the Basilique St.-Aphrodise is a carved fourth-fifth century sarcophagus that serves as a lintel, and a carved tomb of the saint which serves as a font. The W wall in the church of La Madeleine has traces of a Roman rampart. Ask at S.I. for maps and more information.

The Oppidum of Ensérune, an Ibero-Greek settlement of the fourth and third century, B.C. (although the earliest evidence of permanent occupation here dates from the sixth century B.C.) lies on the crest of a ridge some 100 m above the coastal plain. The excavations show three phases of settlement and the remains of a silo terrace consisting of pits cut into the side of the hill along with channels. In addition there are some apse-shaped cisterns, remains of terraced, one-room houses, columns, a fortified wall, and evidence of a once-paved road. Iberian inscriptions (written in a Graeco-Phoenician script) have been found here. Museum in situ.

At Colombiers, nearby, in the rebuilt fifth-century church, is a Visigothic altar of the sixth-seventh century, and a Merovingian sarcophagus of the fifth-sixth century. Broken sarcophagi are lying scattered around the church.

The inner ramparts at Carcassonne, 60 km W of Béziers, were constructed in Late Roman times and exhibit typical features such as large and small blockwork foundations, rubble core, and u-shaped towers astride the wall. Most of this is to be seen on the NE side of the citadel.

Location:
Béziers is near the Mediterranean, S of Montpellier 58 km on the A 9-E 15. Ensérune is 14 km W of Béziers. Take the N 9 for 10 km to Nissan-Lez-Ensérune. Turn right across the Canal du Midi to the oppidum. Signposted.

Colombiers is about 3 km E of Ensérune along an unpaved farm road.

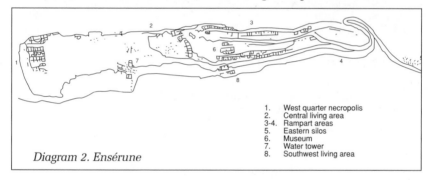

1.	West quarter necropolis
2.	Central living area
3-4.	Rampart areas
5.	Eastern silos
6.	Museum
7.	Water tower
8.	Southwest living area

Diagram 2. Ensérune

Cambous Hérault
Sights:
Neolithic/Copper Age village of Cambous with reconstructed houses, walls, tombs and dolmens. The site was occupied about 3000-2500 B.C. and has 10 km of trails. Guided visits.

Location:
NW of Montpellier 22 km on D 986, then W on D 113 to Cambous. Signposted. 800-m walk to site.

Château de Roussillon Pyrénées-Orientales
Sight:
Ruscino. Fortified site fourth-second centuries, B.C. Pacified by Romans in the first century B.C., it became an urban centre. Slight remains of the small forum oriented N-S, public square with rows of shops (only partially excavated), dwellings, a basilica with bases of columns, steps and an annex. A large sewer cuts across the forum and the basilica to drain into the valley. Work is ongoing here.

Location:

SW of Montpellier and E of Perpignan ca. 5 km on D 617. Turn right onto the C 7, direction Cabestany and Château-Rousillon (*Centre Commercial*) and follow the road back underneath the D 617. The site is about 200 m further on. Signposted.

Les Cluses Pyrénées-Orientales

Sights:

The Port des Cluses is the ruin of a fourth-century frontier gateway between the Roman provinces of Gallia Narbonensis and Hispania Tarraconensis.

Traces of the Roman Via Domitia are visible here, as well as vestiges of two third-fourth century Roman fortifications. Next to the forts is the pre-Romanesque church of St.-Nazaire with three naves. At Les Cluses Haut there is also some Roman road visible near the church, and vestiges of the Roman gate beside the N 9.

Location:

SW of Montpellier and S of Perpignan on the N 9 toward Le Perthus to just S of Les Cluses (ca. 3 km from Le Perthus). Park in the pull-off on the W side of the highway, just S of the Restaurant Laetitia, where there are information signs about the Via Domitia.

Dorres Pyrénées-Orientales

Sight:

Remains of Roman baths on the side of the hill in the village next to a modern swimming pool. Signposted.

Location:

S of Toulouse and NE of Bourg Madame ca. 7 km on the N 20-E 09/D 618.

Elne Pyrénées-Orientales

Sights:

Old Illiberis. There are some Iberian and Roman wall remains in the chapel of San Jordi beside a parking lot which contains a small excavation. With successive occupation since the sixth-century B.C. the entire town lies on top of an archaeological heap.

The Iberian oppidum of Elne was a stopover on the Via Domitia coastal route. Vestiges of Roman houses are from the second century. Elne was declared an Episcopal See in the sixth century.

Location:

Elne is SW of Montpellier and S of Perpignan on A 9, 11 km. The site is in town.

Gaujac Gard

Sights:

St.-Vincent-de-Gaujac. Oppidum and sanctuary occupied periodically between the fifth century B.C. and the sixth century A.D. and later from the tenth-fourteenth centuries. In Gallo-Roman times it was a rural sanctuary. It lies on a hill in the forest and there are remains of a small temple, cistern, wall, and peribolus, as well as excavations revealing a first-third century temple and baths—the latter with hypocaust and drains. There are also vestiges of a curtain wall and further remains of a Medieval stronghold.

Location:

NE of Montpellier and ca. 18 km N of Pont du Gard on the N 86. To find the oppidum, go through Gaujac on D 310, then walk up unpaved road to site. Signposted.

Lodève Hérault

Sights:

The twelfth-century Prieuré Saint-Michel de Grandmont has anthropomorphic rock-cut tombs behind the building. There are also Visigothic tombs, and a fine dolmen on the church property.

In the area there are several other dolmens. The local S.I. will give maps, as some are rather complicated to find.

Location:

NW of Montpellier, take the N 109-E 11, 55 km to Lodève, then go E on D 153 ca. 8 km to Saint-Michel de Grandmont. Signposted.

Loupian Hérault

Sights:

The large Gallo-Roman Villa Les Prés-Bas, of first century, B.C.-fourth-fifth centuries, A.D. is currently being restored. It is reputedly the finest Roman villa in Mediterranean France, and contained the best-preserved mosaics in the region. The excavation is ongoing. Under cover a hypocaust is visible beneath the floor, and mosaics for about thirteen rooms have been restored as far as possible from the later villa of A.D. 375-425. There is nothing to be seen of the earlier, first-century B.C. villa.

Opposite the church of Sainte-Cecile is a fourth-century Paleo-Christian church and baptistry to be incorporated into an archaeological park for the public. Some foundations are currently visible.

Location:

SW of Montpellier. Loupian is reached by leaving the N 113 just before Mèze to (signposted) Loupian. After a few hundred metres, turn left to Gallo-Roman villa. Church is in town.

Lunel Hérault

Sights:

Ambrussum. Fortified site and stopping place on the Via Domitia. The site was first occupied in Neolithic times. The oppidum was defended in the Iron Age, the upper area being occupied from the third century, B.C. to the first century, A.D., with remains of a portico, three groups of dwellings with foyers, galleries, and rooms. The owner's quarters are on two sides of the courtyard.

A building which was probably public (as one side of it is open, with columns every 4 m) lies to the S. The rooms at the back of it were most likely shops.

The lower area was occupied first century, B.C.-third century, A.D. and two houses have been excavated here, although not much remains. These, too, were courtyard style.

A bridge with only one arch remaining out of eleven dates from the first century. South of this ca. 100 m is a well-preserved stretch of paved Roman road which skirted the oppidum. It may have been the Via Domitia.

There are remains of ramparts originally 650-m long and of twenty-five towers, most of which were semicircular, one of them exceptionally large. The best-preserved are to the W, and consist of rectangular blocks of various thicknesses. Interesting site.

Location:

NE of Montpellier on the N 113, 24 km. Leave Lunel on road toward Sommières and turn off right at sign for Villetelle. Follow this road until just before it passes under the autoroute, and a sign on the right (by a Cypress tree) says: *Ambrussan - Site Archéologique, preRomain et Romain.* Continue 1.5 km to site. The bridge is 300 m beyond the Quartier Bas, then walk up right by (modern) military stone to Roman road and oppidum.

Maguelone Hérault

Sights:

The old cathedral of St.-Pierre has a sixth-century sarcophagus which is decorated with Visigothic spirals of leaves. The lintel over the entrance to the church is a Roman military column. There are also two Roman tombs in the Lady Chapel.

Location:

S of Montpellier on the D 986, 9 km to Palavas, then W, 4 km. The cathedral is situated on a sandspit.

Murviel-les-Montpellier Hérault

Sights:

The city takes its name from the walls that were once there. The Gallo-Roman enceinte was destroyed in 737 by Charles Martel. The fortified enclosure of Altimurium here has three walls. (The first is from the second century B.C., the second is from the second century B.C.-second century A.D. and the third is from the second century A.D. on). There is an excavation of a Roman temple of Greek design and possible Roman foundations. This is intended to be an archaeological park in the future.

Location:

A little W of Montpellier on the D 27E. It can also be reached by taking the D 5 SW of the city to Pignan (ca. 9 km), then NW on the D 27 another 3 km.

Nages Gard

Sights:

Oppidum des Castels. Large fortified site inhabited for about 300 years, showing numerous remains of external and internal walls. Some of the fine battlements, 2-3 m (sometimes as much as 7 m) thick and 4.5 m high, with semicircular towers, are fairly intact. It is one of the best-preserved pre-Roman sites in the south of France. Nages I and II of the second and third centuries B.C.

have large fortifications on the ramparts, one with a diameter of 11 m. Nages III, of the first century B.C. was larger but its wall was without towers. Streets are visible, along with a Roman fountain and reservoir. Near the largest tower was a small temple (fanum) from 70 B.C. It is one of the earliest known in Gaul but was destroyed in A.D. 10.

The Roman cistern at the entrance to the village is still used for the fountains. The site was abandoned early in the first century A.D. Open access, and worth a visit.

Location:
NE of Montpellier and W of Nîmes ca. 15 km on D 40/D 37. In the village, turn up rue des Castels which becomes rue de la Fontaine Romaine. After this, site is signposted.

Narbonne Aude
Sights:
Narbo Martius, in the province of Gallia Narbonensis, was founded by the Romans in 118 B.C. and became one of the most important commercial and administrative centres along this coast. Although Roman commerce was primarily conducted by ship, and Narbo Martius was not on the sea, this did not deter the Romans, who proceeded to transform the local marshland into a a great seaport to rival Marseille. It was of sufficient size and well sheltered enough for both military and commercial fleets. Narbonne remained a most strategic site on the Via Domitia until the fourteenth century, when a great storm silted over the lagoons and the harbor, whereupon the city went into economic decline.

After 410, the Visigoths took over Narbonne and made it their capital. By the early eighth century it was captured by the Moors, and retaken by the Franks under Pepin later in the same century.

Visible today is the Horreum, a huge subterranean public Roman warehouse built during the time of Augustus, and giving some idea of the commercial nature of Narbonne's past. Throughout the extensive and seemingly endless galleries each small storeroom has a design carved above it indicating the type of goods that were kept there, such as pottery, perfume, olives, honey, wine, etc. In the north wing are some stones depicting the city as it was 2000 years ago. A poem carved on the wall refers to the pride the people had in their city.

The fortified tower, Donjon Gilles-Aycelin, is built on the remains of the Gallo-Roman ramparts, and a short distance further NE is the Place Bistan where some decorative blocks and Roman columns have been re-erected. S of the square, the museum is supported by a bridge on Roman foundations.

In the Crypte Archéologique of the Basilica St.-Paul Serge, are the excavated remains (seven sarcophagi) of the fourth-century Christian necropolis which can be entered from the N doorway of the church.

S of the cemetery where Avenue de Lattre de Tassigny meets rue Chanzy, there is an ongoing excavation of an area occupied from the first century, B.C. until the third century. In the fourth century a church was built there; it became a burial site in the fifth century and was abandoned by the sixth century.

At the archbishop's palace are some paintings and mosaics from Roman villas in the area, and beside the Ecôle de Montmorency, in the upper part of a 24 m section of the sixteenth-century wall, are Gallo-Roman sculptured and inscribed stones.

The pre-Roman oppidum of Montlaurès dates from the end of the sixth-first century B.C. Excavations in progress and visible are rock-cut foundations of houses which lined a road there. Some of these extend 3 m into the rock with walls only on the front.

See also: Sallèles d'Aude.

Location:

Narbonne is on the Mediterranean coast SW of Montpellier. It is 62 km N of Perpignan. To find the oppidum, take the road out of Narbonne in the direction of St. Pons, following signs for Z.I. Malvezy, Moussan. Pass factory of *COMURHEX*, then turn right immediately at sign: *Oppidum of Montlaurès*, 600 m off road.

Languedoc-Roussillon: Nîmes. Temple of Diana. (Courtesy of Bryan Pryce)

Nîmes Gard

Sights:

Roman Nemausus. Today's city contains some of the finest and most well-preserved monuments from the Gallo-Roman era.

The spectacular and imposing first-century amphitheatre, with a capacity for more than 20,000 spectators, is in the centre of town. It is well-preserved, particularly in the upper parts, with 60 arches around the exterior, and 124 exits which enabled the entire audience to leave within a few minutes. It could be shaded from the sun by a huge awning. In the troubled fifth century it was converted into a fortress; during the Middle Ages it became a feudal castle; in the thirteenth century some 2000 people used it as a township. It was not cleared until the nineteenth century.

NW of the amphitheatre, in the Place de la Comédie, is the impressive Maison Carrée of the first century, probably the best-preserved classical Roman temple around the Mediterranean. It stood in the SE corner of the forum although the exact dimensions of the forum are unknown today. The columns and the architrave are of Corinthian design, with arcanthus leaves dominating. It was used as the town hall, and has now been beautifully restored.

The Jardin de la Fontaine was a Gallo-Roman sanctuary built around a spring pool with semicircular steps; its waters reputedly had healing properties. Here stands the so-called Temple of Diana which has been considered as either part of the second-century Roman baths or, more likely, a library of uncertain date. The park, replete with Roman remains and dominated by the Tour Magne, a 33 m high Roman monument, lies below Mont Cavalier. There are actually two towers, an Iron Age one of ca. 18 m in height built in the third century B.C., and the outer casing dating from the beginning of the first century, B.C.

SE of this, under the walls of the Fort, are the slight remains of a shallow Roman water tank, the Castellum Divisorium, which distributed water brought in via the Pont du Gard aqueduct. It has been calculated that 20-40,000 cu. m of water poured out of it each day to supply the needs of the city. All that is left is a round collecting basin from which ten pipes sent water to the different parts of the town.

The Porte d'Arles (or Porte d'Auguste) is a Roman town gate once part of the wall, consisting of two large arches for vehicles, with two smaller flanking arches for pedestrians. It was built in 16 B.C. on the orders of Augustus. It stands opposite the church of St.-Baudile where rue Nationale meets Blvd. Amiral Courbet.

Ramparts in Nîmes were some of the longest and widest in Narbonensis. In Place des Arènes 90 m of them, along with 2 towers, have been exposed. A round tower and some low walls can be seen on rue Alexandre Ducros in the Jardin de la Clinique St.-Joseph, and in Place Montcalm at rue Porte de France, are the remains of a single, semicircular gate, the Porte de France. Other small sections of ramparts can be seen around the city, including the corner of rue Armand-Barbès and Avenue Kennedy, in rue Montaury, rue du Rampart Romain and rue de Cambret.

See also: Pont du Gard.

Location:

Nîmes lies NE of Montpellier. It is on the A 9-E 15 SW of Avignon.

Languedoc-Roussillon: Nîmes.
Temple of Diana

Nissan-lez-Ensérune
Hérault
Sights:

Here is an on-going excavation of a Roman villa, where fourth-century baths are being uncovered. Found by going out of town on D 162 1.3 km, then turning right and going 1.9 km on a narrow road. Turn in alongside vineyard to excavation.

The Chapelle St.-Christol, dating from the fifth century, was once restored using stones from a Roman villa on whose site the church was built. Part of the ancient necropolis

Languedoc-Roussillon: Nissan.
Fifth-century Chapelle St.-Christol

beside the church is visible; the remainder is under the parking lot. There are Visigothic tombs and an altar base. Found by leaving Nissan on the road to Lesignan and turning right at sign for chapel. Go left at T-junction, and immediately left again.

Location:

Nissan is SW of Montpellier and SW of Béziers 10 km on N 9.

Pépieux Aude
Sight:
Spectacular 5000 year-old Dolmen des Fées (Fades), 25 m long, said to be the longest in France. There are two chambers, one capstone and a long passageway intact. The standing stones have been reinforced. Easy access. Signposted.

Location:
SW of Montpellier and W of Béziers. Go 44 km W of Béziers on the N 113, then NW 5 km to Pépieux. The dolmen is NE of the village and is found by taking the road toward Siran. From Siran, it is 1 km E on the D 168 toward Cesseras. It lies about 200 m off the road on the S side.

Le Perthus Pyrénées-Orientales
Sights:
Excavations have revealed the foundations of the 71-B.C. Trophy of Pompey, built to celebrate Pompey's victory in Spain against Sertorius. (See under Aquitaine: Pays Basque, Urkulu for information on the trophies.) Also here is more of the Via Domitia and Via Augusta (to Spain), and foundations of a Medieval priory which was built over most of the trophy in the eleventh century, with vestiges of the narthex, cloister, outbuildings, and kitchens

Location:
SW of Montpellier and S of Perpignan approx. 27 km. Take the road out of Le Perthus (marked, *Via Domitia*). Go 2.2 km. (Well signposted).

Pont du Gard Gard
Sight:
The massive, magnificent three-tiered aqueduct, 275 m long, 49 m high, which spans the valley of the Gard (or Gardon) was built about 19 B.C., probably on the orders of Agrippa, son-in-law of the Emperor Augustus (although scholars are divided on its date, some considering it late first century A.D.). It crosses the Gard near Remoulins, and supplied Nîmes with water.

Some 35 km of it was built underground like many of the Roman aqueducts. The 41 km-long water conduit to Nîmes carried a daily flow of water to the Castellum Divisorium, whence it was distributed throughout the town. The road over the first tier of arches was added in 1747. Excellent site.

There are several other visible sections of this aqueduct including those at Le Pont Rou which has a well-preserved wall with sections of arcade stretching several hundred metres, and a short, triple-arched bridge at Bornègre, both N off the D 981, and at Baune-Sartanette to the S.

Location:
NE of Montpellier. Ca. 25 km NE of Nîmes on the N 86.

St.-Guilhem-le-Désert Hérault
Sights:
The church of this small village contains a Gallo-Roman sarcophagus, another from the sixth or seventh century and various tombstones. There are numerous megaliths, including dolmens at Thiéres, Azirou, La Rigoule, and Les Lavagnes, as well as menhirs at the Mas de Tourreau and Lacan. See S.I. for maps.

Location:
NW of Montpellier. Leaving Montpellier go W on the N 109-E 11 30 km to Gignac. Then turn right (N) on the D 32/D 27 for the town.

St.-Jean-de-Cuculles Hérault

Sight:
Between here and the delightful little Medieval village of Les Matelles is a picturesque Roman bridge with two well-preserved arches.

Location:
Go NW of Montpellier 15 km on D 986 then E on D 113. Depart Les Matelles on the D 17 E, and after 2.4 km cross a modern bridge. Look for the Roman bridge to the left.

Languedoc-Roussillon: St.-Jean-de-Cuculles. Roman Bridge

Sallèles d'Aude Aude

Sights:
Well-preserved Gallo-Roman village of Amphoralis, dating from the first-third centuries with a Gallo-Roman pottery-making centre. Here was also discovered a children's cemetery of the first century, B.C. Museum in situ.

N of this site are vestiges of a second-century aqueduct.

See also, entry for Narbonne.

Location:
SW of Montpellier, go N of Narbonne on the D 13, 5.5 km to Cusac d'Aude. Proceed W 5 km on the D 1118. Signposted.

Sigean Aude

Sights:
Two km from Sigean lies the pre-Roman oppidum of Pech Maho with remains of ramparts and foundations of rooms. It was occupied three separate times from the seventh-third centuries, B.C. and provides strong evidence of Greek influence in this area. Iberian inscriptions have also been found here.

Location:
SW of Montpellier and S of Narbonne, go about 16 km on A 9 or N 9 to Sigean. To find the site, take the road out of Sigean toward Portel. Pass the traffic circle for entry onto the autoroute and almost immediately take the next road right, signposted: *Clinique La Pinède*. Immediately take the part of the road that forks right and follow it for 800 m to a farm road on the left leading into the vineyards. The oppidum is 250 m after the turnoff onto the farm road. Guided visits can be arranged in summer with the Archaeological Museum in Sigean.

Sommières Gard
Sight:
In the rue de la Grave, only a single arch is preserved of what was originally a Roman bridge of five arches. There is a bridge across the river in town signposted as Roman, but it has been almost completely rebuilt.

At nearby Boisseron another Roman bridge of six arches has been widened in more recent times to take automobile traffic. Signposted in town.

Location:
NE of Montpellier and SW of Nîmes 28 km on the D 40. Boisseron is 2.5 km S of Sommières on the N 110.

Other sights in the area include: **AMÉLIE-LES-BAINS**. Remains of Roman baths are preserved in the modern spa, the Thermes Romains, and can be viewed with permission. Amélie-les-Bains is located SW of Montpellier and SW of Perpignan 17 km on the A 9-E 15 then SW 15 km on D 115. **BALARUC-LES-BAINS**. Excavations of a second-third century Gallo-Roman villa of which a large basilica has been revealed. The dimensions of the structure can be seen from the foundations. Go SW of Montpellier 21 km on the autoroute A 9-E 15, then follow signs toward Sète and take road marked for Balaruc-les-Bains. Site in town. **LUSSAN**. To the N is one of the finest menhirs in the Midi. NE of Montpellier, E of Alès and W of Bagnols 23 km on the D 6. Lussan is 3 km N of the road and the menhir is N off that on a secondary road. **MONTFERRAND**. NW of Carcassonne some 50 km, by the N 113 which leads from Toulouse, are vestiges of some thermes that were part of a villa or inn which was subsequently converted into an early Christian church. **PRADES**. St.-Michel-de-Cuxa. Abbey with Visigothic horseshoe arches and doorways, rare outside of Spain. St.-Martin-du-Canigou. Abbey with tenth-century lower crypt. Nearby are two rock-cut tombs. SW of Montpellier and W of Perpignan 33 km on N 116. St.-Michel-de-Cuxa is 3 km S of Prades on D 27. Signposted. For St.-Martin go SW of Prades on N 116, then 5.5 km on D 116. With a 4-wheel drive, you can reach the Abbey but ordinarily, drive to Castell and walk the rest of the way up a steep road. **ST.-THIBÉRY**. Six arches remain of a (reputed) Roman bridge on the Via Domitia across the Hérault. SW of Montpellier and NE of Béziers 12 km to Bessan on the A 9-E 15, then N, 4 km on D 13. Signposted in town as *Pont Romain*. It is after the old mill (1.1 km beyond the town). **UZÈS**. Near the ducal palace is an early Christian crypt of the fourth century with niches for cult objects. NE of Montpellier, and 16 km NW of the Pont du Gard. **VENDRES**. Ruins on the edge of the marsh here are thought to be of a temple dedicated to Venus. There are also some walls considered to be remains of a villa. SW of Montpellier and S of Béziers approx. 12 km on D 64, then turn S on 37 E.

Map 5. Via Domitia

The **Via Domitia** is the oldest Roman road in Gaul. Originally military, it later became an important line of communication and trade running from Beaucaire on the Rhône River to Le Perthus in the Pyrenees. It was 260 km long and was begun by Cneus Domitius Ahenobarbus who crossed the Rhône with his legions in 118 B.C. and completed his conquest of Languedoc-Roussillon in 118 B.C. A large number of milestones have been found along the road. Although it was abandoned for centuries, parts of this formidable monument are still visible in situ today. The S.I. will give good maps, but the itinerary is as follows:

From Beaucaire (Ugernum) to Nîmes (Nemausus) Beaucaire (see entry), Nîmes (see entry)

From Lunel (Ambrussum) to Castelnau le Lez (Sextantio) is the pre-Roman oppidum (see entry under Lunel). The oppidum of Sextantio has now disapeared. At Castelnau is a facsimile of a military column.

From Castelnau le Lez to Ensérune at Prades de Lattes there is an ancient Roman gate in the process of excavation, an archaeological park on the site of ancient Lattara (to the south in the old part of town near the port), and a military column in the cathedral of Maguelone (see entry).

A portion of the road is visible between Lavérune and Poussan in the Basin of Montbazin, surrounded by the mountains of Gardiole and the hills of Moure (D 185 E, D 119 E and the neighbouring liaison roads). At Murviel-les-Montpellier is an oppidum (see entry). At Loupian is the excavation of a large Gallo-Roman villa (see entry). The Via Domitia crosses the Hérault at St.-Thibéry over a bridge of which several arches are visible (see entry). At Balaruc was a villa (see entry). There is still a bit of the ancient rampart visible at Agde. At Béziers the road is reputedly visible along the Canal du Midi (see entry for Béziers-Ensérune). Ensérune (see entry for Béziers).

From Narbonne (Narbo) to LaPalme (see entry for Narbonne). Pech Maho (see entry for Sigean). Aire de Lapalme at the crossroad of Cabanes of Lapalme has a sign giving information and maps.

From Salses to Elne (Illiberis) Ruscino (see entry for Château de Roussillon). South of here the Via Domitia splits in two: one forked via the coast, the other by the interior. The coastal route crosses Elne (see entry) and passes by Port-Vendres. The interior route goes via Les Cluses (see entry) and continues via Le Perthus (see entry) to meet the Via Augusta at the Trophy of Pompey.

Limousin (Limoges)
Corrèze (19), Creuse (23), Haute-Vienne (87)

The remains of a male Neanderthal were found at La Chapelle-aux-Saints. Prehistoric caves, menhirs, dolmens and Gallo-Roman sites are found throughout the region, which is a tree-covered land of granite hills and a humid climate. The Celtic Lemovices lent their name to the later Roman town on the river Vienne that was to become the present-day capital, Limoges. Remnants of the Merovingian and Carolingian period are best represented by the crypt of the abbey of Saint-Martial at Limoges.

Limoges Haute-Vienne
Sights:

The Roman city of Augustoritum, occupying both banks of the Vienne, was one of the largest in Gaul, but few vestiges remain. The site, a refuge in the fifth century against the barbarian invasions, is near the Pont St.-Martial. The town began to grow in the tenth century around the bones of St.-Martial who, in about 250, evangelized the Celtic Lemovices.

The Rue du Pont St.-Martial leads down to a thirteenth-century bridge built on Roman foundations.

The steps behind the Palais de Justice ascend to the Jardin d'Orsay in which are found a few remains of a large first-century Roman amphitheatre that held 20,000 spectators.

The crypt of the old abbey of St.-Martial, under the Place de la République, was once a necropolis where early Christians were interred. It contains sections which date from the fourth century and accommodates sarcophagi along with a ninth-century mosaic. Enquiry should be made at the S.I. or Municipal Museum for admission. There is also a large piece of second-century concrete masonry from the Gallo-Roman era, and other tombs from the Merovingian and Medieval periods..

Location:

96 km SE of Poitiers and 102 km N of Périgueux on the River Vienne. The amphitheatre is in the NW sector on the rue de L'Amphithéatre.

Monts de Blonds
Haute-Vienne
Sights:

Megalithic circuit leading to the Menhir du Pic, Pierre à Cupules d'Arnac, Dolmen de Rouffignac, Menhir de Ceinturat, Dolmen de Puychaud, Dolmen de la Lue, Dolmen de la Borderie and the Dolmens de la Betoulle.

Location:

The area is S of Poitiers and W of Limoges. An easy way to begin this well-marked, picturesque route is to start from St.-Junien which is some 30 km W of Limoges on the N 141-E 603. From here, take the road toward

Limousin: Monts de Blonds. Dolmen de la Betoulle

Bellac, D 675, and turn off right (NE) after 2.3 km, toward Javerdat 6 km ahead.

From Javerdat, take the D 711 toward Cieux and at the crossroad of the D 9, go left. After 300 m there is a signpost: *Menhir du Pic*. Take the dirt road on the right for 400 m. The menhir is 5.30 m high, was broken in the middle and put upright again.

Continue on the D 9, 3.1 km and turn right toward Arnac. Go 400 m and the Pierre à Cupules d'Arnac menhir is in a field (right), at the entry to the village. It is 3.2 m high.

Return to the D 9, turn right, and take the first road left toward Rouffignac. Pass the hamlet of Les Betoulles and turn right after 200 m on dirt road. Dolmen de Rouffignac is signposted and has three standing stones covered by a capstone.

Return again to the D 9 and turn left. Travel 900 m and turn right. Continue 500 m and then left on dirt road for a further 500 m. The 5.10-m high Menhir de Ceinturat is signposted. Legend has it that if you wish to marry in a specific year, you must throw a stone onto the ledge situated midway up the menhir the first time you see it.

From Ceinturat take road toward Cieux, passing signs for Pierre à Sacrifices de Ceinturat and Abri de la Roche aux Fées, which are natural rock formations. From the latter, turn left after 700 m toward Blond. Just out of Villarajouze is a sign (left): *Dolmen de Puychaud.* Follow blue signs on rocks and trees to left ca. 100 m. The dolmen is small with a broken capstone which is askew, resting on four standing stones. Chamber is visible, but the passageway is in ruins.

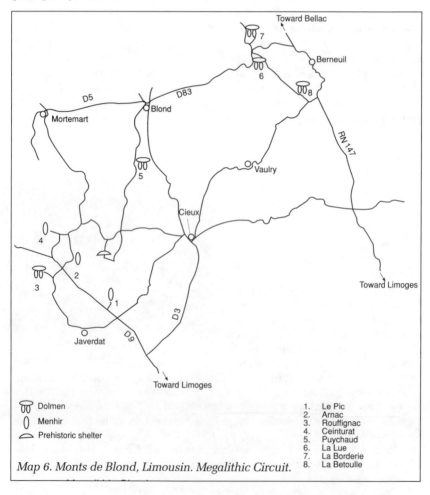

Map 6. Monts de Blond, Limousin. Megalithic Circuit.

Continue up to Blond and turn right on to the D 83. Just before the intersection of D 83 and the roads going to Virat and La Borderie, the restored Dolmen de la Lue may be seen in a field to the right. From Blond to the dolmen is 6.2 km. The capstone, cut in two, originally measured about 5 m x 3.50 m.

Next, take the road to La Borderie for ca. 100 m, then turn right on a dirt road where the Dolmen de la Borderie is signposted. Continue 200 m (at fork, go left) and the dolmen is on the right beside the fence. It has a large capstone on six standing stones.

For the last megaliths on this circuit, coming from La Borderie and La Lue, take the narrow road going through Virat, which later joins the D 2 between Breuilaufa and the RN 147. Ca. 3.5 km from La Lue there are four dolmens, the Dolmens de la Betoulle, standing on the left, forming a trapezoid. three are ruined, but the fourth was restored and has one capstone and six standing stones.

Pontarion Creuse
Sight:
Gallo-Roman necropolis of Sagnes containing 300 cremation graves, some with urns.
Location:
NE of Limoges 82 km. Go on N 141 to Pontarion 59 km, then take the D 13 after crossing the Taurion River, and a path leads through the woods to the site.

St.-Merd-les-Oussines Corrèze
Sights:
Les Cars. Interesting Gallo-Roman site includes rectangular temple with podium and monumental stairs, mausoleum, large vat for water conservation, and second-century baths with hypocausts, marble frag- ments, and mosaic. These are remains of a luxury villa of the second century, aban- doned at the end of the third. At Varieras, nearby, is a Roman bridge.

Limosin: St.-Merd-les-Oussines. Les Cars

Location:
St.-Merd is SE of Limoges and NW of Ussel. From Ussel, go SW on E 70, 9 km to St.-Angel. Then NW on D 979/D 36, 23 km to Millevaches. Turn W on the D 164 for 5.5 km. Site is signposted.

The bridge is W of Les Cars and N of Pérols-s-Vezère.

Saint-Quentin-la Chabanne Creuse

Sights:
Menhir de Pierrefitte, at 4 m, is the highest menhir in the Creuse. The Roman bridge, Pont de Senoueix, across the Taurion has one arch.

Location:
E of Limoges, S of Aubusson and a few km SW of Felletin. From Felletin, go S on the D 992 to Saint-Quentin. The menhir is just off the D 992 toward Les Bordes from the village. After 1 km take the dirt path right some 200 m on foot. For the bridge follow the D 992 toward Gentioux and just before Joux, turn on D 16 toward St.-Marc-à-Loubaud. The bridge is over the river.

Other sights in the area include: **BLESSAC**. Dolmen. E of Limoges and W of Aubusson ca. 4 km on D 941. Leave cafe in village on D 17 in direction of St.-Sulpice-les-Champs. 1 km from the village, a path to the right leads to the dolmen. **BORT-LES-ORGUES**. Dolmen de Vallat. SE of Limoges, go SE of Ussel 30 km on D 982/D 9779 to Bort. Follow signs ca. 6 km on D 922 from Bort toward Lanobre. Vallat is signposted out of here. **ÉVAUX-LES-BAINS**. Vestiges of Roman baths at S.I. NE of Limoges and 44 km from Aubusson. From Guéret go E 31 km on the N 145 to Gouzon. Then continue E on the D 915 ca. 21 km to Évaux. **FELLETIN**. Dolmen de la Croix Blanche. E of Limoges, go S of Aubusson 8.5 km to Felletin. 2 km SE of Felletin, at the sign for the D 10, continue straight ahead and S. 100 m on right, in field, is the dolmen. **MOUTIER D'AHUN**. Ninth-century bridge across the Creuse. There is also a Gallo-Roman stele with inscription incorporated into the façade of the church. NE of Limoges. From Guéret go SE 20 km on D 9.

Lorraine (Metz)
Meurthe-et-Moselle (54), Meuse (55), Moselle (57), Vosges (88)

On the easternmost part of the Parisian basin and the western side of the steep, forested Vosges mountains, Lorraine occupies the valleys of the upper Meuse and the Moselle Rivers. Finds of prehistoric tools show some relationship with the remote past. The area was inhabited by Celts then occupied by the Roman legions who founded their capital on an earlier Celtic site at Metz. Roman roads dissected the area and villas were common. The region was devastated by the Alemani, Franks and Huns. Merovingian cemeteries have also been discovered here.

Audun-le-Tiche Moselle

Sight:

Seventh-century Merovingian necropolis with over 200 stone tombs, some still unexcavated, but those that are, are well marked as to their contents.

Location:

Audun is N of Metz and NW of Thionville. Leave Thionville on the D 14, direction Longwy. After 16 km turn right (N) at Aumetz to Audun-le-Tiche which is 11 km further. The necropolis, a fifteen-minute walk, is on a hill behind the village. Signposted.

Lorraine: Bliesbruck. (Courtesy Siwan Anderson)

Bliesbruck Moselle

Sights:

Here is a Franco-German excavation (independent of frontiers) on both sides of the (originally Roman) road. The site of a first-fourth century Gallo-Roman market town of some 20 hectares, it once had a population of about 2500, and stretched some 800 m along the road. Under excavation for many years, it has revealed the remains of a villa, public baths, heating chamber or praefurnium, a large cult building, iron-smelting and reconstructed pottery workshops, wells, ovens, hearths, graves, a third-century bakery, and devotional wells in honour of gods. There are two distinct areas where the various crafts and trades were practised. Guided tours are possible and can be arranged with the Centre Archéologique beside the site. Currently the museum is on the German side. Small museum in situ.

Location:

E of Metz, Bliesbruck is in the Moselle-Sarre valley near the German frontier. Travel NW of Strasbourg on the A 4-E 52 to Sarreguémines, then SE on the N 62 8.5 km and N, 2 km on the D 82 to Bliesbruck. Alternatively, go E of Metz on the E 25-A 4 for 40 km, then 19 km on the E 52-A 4 and turn N, 10 km on the N 61 to Sarreguémines, and from there to Bliesbruck.

Deneuvre Meurthe-et-Moselle

Sight:

Reconstructed archaeological site of a spring sanctuary dedicated to Hercules. Five basins, two in wood and three in stone, were found here.

Location:

SE of Metz and NW of St-Dié ca. 18 km on N 59 to Baccarat. Deneuvre and the site are signposted from here.

Le Donon Vosges
Sights:

A mountain in the central Vosges, Le Donon has been occupied since Neolithic times. It became a Celtic religious centre, succeeded in Roman times by a temple of Mercury. There is an in situ museum containing Roman objects found here, and in a hollow below the summit there are a number of Roman stelae set in a semicircle. On the Col du Donon, in a clearing in the forest, is a copy of a Roman Jupiter column.

There are some well-preserved sections of Roman road nearby.

Lorraine: Le Donon. Roman Road

Location:

SE of Metz. Go SE of Nancy on the D 59 to Raon l'Étape. From here, turn NE on the D 393, and go 28 km to Le Donon. At Le Donon take the road toward Sarrebourg and about 600 m after the last house, turn right up a small road with two posts at entrance. Park at 1.3 km and walk about twenty minutes to the museum at the top. For the excavations and Gallo-Roman stelae, follow paved road to cobblestone path (back to the right).

For one Roman road, turn left at Raon-sur-Plaine by Restaurant/Hotel de la Poste (just before Donon) and there is a sign: *Voie Romaine*. Take narrow well signposted road for 5 km. By parking lot begins 500 m of fairly well-preserved road through the forest. Highway winds around the mountain and forests, with exceptional views. Another section of Roman road is reputed to be between Moyenmoutier (7 km SE of Raon-l'Étape) and Saales.

Grand Vosges
Sights:

The entire village of Grand is built on the site of the Gallo-Roman town of Granum, with public baths, an extensive drainage system, basilica, theatre, and temple. Here, in this ancient religious centre, the Gallic god of war, and later Apollo, were honoured. The town was destroyed in the fifth century.

Ongoing excavations have also revealed an amphitheatre which is currently being reconstructed. A third-century Roman mosaic, the largest found in France (224 sq. m), is housed in what was a basilica.

There are also subterranean canals which at present can only be seen in groups of 10 or more on Sunday afternoons in July and August, but this may change. Soon to be open to the public is the prison.

Location:

SW of Metz and W of Neufchâtel, Grand is reached by taking the N 74 10 km SW then turning right (N) onto the D 427 for 6.5 km, and right again onto the D 71 for a further 6 km. It is well signposted.

Metz Moselle
Sights:
The city, ancient Divodorum, situated at the confluence of the Seille and the Moselle, dates back to the sixth century, B.C. To the S of the Esplanade Mont St.-Quentin is Saint-Pierre-aux-Nonnains, an early Christian church, that belonged to a seventh-century Benedictine abbey. Supposedly the oldest extant church in France, it was founded on the site of a Roman basilica of ca. 310.

The city is abundant with interesting remains:

The museum of Gallo-Roman archaeology occupies the site of still visible Roman baths.

In the cathedral of St. Etienne (in the choir on the left) is a marble Merovingian bishop's throne fashioned from a Roman column. The large bronze basin in the side aisle, once used as a font, is of Roman origin.

In the restaurant *Flunch* on the rue des Clercs, is a substantial part of a second-century Roman wall at the back of the restaurant. The carpet shop *Tolub* has, in its basement, foundations of Roman ramparts, but permission is needed to enter. There is a large base of a Roman column in the courtyard of the Hôtel de Ville, and the Trinitaires cave contains Roman remains. The Église St.-Martin has some visible Roman wall at its entrance.

In the NE suburbs of Metz, at Vantoux, is the ninth-century chapel of St.-Barthélmy.

Nearby is the Roman Aqueduct of Jouy of which eighteen arches remain, along with a water-storage tank. There are more arches at Ars-sur-Moselle, a little N of Jouy. This aqueduct carried water from Gorze to Divodorum.

Location:
Metz is E of Paris and near the frontier of Luxembourg. The aqueduct is S of the city on N 57, 10 km.

Plombières-les-Bains Vosges
Sights:
The Etuves romaines, or Roman steam baths, are located to the left of the pharmacy, which is nearly opposite the S.I.

The Gradins du Bain Romain, tiered steps used for seating, are also nearby. Guided visits to Roman remains in town can be arranged with the S.I.

Location:
SE of Metz, NW of Mulhouse, W of Colmar and S of Nancy approx. 40 km on the N 57-E 23.

St.-Dié Vosges
Sights:
Celtic camp at Bure. The site from about 70 B.C. – A.D. 352 occupies a long ridge, high above the valley floor, and looks as if it were once a thriving community. To be seen are remains of ateliers, pottery, iron forge, ramparts, fossa, and cisterns. There are a number of stelae denoting Celtic themes. One site appears to have been a place of worship. Each is marked with a description of what it may have been. There is some evidence of Neolithic occupation. Altogether well worth the walk up the forestry road.

Location:

SE of Metz and NW of Colmar on the N 415 about 53 km. Then, leave St. Dié on the N 59 in the direction of Nancy for approximately 2 km. At the entrance to the village of la Pecherie, turn right by sign for the village and Camp Celtique. Continue 1.8 km and at fork, go left and roughly 500 m more to sign on left (by west gate to camp). This is a steep twenty-minute walk. If you continue up the road 800 m more to another sign: *Camp Celtique, Route Forestière*, a path turns back in on the left (with a bar across). This is a twenty-minute walk up a gentle slope to the site.

Sarrebourg Moselle

Sight:

A few km from town is the Gallo-Roman Villa of St.-Ulrich, probably dating from first-third centuries, and partially reconstructed. It is easily visible and accessible.

Location:

W of Strasbourg, E of Nancy and SE of Metz. Take the D 955 from Metz SE 87 km to Héming, then go NE 7 km on the N 4 to Sarrebourg. For the site, leave town on the Nancy/Metz road, cross the metal bridge and take the road toward Morhange. It is signposted (right) beside km stone #41. Go down narrow road 1 km and park beside chapel. Walk down beside chapel (about 100 m).

Other sites in the area include: HOMBOURG-HAUT. In Vieux Hombourg, the old part of town, is a neglected and overgrown Gallo-Roman site with remains of two levels of wall, a possible cistern, and foundations of a rectangular structure. Behind the church cemetery. E of Metz approx. 53 km on the N 3. REMIREMONT. To the NE, above the suburb of St.-Etienne on St.-Mont, are the ruins of a seventh-century monastery, the Pont des Fées (bridging a Gallo-Roman ditch), and the Pierre Kerlinkin (a red sandstone monolith). SE of Metz, W of Colmar. Leaving the station at Remiremont, follow signs for St.-Etienne and then St.-Romary-St.-Mont. Four km from station a road to the right points to Pierre Kerlinkin. Drive 700 m to crossroad, turn left and continue for 5-6 km to top of mountain to the stone. From the same crossroad, go straight and 300 m further there is a sign on the right: *Pont des Fées*. The sign for St.-Mont also points across the Pont des Fées. Cross the bridge and follow trail to ruins at top, roughly 1 km hike. WALSCHEID. Gallo-Roman cemetery "Trois Saints". SE of Metz. Go to Sarrebourg and take the D 44 ca. 5 km to Hesse, then the RF/D 96 about 10 km to Walscheid. To find the cemetery, face the S.I. in the village and go right 2 km, leaving car at entrance to forest. Walk to a crossing and turn right, continue to second crossing and turn right again (2-3 km). Once you reach the second crossroads, it is signposted. There is also a planned walk from the village. Enquire at the S.I.

Midi-Pyrénées (Toulouse)

Ariège (09), Aveyron (12), Haute-Garonne (31), Gers (32), Lot (46), Haute-Pyrénées (65), Tarn (81), Tarn-et-Garonne (82)

This large area bordering the Pyrenees, contains the upper Garonne and the Ariège Rivers, as well as some of the finest sites exhibiting prehistoric art in the Dordogne, which traverses a small section of the region. The grotto at Aurignac, discovered in 1860, gives its name to the first period of the Upper Paleolithic—Aurignacian. The grotto of Gargas in the Haute-Garonne contains 160 hands in negative. At Niaux is one of the most beautifully decorated caves in Europe for both the richness and amplitude of its frescos, while at Pech Merle nearly all the art forms of the Paleolithic are represented within a single space.

The capital, Toulouse, was first an Iberian site and then a Celtic village-port on the river, and capitalized on the ancient trade route from the Mediterranean to the Atlantic coasts. The Celtic village (Tolosa) had a sacred pool which in 106 B.C. was drained by the Romans, who confiscated the coins and sacred objects contained therein. It was the capital of the Visigoths from 419 to 507 and then came under the hegemony of the Franks in 628. The region is rich in thermal springs, prehistoric grottos, and Roman remains.

Alzen Ariège

Sight:
Tenth-century chapel of Ste.-Croix, under restoration, situated high on a cliff, contains one nave with two side chapels (very small) and a small wooden balcony above the entrance.

Location:
S of Toulouse and E of St.-Girons approx. 27 km on D 117 to La Bastide. Go 2.5 km more to Montels and turn S, for Alzen on D 221, then D21. Pass through town and chapel is 400-m walk on fairly steep path. Signposted.

Midi-Pyrénées: Alzen. Tenth-century chapel of Ste.-Croix

Auch Gers

Sights:
In the proximity are three Gallo-Roman towers (*piles*). Take N 124 toward Mont de Marsans, then proceed right about 11 km from Auch and turn in on road just E of Ordano-Larroque, signposted: *La Roque*. Go 1 km and the tower, containing niches for statuary, is on the right in a field.

Continue on the same road toward St. Lary and when you arrive at the Auberge of St. Lary (on left) the top of the Gallo-Roman tower can be seen from the garden. It is in the woods. To reach it, continue past auberge and take the first road left marked: *Martet* (about 200 m before reaching the D 930). Go to the second house (yellow) and walk up between the fields toward the woods. The tower is not visible from the house and is not very easy to find. There is another tower S of the D 374, and this is reached by going to St.-Jean Poutge and turning left (S) on the D 939. Turn left again after 4.7 km at water tower, and the sign for the D 374 Biran, 4 km. After 500 m the Roman tower is on the left in a cornfield. It has a large niche for statuary and is easy to find.

In the town of Auch there is another Gallo-Roman tower in the rue des Penitants Bleus, near the cathedral.

The cathedral of Ste.-Marie has a crypt with the seventh-century marble sarcophagus of St. Léothade. The sacristan will unlock the crypt on request.

Location:
Auch is W of Toulouse 78 km on the N 124.

Midi-Pyrénées: Auch (near St.-Jean Poutge). Gallo-Roman Pile

Buzeins Aveyron

Sights:

A circuit of dolmens has been put together by the local villages, and consists of twelve sites of dolmens, gallery graves, and tumuli in varying states of repair.

Location:

Buzeins is NE of Toulouse and E of Rodez to the N of the N 88 some 10 km W of Séverac. A circuit map is available in the village.

Cabrerets Lot

Sights:

In the adjacent valley of the Sagne is the Grotte de Pech-Merle. It contains stalactite caves with painted or incised figures (from the Aurignacian period) of mammoth, bison, horses, handprints in negative, human figures, and stylized outlines. In one chamber are the footprints of a man or woman and child. This is a prehistoric site with evidence of human symbolic behaviour some 20,000 years ago. The number of visitors is limited. Museum in situ.

Location:

N of Toulouse, E of Cahors 25 km to Vers on the D 653, then 14 km on the D 662. From here go N 4 km on the D 41 toward Cabrerets and the cave. It is on the right bank of the Lot.

Gourdon Lot

Sight:

The Grottes de Cougnac, about 2 km from the village, display 19,000-year-old paleolithic cave drawings including ibex, elephants, and human figures.

Location:

Gourdon is N of Toulouse and SE of Les Eyzies. It is ca. 48 km SE of Montignac on the D 704.

Limogne Causse Lot

Sights:

In this area is an abundance of megaliths including the Dolmen de la Borie du Bois near Laramière. At Limogne take D 24 SE, then pick up the D 55 E toward Laramière. Just after a right turn toward Vidaillac, the dolmen can be seen to the right of the road.

Another, the Dolmen des Quartous, on a small promontory, is found by leaving Montricoux (12 km SE of Caussade) on a rural road toward Pénayrol.

The Dolmen du Rouzet is 15 km S of Montricoux and on the right bank of the Vère, E of the village.

To the SW is Caussade on the D 926. From here proceeding SE 6 km, pick up the D 75 E. Pass St.-Cirq and about 4 km after Pradals is a dolmen on the left.

From Larroque go SE on D 964 and after 8.5 km take the left fork D 1 to Le Verdier. There is a dolmen on the left of the road, just before the town, and another just S of Vieux, 3 km farther on.

Location:

Limogne is E of Bordeaux and E of Cahors. From Cahors go 36 km SE on the D 911.

Mas d'Azil Ariège
Sights:
The Grotte of Le Mas d'Azil (from which is derived the name of the Azilian culture of the Mesolithic) contains prehistoric rock drawings in galleries which are not open to the public. Much of the cave can be explored, however. There are finds here from the Magdalenian period of about 12,000 B.C. and the Neolithic of about 6000 B.C. The site served also as a refuge for early Christians, Cathars and later, Huguenots.

There are several dolmens in the area, the most accessible of which, the Dolmen du Cap del Pouech, is signposted in the village. It has four standing stones and a large, worn capstone. There is a second one beyond on the same road. Another is located at Camarade-Les Moulis and another, the Dolmen de Coudère, is located at Gabre. Ask locals for directions, as these stones are somewhat hard to find.

Location:
Mas d'Azil is S of Toulouse and NE of St. Girons 7 km on the D 117 then NE on the D 119. Well signposted.

Montmaurin
Haute-Garonne
Sights:
The site was important in Gallo-Roman times, the most notable discovery being a large, first-century Gallo-Roman villa, embellished in the third and fourth centuries. Displayed are a reception area,

Midi-Pyrénées: Montmaurin

temple, baths, resi-dential rooms and living quarters, garden, fish ponds, peristyle and outbuildings. The entire edifice was destroyed by fire around 375-380. Excellent site.

Nearby at Peguilhan in the chapel of Bétis are Gallo-Roman sculptures.

At La Hillère, E of Montmaurin, a chapel in a cemetery displays a large polychrome mosaic dating from the fourth century. Beside the road, excavations have revealed a fourth-century water sanctuary with temples, fountain, baths and a market. It is linked to a cult that worshipped water.

Location:
SW of Toulouse and E of Tarbes. The site can be reached by going NW of St.-Gaudens on the D 9 to Lannemezan, ca. 15 km, then W on the D 9 for 4 km. Well signposted. Peguilhan is N of Montmaurin and NE of Boulogne-sur-Gesse some 8 k on the D 632/D 90. To reach La Hillère, take the D 9 SE and turn left (N) on the same road leading to the Gorges de la Save. The site is on the right, just before the Gorge.

Montoulieu-St.-Bernard Haute-Garonne
Sight:

Gallo-Roman swimming pool, on private property but available to be viewed (a gratuity to the owner is in order). Enclosed with a wall, the pool is lined with marble slabs and seats. There is part of a hypocaust beside it.

Location:

SW of Toulouse, go W of Martres-Tolosone on the road toward Aurignac and Montmaurin (D 10). This site is 1.2 km off the D 10 on the D 8 and easy to locate. Signposted.

Montréal Haute-Garonne
Sights:

There is a large excavation of a second-fifth century Gallo-Roman villa 1.5 km SW, at Séviac. To be seen are baths, peristyle, courtyard, rooms (one with an underfloor and water heating), mosaics, water channels, foundations of a pool, drains, hypocaust with furnace and wall ducts, a third-century wine press, and a Gallo-Roman outer wall. A Paleo-Christian chapel and baptistry, and necropolis with sarcophagi date from the fourth-fifth centuries. Dating from the sixth-seventh centuries are several Merovingian dwellings.

Nearby is the Eglise de Genens which has seventh-eighth century sculptures above its porte romane.

Location:

NW of Toulouse, go W to Auch, then NW 44 km on the D 930 to Condom. Next, go W 15 km on the D 15. From Montréal continue W on D 15 for 2 km. Signposted.

Moulis Arièges
Sight:

Roman tower (*pile*). Probably a religious monument placed along the Roman roads. Rectangular, made of brick with a niche at the top, it may have contained a statue of Mercury, who protected travellers and merchants. Some vestiges of Roman road were discovered in front of the monument, but nothing is now apparent.

Location:

SW of Toulouse and SW of St.-Girons 5 km on D 618. Signposted and situated on the edge of a cornfield next to the cemetery before reaching Luzenac. Visible from the highway.

Roquebrune Gers
Sight:

Vestiges of a very small partly destroyed building, remains of a large, third-century shrine with three niches inside for statuary (on three remaining walls). Ca. 6 m high, with base 5 x 4 m.

Location:

W of Toulouse, SE of Bordeaux and NW of Auch 30 km on the N 124 then S. At sign for Roquebrune go W of D 34, S of Vic-Fezensac. At village turn left by church. After 2.1 km turn right by restored old house. Sign says: *Montjoi*. Go through woods and turn left at bottom of hill at second sign for *Montjoi*. After 500 m, Roman remains are in the field to the right.

St.-Bertrand-de-Comminges Haute-Garonne

Sights:
Here is the Gallo-Roman Lugdunum Convenarum, capital of the Iberian Convenae, founded in 72 B.C. Herod Antipas and his wife Herodias, the murderers of John the Baptist, may have died here. The town first established on the hill spread to the plain below, and appears to have been destroyed in the sixth century by the Burgundians, but revived in the twelfth century.

On the left on the hill are the remains of a Roman theatre with houses built into the stage. Currently, it is only partially excavated.

Lower down there is a Paleo-Christian basilica of the fifth century, with sarcophagi, forum baths, a temple, the north baths, a military camp, a circular monument marking a crossroads, a market, and a square with portico. Excavations are ongoing.

Close at hand are the impressive Grottes de Gargas with prehistoric rock paintings, and some 160 hand impressions, some deformed. The tour of the cave is 45 minutes.

Location:
SW of Toulouse 105 km and SW of St. Gaudens on the road toward Luchon some 15 km on the D 8/N 125. The town is 2 km W of Valcabrere. For the Grottes de Gargas go 6 km from St.-Bertrand. Well signposted.

Salies du Salat Haute-Garonne

Sight:
Grotte Préhistorique de Marsoulas with rupestrian paintings and engravings of horses and bison, as well as anthropomorphic figures.

Location:
Salies is SW of Toulouse ca. 70 km on the N 117-E 80/D 117. To reach the caves, take the road toward Cassagne, following signs for Marsoulas. Signposted. From the bridge in Salies to the Grotte is 2.3 km.

Tarascon-sur-Ariège Ariège

Sights:
About 4 km SW of Tarascon is the Grotte de Niaux, with several km of galleries. It is most famous for its well-preserved drawings of animals of the Magdalenian period, including bison, horses, deer and ibex in profile in a huge chamber some distance from its entrance. Visits are controlled and not more than twenty persons are allowed in at a time.

The Grotte de Bedeilhac is 5 km NW of Tarascon. The huge entryway to the cave leads to galleries containing paintings and engravings from the Magdalenian period. Represented here are bison, horses and deer. The main gallery is 1 km in length.

Just under 9 km N of Tarascon on the N 20-E 09 is the Pont du Diable, restored in the second, ninth and fourteenth centuries.

Location:
S of Toulouse near the Spanish border and S of Foix ca. 16 km on the N 20-E 09.

Toulouse Haute-Garonne
Sights:
Here are found the scanty, overgrown ruins of a second-century amphitheatre. Some of the remains of twenty-seven pillars stand over 6 m. Directly behind the podium, there is evidence of a room which is believed to have been for gladiators. Take the direction Hôpital Purpan from town, and follow signs for Arènes Romaines (which is near the hospital).

Under the Institut Catholique is a Roman wall which is open to visitors.

In front of the S.I. (which is in the back of the Hôtel de Ville) in a small park, are remnants of a Roman wall and a Roman tower.

The few vestiges of the Gallic oppidum of Vieille-Toulouse lie some 11 km S, off the D 4 and D 95.

Location:
Toulouse is the capital of the region and is situated on the right bank of the Garonne River. The amphitheatre may be seen to the NW of the city, to the E of the D 2 before it crosses the river Touch. Or, take the direction Hôpital Purpan from town and follow signs for Arènes Romaines.

Valentine Haute-Garonne
Sights:
Excavation of Gallo-Roman fourth-century villa, somewhat overgrown, with pool, columns, hypocaust, water conduits, remains of various structures, foundations, marble columns, and rooms. 50 m SW are traces of a fourth-century temple, walls of a Paleo-Christian chapel, and several tombs from fourth-thirteenth centuries.

Nearby, at Labarthe-Rivière, is a Gallo-Roman funerary monument.

Location:
Valentine is SW of Toulouse and SW of St.-Gaudens 2 km. Take the road out of St.-Gaudens in the direction of Luchon. Pass the village of Valentine and turn right beside the water tower on rue du Château d'eau. Continue ca. 300 m to excavation on both sides of the road.

Labarthe-Rivière is 3 km S of Valentine (signposted in village). Go into Labarthe, cross railway tracks and 800 m further on, opposite the gas station, is the monument on the right.

Vals Ariège
Sights:
A very ancient settlement with a striking rupestrian church. At the top of the stairs that enter the building through the rock, there is a Carolingian nave, improperly referred to as the crypt. This part of the church is pre-Romanesque. There is an eleventh-century apse and eleventh-twelfth century frescos on the vaulted ceiling.

Excavations taking place around the church reveal prehistoric remains, a Gallic temple, and Merovingian houses.

Location:

SE of Toulouse, W of Carcassonne and N of Foix 14 km on the N 20-E 09 then right (E) on the D 12, 4 km to join the D 119 for 3.5 km. Then fork left (NE) on the D 40 to Vals.

Other sights in the area include: **CAHORS**. In town to the W of the Place Thiers is the Porte de Diane, an archway of a Roman bath. Source of a spring, worshipped by both the Gauls and the Romans, it still supplies Cahors with drinking water. N of Toulouse. Cahors is S of Limoges some 200 km on the N 20-E 09. **CONQUES**. Roman bridge across the river Dourdou. NE of Toulouse and N of Rodez 35 km on D 901. **LECTOURE**. The town developed from a Gallo-Roman settlement, and much of the old ramparts still remain. NW of Toulouse and N of Auch 35 km on N 21. **LUZECH**. N of the village are the ruins of the Roman oppidum of Impernal. N of Toulouse and W of Cahors, take the D 8 W following the valley of the Lot 19 km to Luzech. Impernal is across the river, signposted. **MARENS-LES-VALS**. Very early romanesque chapel, possibly pre-tenth century. S of Toulouse and S of Ax-les-Thermes 8 km on N 20-E 09. Signposted. **MARTRES-TOLOSANE**. Some highly decorated Paleo-Christian sarcophagi of fifth-sixth centuries, some Carolingian, in and around the church. May be moved to the museum in the future. SW of Toulouse on the N 117-E 80 ca. 52 km. Village is signposted. **RODEZ**. In the cathedral of Notre-Dame are two marble sarcophagi of bishops of fifth and sixth centuries and a tenth-century altar table. SW at Vors is the reconstructed source from which began the Gallo-Roman aqueduct which fed Rodez. NE of Toulouse, and N of Albi 70 km on the N 88. For Vors, follow the N 88 S to T-junction with N 911. Turn right (W) and go 11 km to where the N 88 goes SW. Vors is just to the NE of this turn on a minor road. The source is in a field below the village, on the left entering from Le Lac.

Nord-Pas-de-Calais (Lille)
Nord (59), Pas-de-Calais (62)

The Celtic Atrebates inhabited the region and gave their name to Arras and to Artois. The north of the territory was occupied by the Morini. One of their ports was Bononia, today Boulogne, from which they carried on commercial activities with Britain. In 57 B.C., Caesar conquered the tribes of the area.

Bordering the English Channel, this flat, agricultural country, criss-crossed by canals, has its major centre at Lille. There are also some prehistoric megaliths in the vicinity, especially in the Douai area. The largest Celtic oppidum in northern France is at Etrun a few kilometres west of Arras. Roman remains, while not plentiful, exist in a few areas. This was a barbarian invasion route from the east, and some excavations of Iron Age sites show severe destruction and burning.

Arras Pas-de-Calais
Sights:
The tenth-century underground galleries in the limestone under the town are open for guided visits. Throughout the Middle Ages during periods of invasion and war, they provided shelter to the local people, and acted as a refuge up to World War I when they were used by British forces as a hospital.

At nearby Etrun is a large first-century B.C. Iron-Age oppidum. There is little to recommend a visit, however. Only some of the tree-covered earthen ramparts that once surrounded the camp have survived.

Two menhirs and a dolmen are situated not far away.

Location:
Arras is SW of Lille some 43 km. See S.I. in Town Hall for visits to the galleries.

Etrun is W of Arras 8 km on N 39 on the road toward St. Pol. Continue through Pont du Gy, turn right and the earthworks are 150 m ahead.

For the menhirs, continue along the N 39 from Etrun, 3 km, then turn right toward Mont-St.-Eloi and the D 341. Turn left (toward Bruay) and go 1.1 km from the edge of town to where a road leads off, left, at an angle. Follow this road for 1.3 km. The menhirs are in a wheatfield on the right.

For the dolmen at Fresnicourt-le-Dolmen, continue on the D 341 from Mont-St.-Eloi to Estrée Cauchy. Enter the village and take the first road right (N) for 2.8 km to stop sign. Turn left and proceed 600 m to rue du Dolmen (left). 100 m up this road and the dolmen, Table des Fées, is on the left. It has a large capstone which lies askew on four large standing stones and is somewhat collapsed, leaning against a tree. Some of the passageway stones are standing.

Bavay Nord
Sights:
Remains of the second-century Roman town of Bagacum, stand at the intersection of several Roman roads. One of the largest cities of what was then Roman Belgium, it was the capital of the Nervii and began to decline at the end of the third century. A vast urban complex has been found with pillars, arcades, forum shops, underground

Nord-Pas-de-Calais: Bavay. Cryptoporticus

room and gallery, basilica, portico (above the cryptoporticus), ramparts, artisanal area, and baths. Museum in situ.

Location:
Bavay is SE of Lille, near the Belgian border and E of Valenciennes 20 km on the N 49. Excavations are in the west part of the town, signposted.

Douai Nord

Sights:

In the Jardin de la Fonderie, off Place Saint-Amé, the modern walls incorporated stones of the Carolingian epoch. On the site of an eighteenth-nineteenth century cannon-foundry, remains of a wooden building were discovered, which may have been a count's residence.

Just S of the city in the Valley of the Sensée is a circuit of megaliths. It includes a polissoir at Féchain, menhirs at Brunémont, Oisy-le-Verger, and Lécluse, a cromlech at Sailly-en-Ostrevent, and a dolmen at Hamel.

Location:

Douai is S of Lille. Take the Autoroute E 15-A 1, 22 km toward Lens and leave it at exit #11/12 going E to the town. The site is located in the town centre and the S.I. will provide a town map.

For the circuit leave Douai to begin at Aubigny-au-Bac on the N 43 S. Take the road from here toward Féchain to see the polissoir in the square. Broken when removed from its original site, it now consists of a piece 1.10 m x 1.90 m, weighing some 4 tons. The sixteen grooves on the top served as polishers for silex axes.

Return to Aubigny and go toward Brunémont on G 121 to see the Menhir qui Pousse. It is 1.50 m high and access can be gained from the parking lot on the beach.

Take the D 21 to Oisy-le-Verger and follow the road that goes between the campground and the lake. The menhir Gros Caillou du Vieux Marais is signposted.

From here continue on the D 21 to Palluel and at T-junction (where menhir Gros Caillou du Vieux Marais is signposted) turn left toward Palluel and follow signs to Hamel. Take the road out of village marked *Tortequesne*

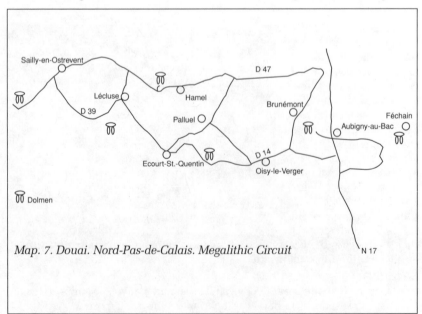

Map. 7. Douai. Nord-Pas-de-Calais. Megalithic Circuit

(D 47). From the stop sign, go 1.4 km to a spring on the right of the road. The dolmen Pierre Chavatte is 8 m above this. Two large standing stones and capstone.

Continue along the same road (D 43) to Sailly-En-Ostrevent to see the Cromlech Les Bonnettes de Sailly. Once at the town, turn left at the church T-junction, and then right after crossing a small bridge. Immediately afterwards, turn left onto a dirt road. Travel 1.6 km and turn right, just before the road crosses over the motorway. After 400 m are the five standing stones, shaped as if they are wearing bonnets. They are on top of an unexcavated tumulus on the right.

Other sights in the area include: LABOURSE. The church of St.-Martin dates from the ninth century and is said to be the oldest sanctuary in northern France. SW of Lille and 12 km NW of Lens on the E 15-A 26. VALENCIENNES. At nearby Famars are the remains of Fanum Martis, a Roman fortress which is flanked by round towers. It is on private property behind the church, and permission to enter is required from the Mairie. Valenciennes is SE of Lille, near the Belgian border. Famars lies about 5 km S off the D 958.

Basse-Normandie (Caen)
Calvados (14), Manche (50), Orne (61)

Distinctive features of the region are the Cotentin peninsula jutting out into the Atlantic in the northwest, and the flatlands around the capital, Caen. Archaeologically, sites are relatively few as the area appears to have been little inhabited before the fourth millennium B.C. Neolithic and Bronze age dolmens and menhirs exist but are not numerous. Inhabited by Celts, the region has preserved some remains. It prospered for a time under the Romans until the barbarian invasions. Devastation of the area began anew in the ninth century with Viking raids. The Norsemen then settled the region in the early tenth century.

Bierre Orne

Sight:

Camp Celtique de Bierre (or: de César). One of the rare defensive camps in the West, constructed about 850 B.C. in the late Bronze or early Iron Age. The drystone walls are well-preserved. The central enclosure encompasses about 100 x 250 m but the entire site covers an area of about 4 hectares, and originally dates back to the Neolithic.

Location:

SE of Caen and NW of Argentan 10 km on N 158, then E on D 245.

Basse-Normandie: Bierre.
Camp Celtique de Bierre

Colombiers-sur-Seulles Calvados

Sight:

A large stone cairn from the Neolithic period lies in an isolated grove of trees. It presents a unique and complex method of construction with megalithic chambers and its unusual external features. Its purpose is unknown.

Location:

NW of Caen and E of Bayeux just over 12 km on the D 12. Go E of Colombiers 6 km on D 176 to Reviers, and the site is just S of the road.

La Haye-du-Puits Manche

Sights:

On nearby Mont Castre are remains of a Gallo-Roman watchpost. On the summit of Mont de Doville are vestiges of Gallo-Roman La Vigie (lookout station).

Location:

W of Caen and S of Cherbourg 20 km to Valognes on the N 13-E 03, then S, 26 km on the D 2/D 900. Mont Castre is about 4 km E on the D 903. Turn right after first railroad crossing on N 903. Pass mill and ruins of church and cemetery and go by footpath to site. Mont de Doville is N of the town on D 900 some 5.5 km. S.I. will provide a map.

Montmerrei Orne

Sight:

Dolmen La Pierre Tournoire. Recessed, below ground surface in the forest, with a very large capstone (about 3.5 x 3.5 m) resting on two stones.

Location:

SE of Caen and SE of Argentan 14.5 km on N 158. Turn off N 158 onto D 16 at Mortrée. Continue to village and turn left opposite Mairie at sign for Noës. 2.3 km from this turnoff there is a faint yellow arrow on road pointing left to a small path. Dolmen is ca. 75 m along.

Mont St.-Michel Manche
Sight:
The first humble church was consecrated here in 706. In 906 a Benedictine abbey was founded by Richard I Duke of Normandy. Notre-Dame-sous-Terre is a tenth-century pre-Romanesque crypt beneath the larger eleventh-century Romanesque church. It can only be visited with a guide.
Location:
SW of Caen and close to St. Malo on the coast of Bretagne. Signposted.

Portbail Manche
Sights:
The eleventh-century church of Notre Dame has remains of a third-fourth century baptistry. The S.I. will arrange visits.

The Abbey of Lessay was built on the ruins of a Roman villa, of which the hypocaust has been excavated.
Location:
W of Caen, go SW of Cherbourg 39 km on the D 904 to Barneville-Carteret. Portbail is ca. 7 km S, near the coast.

Valognes Manche
Sights:
The Vieux-Château is a relic of Gallo-Roman Alauna. Excavations have revealed part of the public baths with sections of wall, some 12 m high, that may be seen along with water channels and pools. The town was destroyed at the end of the fourth or beginning of the fifth century by invaders, and it was left abandoned throughout much of the Middle Ages. Merovingian artifacts may be seen in the crypt of the library.
Location:
SW of Caen and S of Cherbourg 20 km on the E 03-N 13. To find the site, follow the road in town marked: *Piscine* up to a small road along the front and to the right of the swimming pool. The ruins are a few metres beyond.

Other sights in the area include: FONTAINE-LES-BASSETS. Pierre des Veuves, small quadrangular dolmen resting on a sandstone block. SE of Caen and NE of Argentan 13 km to Trun on D 916, then W on D 13. GIEL-COURTEILLES. At 100 m from the Pont de la Villette, between Ménil-Jean and Giel, and 5 m from the river, the Menhir de la Longue Roche is a 3 m-high block of sandstone. SE of Caen and W of Argentan 13 km on D 15 to Habloville, then S. HABLOVILLE. Pierre des Bignes, dolmen. Large granite table supported by six stones. SE of Caen and W of Argentan 13 km on D 15. SILLY-EN-GOUFFERN. La Pierre Levée (Pierre aux Fées). Largest menhir of the department of Orne, 5.40 m high. SE of Caen and E of Argentan on N 26 7.5 km, then S, 4 km on D 16.

Haute-Normandie (Rouen)
Eure (27), Seine-Maritime (76)

The chalk subsoil rises to an elevation of about 250 metres while some of the perpendicular cliffs on the Atlantic coast stand as high as 100 metres. The Seine Valley cuts a swathe through the region to the sea. From a Celtic settlement, the capital city of Rouen became the Roman Rotomagus. Normandy was conquered by Caesar's lieutenant, Sabinus, in 56 B.C. and in the third century the region was laid waste by barbarian hordes. There is evidence of Gallo-Roman occupation but relatively little of prehistoric people. After the victory of Clovis at Soissons in 484, the territory fell under the sway of the Franks. In 912, the town of Rouen became the ancient capital of the duchy of Normandie under the Viking king, Rollo, ancestor of William the Conqueror.

Evreux Eure
Sights:
At Le Vieil Evreux is the large pre-Roman settlement, and sanctuary of Gisacum. Gallo-Roman ramparts in town are on the Promenade des Remparts. Beside the calvary, on rue du Théâtre Romain, is located the second-century theatre, which had capacity for about 4000. There is little to see at present. Much overgrown.

One km W are the baths. Beyond the Salon de Fêtes take the small dirt road up to the trees. The baths are enclosed and a key must be obtained from the Mairie. They can be seen from outside of the fence, however.
Location:
SE of Rouen and SE of Evreux 8 km off the N 13. The site is 3 km S of Route 13.

Lillebonne Seine-Maritime
Sights:
Lillebonne, capital of the Gallic nation of the Calètes, became prosperous Juliobona of Gallo-Roman times. Before the silting of the river, it was a port. Remains of a first-century amphitheatre-theatre with an estimated capacity of over 6000 have been excavated here. Dating from Hadrian, ca. 120, it was altered in the second century, used as a fort during barbarian invasions, and later as a quarry. Although all that remain are walls for supporting tiers of seats, this is nevertheless an impressive site.
Location:
W of Rouen. The town is located at the mouth of the Seine on a small inlet 30 km E of Le Havre. The amphitheatre is opposite the Hôtel de Ville.

Rouen Seine-Maritime
Sights:
The neo-Romanesque church of St. Gervais has, under the choir, a fourth-century Carolingian crypt, a relic of an earlier church. Not far away is the tenth-eleventh century château of Robert le Diable, father of William the Conqueror, who died in 1035.
Location:
Rouen is NW of Paris on the E 05-A 13. The church is to the N of the Hôtel Dieu. The château is just SW of Rouen ca. 15 km off the Motorway A 13. It is visible from this motorway. Take the exit for Le Mans and double back to where the road goes right, and turn right again before going under the freeway. Signposted.

Other sights in the area include: JUMIÈGES. In the church of St.-Pierre of the great Benedictine Abbey of Jumièges are two bays and a porch remaining from the Carolingian church. W of Rouen ca. 24 km on the D 982. Then take the D 143 to Jumièges.

Pays de la Loire (Nantes)
Loire-Atlantique (44), Maine-et-Loire (49), Mayenne (53), Sarthe (72), Vendée (85)

Situated partly on the Atlantic Coast and traversed by the Loire River with its capital at Nantes, probably the Celtic Nannetum, the area is rich in archaeological sites. Numerous grottos (some decorated) sheltered prehistoric humans. The region contains thousands of megalithic monuments in varying states of repair. The 20-m-long dolmen at Bagneux (Saumur) is one of the finest in the country. The area is also rich in Gallo-Roman sites and Medieval mottes or defensive towers, some constructed in the tenth century.

Angers Maine-et-Loire

Sights:

This was once a Roman town with baths, circus, amphitheatre and, in the third century, defences. An ongoing excavation in the château reveals Gallo-Roman vestiges of a temple or sanctuary, and fortifications from Gallic wars dating back to 57 B.C.

On the lower side of Rue Donadieu-du-Puycharric are remains of the third-century town wall.

Some 15 km E, on the S side of the river is the Abbaye de St.-Maur-de-Glanfeuil. There is an excavation here of a fourth-century Roman villa which has revealed a temple and bases of columns. In the Chapelle St.-Martin is a Carolingian cross.

Location:

Angers is NE of Nantes 89 km on the A 11-E 60.

Aubigné-Racan Sarthe

Sights:

Gallo-Roman ensemble of Cherré, situated in the curve of the Loir, is overlooked by the pre-Roman oppidum, Camp de Vaux. The site includes remains of a temple, baths, theatre, cavea, forum, and vestiges of an eighth-fifth century, B.C. necropolis. Ongoing excavations.

Location:

NE of Nantes and SE of La Flèche 20 km on D 306 to La Lude, then E on D 305 6.5 km toward Vaas and S ca. 3 km to site. Signposted.

Bazougers Mayenne

Sight:

Menhir la Hune. A polissoir from Neolithic times, with three grooves on its north face, was erected as a menhir 5.60 m high.

Location:

NE of Nantes and SE of Laval. Go SE of Laval on D 21 to Parné-sur-Roc but before entering town turn left (N) on road toward Bazougers. 350 m after railroad crossing, turn right toward le Frêne and the menhir is on the left in a field. It is visible from the road.

Brécé Mayenne

Sights:

Dolmen and two menhirs. Dolmen du Petit Vieux-Sou, 11 m long. Menhir la Pierre St.-Guillaume, 4.30 m high (upside down), and Menhir Pierre St.-Siviard, 2.90 m high.

Location:

NE of Nantes and NW of Mayenne some 2 km S of Gorron. To find the dolmen depart Brécé SE on the D 503 to just past the church of Favière. Turn right, passing Ferme la Petite Reinère, la Louverais and at the Ferme de la Rivière turn left, walk 300 m to Ferme du Petit Vieux-Sou, then veer right for 180 m and the gallery grave is in the woods on the left.

For Pierre St.-Gillaume take the D 33 out of Gorron (2 km NW of Brécé) and 80 m after Ferme de la Garde, the menhir is on the left, 10 m from the road. For Pierre St.-Siviard continue on N 806 toward Ambrières and just before it is crossed by D 132, leave the road and go left on a path 300 m on foot to the megalith.

Chantrigné Mayenne

Sights:

Menhir le Grand Coudray 1.80 m high. Dolmen la Hamelinière, 12 m long.

Location:

NE of Nantes and N of Mayenne. For the menhir, go E of Ambrières-les-Vallées toward Chantrigné and just after crossing the river, turn left toward Ferme et Manoir du Grand Coudray. 200 m past farm and 25 m before the transformer is the menhir. To find the dolmen, go out of Chantrigné on the D 33 and the dolmen is nearby, on the left.

La Chapelle des Marais Loire-Atlantique

Sights:

Le Riholo. Tomb (3500-3200 B.C) with lateral rooms and a terminal room, mostly collapsed. La Roche aux Loups (Bas-Bergon) has three standing stones and a large capstone, and is a jaunty little dolmen in a field with cows.

Location:

La Chapelle des Marais is W of Nantes and N of St.-Nazaire 16 km. For Le Riholo, go out rue du Gué, past cemetery 1.3 km to stop sign. Turn left and follow 1.5 km to just before road forks. Dolmen is signposted (right) but sign faces the wrong way. Go up wooden steps and walk 30 m to dolmen.

From La Chapelle des Marais take road to Bas-Bergon to see La Roche aux Loups. From edge of town go 2 km and dolmen is signposted left. Follow path 500 m and turn right. Dolmen on left, just after trees, in field.

Chatillon-sur-Colmont Mayenne

Sights:

Menhir la Chaire, 2.10 m high. Dolmen le Haut-Rocher, 7 m long.

Location:

NE of Nantes and W of Mayenne. Take the D 5 NW of Chatillon and 100 m past the transformer, crossing the river, take a right toward the Ferme de la Chaire. After 900 m, the road goes right to the farm, but continue on 250 m, past a road left, and continue another 400 m to the menhir, which is on the right. The dolmen is 200 m coming back from the menhir toward the farm.

Conneré Sarthe

Sights:

Pierre-Couverte, a large passage grave and Pierre-Fiché, a pierced menhir.

Location:

NE of Nantes and E of Le Mans approx. 25 km on the N 23.

Couesmes-en-Froulay Mayenne

Sight:

Menhir de Montcorbeau, 2.40 m high.

Location:

NE of Nantes and NW of Mayenne. Take D 132 NW of Couesmes toward Vaucé. Cross river and turn right toward Château de Montcorbeau. Menhir is in the field on the right, shortly after the turn.

Crossac Loire-Atlantique

Sight:

Dolmen la Barbière. Tomb with corridor. Large capstone supported by three stones, but passage stones askew. Indistinguishable engravings on one stone lying down.

Location:

Crossac is NW of Nantes and N of St.-Nazaire some 15 km on D 50/D 16. The dolmen is 1 km S of town on the D 4 on the left (E). Signposted.

Ernée Mayenne

Sights:

Allée Couverte la Contrie and Dolmen la Tardivière.

Location:

NE of Nantes, W of Mayenne and SE of Fougères. Take the D 220 out of Ernée and at sign, left, for Ferme de la Contrie, turn left but do not turn off to the farm. 20 m from the main road, walk in left to dolmen. For the Tardivière, continue on D 220 and go right to Ferme la Tardivière. The dolmen is on the left turning up the road toward the farm itself.

Evron Mayenne

Sights:

In the vicinity are several interesting sites:

Le Rubicaire, Gallo-Roman castrum ca. 2 km N of Ste.-Gemmes-le-Robert on the D 20, signposted in the village and on road as: *Camp Romain de Rubicaire*. Small earthwork, fortified site roughly 75 x 60 m in dimension and up to 2 m high. Overgrown. Dirt track leads into the centre, 100 m off the road.

Dolmen des Erves, restored. Go SE of town to Ste.-Suzanne where D 143 is signposted after a few hundred metres . Camp de Beugy and Dolmen des Erves are signposted on the D 143. The dolmen is right beside a farmhouse and has two very large capstones over the chamber and portico, giving the appearance of a double dolmen. It is one of the oldest in the area, dating back 6000 years. The remains of about fifteen people (one of them incinerated) were found here.

Camp de Beugy—a few metres beyond the signpost for Dolmen des Erves are two adjoining camps with earthwork walls of ca. eleventh century. One was constructed by William the Conqueror while he was besieging the other!

Allée Couverte des Iles. Collapsed dolmen. From the Dolmen des Erves go up further on D 143 to crossroads. Turn right (Ferme des Séradières to the left) and after 500 m there is a road to another farm on the left but go 80 m on a path to the right to find the gallery grave.

Location:
Evron is SE of Caen and SE of Mayenne 24 km on D 35/D 7.

Gennes Maine-et-Loire
Sights:

There are two churches here that incorporate fragments of brickwork earlier than the tenth century. The church of Saint-Vetérin has a seventh-century wall. It was largely rebuilt in the thirteenth and fourteenth centuries. The church of Saint-Eusèbe contains numerous Merovingian tombs.

Less than 300 m SW of the village is the second-century theatre-amphitheatre built into the side of the hill. About 20 m further on is part of the circular covered wall of the arena. Plans are to use this as an open-air theatre in the future.

Pays de la Loire: Gennes.
Dolmen de la Madeleine

About one km S is the large Dolmen de la Madeleine with enormous capstones and standing stones. An oven is constructed inside.

In the vicinity are many menhirs and dolmens, and the S.I. in town will supply maps. Some of the best-preserved are as follows:

Dolmen de la Pagerie. From Gennes take the road toward Louerre. Turn right at the last house and follow this small road for 600 m. The large dolmen is on the right. The first capstone measures 1.20-1.50 m. The entrance is preserved.

Le Tertre de Bouchet. Menhir 3.60 m high. At Bouchet, just SW of Gennes, along a small dirt road. Ascend the steep section of the hill between the houses and at the top follow the pathway 200 m to the right.

Dolmen de la Forêt. Continuing on the dirt road from Bouchet toward the W ca. 900 m further, there is a dolmen with its entrance preserved.

Menhir of Bois Gilbert. 1500 m from Gennes, along the road toward Coutures is a 3.25 m-high menhir.

Menhir of Nidevelle. Leaving the village on the route toward Coutures, turn left. 200 m beyond is a menhir 5.5 m high.

Menhir of Cumeray. From Thoureil NW of Gennes, take the road toward St.-Georges-des-7-Voies. After 1500 m turn left into the woods for 188 m. The 3.30 m-high menhir is on the left.

Menhirs of St. Gondon and La Butte aux Houx. From Thoureil NW of Gennes, follow the road to St.-Georges for 500 m. Turn right at the cross. Immediately after the house of St.-Gondon, go left. At 100 m, above a sandstone escarpment, there is a menhir 2.70 m high. This is the first of a series of menhirs aligned toward the west. The second and the third are at 98 m, and the fourth, 78 m further on. After 44 m is the fifth, and the sixth (lying down) is at 145 m. The seventh is that of Mezan which can also be reached by going W from the S.I. of Gondon toward the woods. It is 900 m from the S.I.

Menhir La Filoussiere. Go the same way as for the Menhirs of St.-Gondon, but continue on the road for 900 m. After the orchards of Marchais Clair, take the first path to the right into the woods. 400 m further on is a menhir 4.80 m high, 25 m to the left of the path. Dolmen la Bajoulière. From Thoureil, NW of Gennes, travel in the same direction as for St.-Gondon Menhirs but continue 2 km to the house on the left and the transformer. Turn left, continue for ll00 m. Completely excavated and restored, it is a hemicycle of small blocks and presents a more complex entrance than usual. The capstone has been estimated at 70 tons.

Dolmen l'Etiau. From St. Rémy la Varenne NW of Gennes go to the village of Bourge-Dion, 3 km to the SW. Continue 700 m past and take the road to the left, going toward Couture for 120 m. The dolmen is signposted at 200 m on the right. There are remains of an entranceway. Inside are multiple grooves which are perhaps the mark of magic-religious rites.

Dolmen la Caillère. From the château of Montsabert, l km S of Bourg-Dion, proceed 150 m in the direction of Coutures. Take the road to the right. The dolmen is beside the road after ca. 400 m.

Dolmen de Piau. From Chemellier, W of Gennes, take the road toward Coutures for 45 m, then take the right fork in the direction of Gennes. After 600 m turn right between houses. At the foot of the slope, turn right into the woods. 30 m before leaving the woods, look to the right 25 m from path.

Dolmen d'Avort. From Gennes take the road to Louerre for 4.8 km. The dolmen can then be seen 80 m to the right, almost facing the Fontaine Maléfique of Avort beside the road to Milly. Remains of entranceway.

Dolmen le Corbeau. This is signposted on the road from Deneze toward Louerre. At 400 m to the north of the village of La Bournée. On the bank of the crossroad, is a polissoir.

Dolmen la Pierre Peteuse. Going toward Deneze, 500 m N of Pre Godin, W of Saulgre, at 30 m is the gallery grave.

Dolmen Saulgre. At the eastern exit of the village of Saulgre, on the road going N, 300 m to the left is another dolmen.

Dolmen de Chavais. From the village of Chavais en Deneze, proceed 400 m S on the road to Cunault. Take a left on the farm road for 500 m. Remains of a dolmen, partially destroyed in order to use the capstone for the bridge in Varennes. (It was ostensibly pulled by oxen for 5 km).

Dolmen Ruisseau d'Enfer. At 150 m from Ruisseau d'Enfer on the left bank of the stream at the village of Pompierre, 3.5 km S of Chenehutte, is a triangular-shaped dolmen, but difficult to find in the woods.

Location:
Gennes is E of Nantes by the Loire River, about 27 km SE of Angers on route 451.

Houssay Mayenne
Sights:
La Baronnière. two menhirs, 3.50 m and 2.90 m high.

Location:
NE of Nantes, N of Houssay, S of Laval and off the D 112 between Houssay and Origné. From Origné go S and turn right (W) at sign: *Ferme de la Baronnière*. Follow road 700 m and continue on foot another 700 m; menhirs are on the right, just before T-junction.

Jublains Mayenne

Sights:

Ongoing excavations of the original Gallic village, later Roman Noviodunum. The Celtic Diablintes minted coins here and constructed a wooden sanctuary which was replaced with a Roman stone temple around A.D. 68. The large podium of the cella remains today. Also from Roman times are vestiges of a fortress, a theatre and thermal baths (under the large church, the structure and grounds of which reveal evidence of the ca. 60 m wide baths enclosed by galleries and several small rooms).

Pays de la Loire: Jublains. Fortress

The site was abandoned in the fourth century during the barbarian invasions.

Location:

NE of Nantes and NW of Le Mans 63 km. 13 km SE of Mayenne. All sites are in town, and well signposted. Worth a visit.

Laval Mayenne

Site:

Notre Dame de Pritz just outside of Laval dates from the seventh-ninth centuries. Beside it is a stele, a small rounded menhir-like stone with marks on it, known as the Lech Celtique.

Location:

NE of Nantes, go N out of Laval on the D 104, 300 m past sign indicating the city limits, where there is a small church on the right. Go in at the gate and 40 m on the left beside the church is the stele.

Le Mans Sarthe

Sights:

To the west near rue Denfert-Rochereau, rue St.-Hilaire and rue de la Port St. Anne (which run round the west side of the old town) are remains of the Gallo-Roman town walls of the third and fourth centuries. Inside the cathedral in the SW corner, there is a menhir of red sandstone.

The former abbey church of Notre Dame de la Couture in the old town has a crypt under the choir, reputedly dating from the tenth century. It has some reused columns, and beneath the altar is the seventh-century tomb of St.-Bertrand, founder of the church.

At nearby Allonnes stand the vestiges of the temple of Mars Mullo, sometimes referred to as the Tour aux Fées. This sacred place (cella), once surrounded by colonnades, appears to have been a site of pilgrimage.

Location:

Le Mans is NE of Nantes and SW of Paris ca. 105 km on the A 11-E 50. Allonnes is found by leaving the city to the SW on the D 147, E.

Montaudin Mayenne
Sights:
2.8 m high Menhir la Boussardière and Broussault gallery grave, 6 m long.
Location:
NE of Nantes and E of Fougères. For the menhir take the D 224 from Larchamp and cross the N 799. 800 m from the crossroad, the road leads left to the Ferme de la Boussardière. Go 200 m further on the D 224, and the menhir is on the left.

For the dolmen take the D 521 S of Larchamp. 150 m before meeting the road going left toward Ernée there will be a sign (on the right) for the Ferme de la Béhourrie. Opposite is a path going into the woods. Walk in and turn right immediately. Continue 100 m, and 40 m further to the left stands the dolmen.

Montenay Mayenne
Sights:
8-m-long gallery grave de la Perche, and Polissoir La Pierre St.-Guillaume.
Location:
NE of Nantes and W of Mayenne. SE of Ernée. From Montenay, take the road SE toward Lasnerie. Pass crossroads of D 209 and cross river, then follow the left fork toward Ferme de la Perche. At junction of roads leading to La Perche, La Ménardais and la Dargentière farms, go straight on foot to where three roads join. Continue straight on for 320 m and at the fork, turn left and proceed 280 m to the dolmen, 60 m in to the right.

To find the polissoir go SE of Montenay toward Lasnerie. Turn left toward Ferme de la Berthellière, continue 600 m then 200 m R to farm. A further 150 m to the site.

Niort-la-Fontaine Mayenne
Sights:
Dolmen le Bignon and Menhir Pierre Robert. Also close by is the Dolmen la Guichardière, with two capstones.
Location:
NE of Nantes and NE of Mayenne and W of Lassay. Take the D 219 out of Niort toward Melleray. Turn left to Hameau du Bignon and continue past the Ferme de Bignon 150 m, then turn right at the crossroad. After 250 m the dolmen is on the right.

Continue through the woods to next crossroad and the 2.6-m-high menhir is on the left. From the farm (500 m from the road), it is a walk of some 550 m. For the Dolmen la Guichardière take the D 202 (Chantrigné to Melleray), and 1.8 km before Melleray turn right to Ferme du Gué. Walk 400 m to farm, cross stream and continue ca. 300 m. The dolmen will be on the left.

Pornic Loire-Atlantique
Sights:
La Boutinardière, passage grave. The passageway is in ruins. Leave Pornic on D 13 to the SW. Go 1500 m to Place du 14 Juillet, and turn right.

400 m further, park the car near the cliffs and follow the path 500 m to dolmen.

800 m W of this is La Joselière, dolmen with corridor, recently restored. It has two lateral rooms and a long, rectangular chamber at the end of the corridor. A large stone covers each of the side chambers and the end of the corridor. Follow the D 13 to La Fontaine-Breton. Turn right toward the sea, and then left. The dolmen is near the coast 300 m away.

The Cairn of Les Mousseaux (1 km W of Pornic) dates from 3500 B.C. Take Avenue du Géneral de Gaulle and turn left on rue Mermoz, then right on rue du Chemin de la Motte. It is signposted on the left. Moulin de la Motte has only vestiges of a huge tumulus, once 70 m long and 30 m wide. It is just a few metres E from Les Mousseaux, but on private property. Other nearby dolmens have disappeared.

Location:
Pornic is SW of Nantes approx. 41 km on the D 751, on the coast.

Poulay Mayenne
Sights:
Polissoirs les Landes. Two stones with three polishing grooves.
Location:
NE of Nantes and NE of Mayenne. Take the N 816 toward Montreuil and 200 m before the Ferme les Landes, walk in left, then immediately left again at fork in path. Pass two oak trees and the polissoirs are 30 m to the right.

St.-Aubin des Châteaux Loire-Atlantique
Sight:
Menhir La Louée, 3.50 m high. Many legends exist about this, one of which states that when Gargantua was sitting on the belfry of Ruffigné with one foot at St.-Aubin and the other at Sion, this 'pebble' fell from his left shoe.
Location:
N of Nantes and W of Châteaubriant 10 km. In St.-Aubin take the D 34 toward Sion and almost immediately turn left toward La Chapelle. 150 m further at the crossing of three roads, take the centre road. The menhir is 300 m on the right, in a field.

St.-Lyphard
Loire-Atlantique
Sights:
Pierre Druidique de Kerbourg. 8-m long tomb with corridor and chamber. Four stones cap the corridor. Some stones misaligned, but it is a good specimen. A second, smaller tomb, collapsed, lies just beyond.

Pays de la Loire: St.-Lyphard.
Pierre Druidique de Kerbourg

Location:
NW of Nantes and NW of St.-Nazaire 20 km to Guérande. Then take the D 51 for 6 km toward Kerhinet. Signposted on the right.

St.-Mars-la-Futaie Mayenne
Sight:
Dolmen la Louvetière. 12 m long.
Location:
NE of Nantes and NE of Fougères. Take the D 534 from St.-Mars 300 m past the crossroads with D 116, to a transformer. 250 m beyond this and 60 m in to the right is the dolmen.

St.-Nazaire Loire-Atlantique
Sights:
In town is a menhir standing alongside a dolmen, the latter consisting of two stones ca. 2 m high, supporting a 3.30-m capstone in the rue du Dolmen leading NE from the Place Marceau.

The fine Tumulus of Dissignac covers two dolmens constructed side by side. Both have 11-m corridors, and the smaller one has engravings on the capstone. Nearby is a cromlech.
Location:
St.-Nazaire is at the mouth of the Loire, NW of Nantes about 45 km on the E 60-N 171. From St.-Nazaire take the D 92 W toward Pornichet. At edge of town is a large traffic island. Go around this and keep following signs to Pornichet, then go right at second street after the island, marked: *Tumulus* (beside Promocash). Follow road 1.4 km to tumulus, which is signposted.

For the cromlech, on the main road to Pornichet, take the road left, directly opposite the road to Dissignac, signposted: *St. Marc/Mer/Cromlech*. Go 1.7 km and the cromlech is on the right.

St.-Philibert-de-Grand-Lieu Loire-Atlantique
Sight:
The restored abbey church offers a rare example of ninth-century Carolingian architecture in its interior. The crypt was once the resting place of St.-Philibert, whose remains, now at Tournus in Burgundy, were moved to protect them from Viking raids. Guided visits by appointment.
Location:
SW of Nantes ca. 17 km on the D 178/D 262.

St.-Pierre-la-Cour Mayenne
Sights:
Menhirs of La Pierre Bouillante consist of 3.50-m and 1.80-m-high stones. They stand 50 m apart in the woods of Essart.
Location:
NE of Nantes, W of Laval and E of Vitré. Take the D 576 out of St.-Pierre toward Port Brillet. Go to transformer and walk in beside it 750 m to a

stream, then turn right and the first menhir is 150 m straight ahead. The second is 50 m further on.

Ste.-Gemmes-le-Robert Mayenne

Sight:
Gallery grave, les Pierres Jumelles. 8 m long. See also, Evron.

Location:
NE of Nantes and SE of Mayenne. From Ste.-Gemmes go NW on D 552. Turn left at road to Ferme de Richebourg and then 300 m to farm. Continue for another 350 m, turn right at large rock. Dolmen is 3 m to the right.

Saumur Maine-et-Loire

Sights:
The Dolmen de Bagneux, an excellent example, is 20 m long, 7 m wide with four capstones and sixteen large standing stones weighing approximately 500 tons. It is located in the garden of a private house, visitable for a small fee. Signposted.

Location:
E of Nantes, SE of Angers and SW of Tours 63 km on the E 60-N 152. Bagneux is 2 km SW of Saumur on the N 147, and the site is on rue du Dolmen, 400 m off the main street of Bagneux.

Other sights in the area include many more dolmens and menhirs. Only the more accessible ones are given here. BAUGÉ. Dolmen de la Pierre Couverte. E of Nantes and E/NE of Angers, N of Longué 15 km on D 938. Leave Baugé on D 141 and after 3.5 km, the dolmen is just to the left of the road. LA BIGOTTIÈRE. Menhir le Faix du Diable. 4.30 m high. NE of Nantes and N of Laval. SE of Ernée. 3 km from Andouillé on the D 104, turn right. The menhir is 50 m from here. CHAILLAND. Menhir de Clivoy, 3 m high. NE of Nantes and NW of Laval. From Chailland take the d 548, S for 2 km, passing (left) Ferme de Clivoy and then passing a km marker on left. A menhir is 70 m beyond on the left, 20 m off the road. GORRON. 4.30 m-high Menhir la Roche. NE of Nantes and NW of Mayenne. Take the D 5 out of Gorron 800 m. Pass Ferme de la Roche and go 200 m to stream, then another 100 m right, along stream to find the menhir. See also entry for Brécé. HERCÉ. Dolmen de la Pierre. NE of Nantes and NW of Mayenne. Just W of Gorron. From Hercégo go S toward Colombiers-du-Plessis. Turn left (E) toward Ferme de la Pierre and walk in 300 m around farm. Dolmen is 100 m beyond. ILE D'YEU. At the NW tip of this island is Dolmen de la Planche à Puare. It has a central corridor with two chambers, one on each side of the passage. Ile d'Yeu is located SW of Nantes and about 40 km NW of Les Sables d'Olonne, in the Atlantic. MOUZILLON. A Gallo-Roman bridge crosses the river Sanguèse S of the church here. SE of Nantes 24 km on N 249, then S, 4 km on D 763. NANTES. Near the cathedral to the N, is the Porte St.-Pierre next to which, in the gardens, are remains of the Gallo-Roman wall beside the Cours St.-Pierre. SW of Paris about 385 km on the motorway. PONTCHÂTEAU. Menhir Fuseau de La Madeleine (The Magdalene's Spindle). NW of Nantes and 18 km NE of St.-Nazaire. It is on the E 60. 3.5 km W of Pontchâteau, take the D 33 and turn left just after the calvary. The menhir is in a field 200 m further on the left. Signposted. **St.-Père en Retz.** Menhir de Pierre Le Maz is over 4 m high. Another stone is lying beside it. S of Nantes and 10 km N of Pornic. From St.-Père go S on the D 58 then take the D 5. After 1 km go right, pass La Pauvedrie and La Caillerie and the menhir is on the left of the road. **St.-Pierre-des-Nids.** Menhir la Pierre au Diable 3.90 m. NE of Nantes and NE of Mayenne. From Mayenne, take the N 12 to Pré-en-Pail, then go S on the D 204, turning left (E) to Ferme de la Poupinière. From farm go on foot 600 m. **St.-Rémy-la-Varenne.** Dolmen de la Bajoulière. 2 km S of the Loire between Angers and Saumur, the dolmen is situated to the N of the village of Fontaine at the extreme SW of the commune of St.-Rémy-la-Varenne.

Picardie (Amiens)
Aisne (02), Oise (60), Somme (80)

This is primarily an agricultural region of low hills and valleys, but with a short stretch of coastline. The capital, Amiens, was the chief town of the Germanic Ambiani. Prehistoric finds have come from all over and from all epochs, forming a rich collection housed in the museum in Amiens. The Somme valley is particularly notable for Paleolithic tools dating back some three quarters of a million years. the region was an invasion-or-migratory route for peoples from the east, and many bronze weapons have been found throughout the area.

By the time of the arrival of the Romans, the region was well-dotted with enclosures whose purposes are unknown. The smallest of these measured only two metres across, perhaps funerary monuments, and the larger ones were possibly for the enclosure of animals. With the Romans, the situation changed as large farms or villas developed for the exploitation of the land. In situ sites are generally Gallo-Roman or Medieval.

Amiens Somme
Sights:
SE of the city, in the suburb of Cagny-la-Garenne, is the excavation of a Lower Paleolithic encampment dating as far back as 450,000 years. There is a cliff beside which the river Avre used to run, showing stratification. Informative signs about geology and early humans at the site. Several hundred stone tools have been found here.

Location:
Amiens is N of Paris on the N 29-E 44. For Cagny, go SE of Amiens by following rue Jules Barni from Place Alphonse Piquet (with large tower). Turn right on rue de Cagny (the S.I. will give a map). Go through Cagny and turn right on rue de la Garenne, then first right (at top of hill). The archaeological park is on the left, opposite the cemetery. Walk 200-250 m up a dirt (and sometimes muddy) road.

Caply Oise
Site:
The Gallo-Roman archaeological site has a first-second century theatre that was part of a town of 10,000 inhabitants. Traces of an oppidum have been found nearby on a hill. A cave with niches from the end of the first century is situated in a field opposite, but there is not a great deal to see.

Location:
S of Amiens 32 km on N 1 to Breteuil, then continue a little further S on the same road. It is signposted off the N 1 just N of the village.

Champlieu Oise
Sights:
Gallo-Roman remains here include one first-century temple super-imposed upon another. It lies to the north of the highway that is part of the old Roman road, Chaussée Bruhenaut, that ran from Senlis to Soissons. To the south is a second-century theatre, 70 m in diameter, with a capacity of about 3000-4000 patrons. Remaining are the three first rows of tiered seating, part of the foundations of the stage, and six public entrances. Further S, beyond the theatre, is an

Picardie: Champlieu. Ancient Church

unexcavated palaestra and adjoining it the public baths with atrium, frigidarium, tepidarium, caldarium, and hypocaust.

Nearby, just outside the village, is a very small Romanesque church built on earlier foundations. Behind, overgrown, are remains of an early Christian cemetery and catacombs. There are also ruins of a later church that was attached to the Romanesque structure.

Location:
SE of Amiens and NE of Paris on the edge of Compiègne Forest. From the A 1-E 15 take exit #10 and go E to Compiègne then S on the D 332 ca. 8 km to the turn off right (W) to Champlieu. The site, on both sides of the road, lies S of the Forêt de Compiègne and just N of the village.

Naours Somme
Sights:
Les Grottes de Naours. A maze of about 2 km of underground streets, three chapels, stables, store-rooms, and living quarters have been excavated. The height is between 1.6 and 2.0 m. Hand-excavated, the 300 chambers were used by the local inhabitants for storage and living during times of invasion, apparently first during the Germanic invasions of the third and fourth centuries, and then again in the ninth when the Vikings ravaged the countryside. They were used over and over in local conflicts and finally during World War II both sides housed troops and stored material in them.

Location:
13 km N of Amiens on the N 25 to Talmas, then left (W) 3 km on the D 60. Signposted in town.

Senlis Oise
Sights:
Ancient Gallic and later Roman site of Augustomagus. On the western outskirts of the town at the far end of rue de Beauvais are the remains of the 90 x 70 m first-century Roman amphitheatre. The walls still stand over 2 m high but now only a few tiers of seats remain. The site is on private property and can only be visited in guided groups arranged through the S.I.

Vestiges of the third-century Gallo-Roman wall with its remaining towers run beside the château but are mostly hidden among private properties. Some parts are visible near the S.I. In the crypt of the Musée d'Art are relics of a Gallo-Roman house along with foundations of the wall. Rue de la Treille has the "Fausse Port," a gate of the Gallo-Roman ramparts.

Location:
S of Amiens and N of Paris 26 km on the A 1, situated on the Nonette River.

Soissons Aisne
Sights:
On the far bank of the Aisne are the remains of the Abbey of St.-Médard, with a ninth-century Carolingian crypt. Several tombs are found here including those reputed to be of Clothair (d. 561) and Sigebert (d. 575), son and grandson of Clovis. There are also a couple of tombs outside, 3 m below ground surface. There are various excavations roundabout.

Picardie: Soissons. St.-Médard Crypt

Location:

SE of Amiens and NE of Paris 61 km on the N 2. The abbey is in the NE part of town, near a seminary. The S.I. will give directions.

Other sights in the area include: **BEAUVAIS.** E and S of the cathedral, beside the Galerie Nationale de la Tapisserie, are relics of third-century Gallo-Roman walls. There is also a vestige on rue Beauregard beyond the remains of the eleventh-century church of St.-Barthélemy, which originally abutted the wall. S of Amiens and N of Paris 60 km on N 1.

Poitou-Charentes (Poitiers)

Charente (16), Charente-Maritime (17), Deux-Sèvres (79), Vienne (86)

The area consists of a fertile plateau, through which runs a sill of ancient rocks, the Hauteurs de la Gâtine, rising to 285 metres. Around La Rochelle on the Atlantic coast is considerable marshland. The countryside contains many dolmens and prehistoric grottos, and some of the cities have fine examples of Roman remains. The present capital at Poitiers was conquered by the Visigoths and then by the Franks. It was in this vicinity, in 732, that Charles Martel repulsed a Moorish invasion from Spain.

The name "Poitiers" ostensibly derives from the Pictaves of Gallo-Roman times but little remains of their sojourn here. Saintes, the capital of the Santons, seems to have been a prosperous town when Caesar conquered Gaul. Judging from its monuments, it was again prosperous under the Romans.

Ardillières Charente-Maritime

Sight:

Dolmen de la Pierre Levée has a rectangular chamber 2.15 m long and 1.40 m wide. Its capstone is intact.

Location:

SW of Poitiers, SW of Niort. From Rochefort near the coast go 13 km N on the D 5 and Ardillières is just E of Ciré.

Les Arènes Charente-Maritime

Sights:

Thénac. Currently under restoration, the small Roman theatre offers little to see except the outlines in the ground, some stones and some entranceways. Much has been removed, probably for use in the local villages. This may have been a rural theatre or even a training ground for gladiators for the amphitheatre in Mediolanum Santonum, a short distance to the north.

Location:

SW of Poitiers and ca. 5 km S of Saintes on the N 137. Thénac is W of Les Arènes on the D 138. The theatre is marked right (N) just out of Les Arènes. From highway N 137 go left 700 m following signs. Theatre-remains are on the left.

Béthines Vienne

Sight:

A Roman bridge over the Salleron stream is crossed as you enter Béthines on the D 32 from St.-Savin. There is a playground beside it—a good place from which to view the bridge.

Location

E of Poitiers 42 km on the N 151 to St.-Savin, then SE 8 km on the D 32.

Bougon Deux-Sèvres

Sights:

Tumulus of Bougon. Important megalithic ensemble claimed to be the world's oldest funerary monument consists of five tumuli dating back to about 4500 B.C. and abandoned about 2000 B.C. A wall separates two of the tumuli from the others, perhaps also dividing the sanctuary into two zones. About 300 skeletons were found here, indicating that these were collective tombs, probably for important persons. Impressive site. Museum in situ.

See also entry for Sanxay, which is close by.

Location:

SW of Poitiers 22 km on N 11, then S on D 5 just after La Villedieu, following signs for Bougon. Well signposted.

Chassenon Charente

Sights:

Religious springs on the site of second-century Cassinomagus, with parts of the walls still standing around the sacred area. The main visible structures is the large thermae with hypocaust, multi-temperature rooms, palaestra, water conduits, and a large pool.

About 200 m north of the baths complex are the foundations of a temple awaiting excavation. At present there is little to see. Museum in situ.

Location:
S of Poitiers, some 46 km W of Limoges on the N 141, past St.-Junien to Chabanais, then turn left (S) 4.5 km on D 29 to Chassenon. Well signposted.

Châteaubernard Charente
Sight:
Dolmen de la Pierre Levée, also known as Dolmen de la Combe des Dames. The capstone, once fallen to the ground, has been reset on its supporting stones.

Location:
SW of Poitiers and just S of Cognac on the D 24. Turn left by the Mairie, and follow the road around to rue de la Pierre Levée. The dolmen is on the right.

Châtellerault Vienne
Sights:
At the ruins of Vieux Poitiers, the most prominent site is the second-century theatre, with a corner wall of the cavea and proscenium standing over 20 m high. Estimated seating capacity is 10,000.

Beside the theatre is a lapidary with a small, inscribed menhir discovered in the theatre, along with some stone sepulchres. About 400 m away are Gallo-Roman potters' ovens. The town seems to have been destroyed by fire in the second century.

Location:
Châtellerault is some 30 km NE of Poitiers on the E 05-A 10. To reach the site proceed S of Châtellerault toward Limoges and Chauvigny. After passing aerodrome, turn right toward Cenon. From here take road left toward Chezelle. Ruins on hill to the left. Signposted.

Chauvigny
Vienne
Sight:
At nearby St.-Pierre-les-Eglises there is a simple pre-Romanesque church in the Merovingian cemetery. Its small ninth-tenth century apse has some frescos that are considered to be the oldest in the region of Poitou.

Poitou-Charente: Chauvigny. St.-Père-les-Eglises

Location:
Chauvigny is E of Poitiers 23 km on the N 151. Leaving Chauvigny on the D 749 S, a couple of km S on the right is a small sign: *Les Eglises. Eglise Romane.* Church is at the end of a small road.

Civaux Vienne
Sights:
The 90-sq. m Merovingian necropolis on a hill in town dates back to the fourth century and is part of a larger ancient cemetery that at one time contained thousands of tombs. Various types of graves are in evidence. Its origins remain obscure. Parts of the walls are Gallo-Roman.

Dolmen of Loubressac with few standing stones and headstone collapsed into the cavity is a poor specimen.
Location:
SE of Poitiers 36 km on N 147 to Lussac, then N ca. 6 km to Civaux. The dolmen is situated ca. 3 km on D 114 toward Mazerolles on the right side of the road. Signposted from D 749.

Civray Vienne
Sight:
Dolmen de la Pierre Pese with enormous capstone (eroded), supported by three standing stones.
Location:
S of Poitiers approx. 50 km on N 10 to Les Maisons Blanches. Turn E on the D 148 and dolmen is signposted, left, just before railway bridge over the road (3 km from the turn-off). Drive up small road left, ca. 100 m and turn left again. The dolmen is almost immediately on the left up a small path in the woods.

Cognac Charente
Sight:
Séchebec dolmen with two enormous capstones and nine standing stones is a good specimen dated from between 2400 B.C. and 1800 B.C.
Location:
Cognac is SW of Poitiers and E of Saintes 24 km. To find the dolmen, take rue de la République in town (signposted: *Champ de Four, autres directions*). It becomes rue de l'Echassier. Dolmen is on the left beside apartment building, presenting an interesting contrast.

Le Douhet Charente-Maritime
Sight:
Remains here of a first-century Roman aqueduct feeding into pools in the château gardens. Originally it went from Fontcouverte to Saintes but as that city grew, it was extended to Le Douhet and Vénérand. It is one of the few places where a Roman aqueduct is still in use in France. It can be seen at ground level just E of Le Douhet, signposted off the N 150. From here to the château, 1 km of it is still in use.

Location:
SW of Poitiers and N of Saintes ca. 10 km on the N 150, just S of St.-Hilaire.

Fenioux Charente-Maritime
Sight:
The first, ninth-century, church here was Carolingian, and the walls of the nave and the narrow openings known as *fenestrelles* survive, the latter characteristic of the Carolingian period. Partially renovated for the first time in the eleventh or twelfth centuries. An anthropomorphic tomb may be seen beside the Lanterne des Morts (twelfth-century graveyard lantern).

Location:
SW of Poitiers and N of Saintes on D 114 to St.-Savinien, then NE on D 18 to Fenioux.

Fontcouverte Charente-Maritime
Sight:
Four or five large arches of a Gallo-Roman aqueduct, 2 of which are reasonably intact, the remainder greatly deteriorated.

Location:
SW of Poitiers and in a NE suburb of Saintes. Take the N 150 N out of Saintes and after city limit sign turn left and go into Fontcouverte. Follow signs for Golf club. To see the aqueduct remains you must enter the Golf club by the gate marked: *Acces aux arches* and follow signs for that and for *promeneurs* (walkers). The vestiges are ca. 700 m beyond the gate.

Jarnac Charente
Sight:
Dolmen de la Pierre Levée, consisting of large stones but with capstone collapsed into recess, and others completely askew.

Location:
SW of Poitiers and E of Cognac 15 km on N 141. Take the road SW out of Jarnac toward St.-Même-les-Carrières. Go through village onto D 90 toward St.-Preuil. From edge of village continue 1 km and turn right onto dirt path for 400 m. The dolmen is on the left.

Loudún Vienne
Sites:
There are eight dolmens in varying condition in the vicinity.

Location:
NW of Poitiers and ca. 13 km NW of Loudún on N 147. At sign on the right for Dolmen de la Fontaine du Sol, turn in 300 m. There is one on either side of the road. On the same road, ca. 10 km from Loudún, turn left at Vaon toward Lantray and sign for dolmen. Go through village ca. 350 m and turn left again at sign for dolmen. It is visible in a field on the right, beside a tree, about 300 m further on.

For the other five, take the D 759 W, 5.5 km, then head S on D 19 after Arcay 3.9 km where the road splits, take the right fork and after the railway track the dolmen is on the left. Continue on the road toward Chassigny and Leugny and at T-junction in Chassigny, go left then right at the end of the village on Route de la Grève. Follow this until a sign appears on the right for St.-Laon and after 800 m the dolmen is on the left in a field. The third is found by taking the D 759 further W to Thouars but just before the town is the turnoff (S) on D 37. After ca. 6 km there is the dolmen just W of the road and another W of Taizé, 4 km further S near Auboue. There is yet another on the S side of the D 37 E of Thouars, just N of the D 65 between Puyraveau and Thouars.

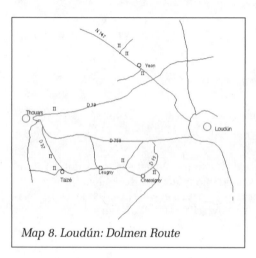

Map 8. Loudún: Dolmen Route

Melle Deux-Sèvres

Sights:

The Roman town of Metallum was selected to be the site of a Carolingian mint because of the nearby argentiferous lead mines (that were exploited in the fifth and sixth centuries). Open to visitors, these mines date back to Merovingian and Carolingian times, but they were closed in the tenth century after 500 years of exploitation.

A herbal garden has been developed at the site, with plants used in Carolingian times for medicine and dyeing. A guided tour of the mines can be arranged at the site.

Location:

50 km SW of Poitiers on the D 950. Signposted in town *Mines Argentifères*.

Plaisance Vienne

Sights:

There is a Merovingian tomb surmounted by a calvary in the middle of the cemetery here. Three km away along the road toward Adriers, is the Dolmen de Chiroux. Just before the road is crossed by the N 147, it is situated to the left, going S.

Location:

Plaisance is some 43 km SE of Poitiers on the N 147-E 62 to Moulismes, then E, 5 km on the D 12.

Poitiers Vienne

Sights:

In town there is a broken dolmen, the Pierre Levée, as well as the restored Baptistry of St.-Jean which is dated to the fourth century and considered one of the oldest Christian monuments in France. It is rectangular in shape and once had a baptismal pool in the centre. After the seventh century, this was filled in and baptism was performed by pouring water on the head. The E apse is seventh century and two small lateral apses are sixth-seventh century.

The arches, marble columns and capitals are Roman, as are the frescos on the dividing walls. The Hypogee Martyrium, an underground funerary chapel of the seventh or eighth centuries, has been closed to the public. In the rue des Arènes slight remains of a large Roman amphitheatre are visible.

To the left of the N 10 just outside the city are the Arcs de Parigné, remains of a first-second century Roman aqueduct. Vestiges are also visible at St.-Benoit in the courtyard of the château, and from the rue de l'Ermitage.

About 9.5 km S of Poitiers on D 4, at Ligugé, Gallo-Roman remains have been found in front of the doorway of the church and under the nave, along with the vestiges of a fourth-century martyrium, the apse of a fourth-century basilica and some fifth and sixth-century Merovingian tombs. Excavations near the church show remains of a Gallo-Roman villa and of a seventh-century basilica, with crypt.

Location:

Poitiers is SW of Paris and S of Tours on the E 05-A 10. The Roman aqueduct is on the N 10 SW of the city. Ligugé is 9.5 km S of town on the D 4. St.-Benoit is just S of the city on D 741.

Ruffec Charente

Sights:

Several megaliths stand SW of the town some 16 km on the N 10.

There is a large monolith to the N of the D 736 between Charmé and Husson. Go 1.3 km from Charmé and turn right into vineyard on dirt path. The stone is ca. 500 m from the road.

Two dolmens are found by taking the D 32 from Charmé to Ligné, 4 km. Dolmens are signposted in Ligné, beside the cemetery. Follow the D 61 and they are signposted again, right, just beyond the village of Villesoubis. The first dolmen has an enormous cracked headstone on ten standing stones, and the second has a very large capstone on four standing stones. Both have remains of passageways or another chamber. They are situated side by side between Ligné and Mansle and are signposted.

The necropolis of Forêt de Boixe has the remains of a fourth-millennium dolmen but only the capstone, lying on the ground, remains today. Deep grooves on it suggest its use as a sacrificial stone.

Location:

Ruffec is S of Poitiers and N of Angoulême on the N 10. Charmé is reached by going SW of Ruffec about 11 km on the D 736. Mansle is S of Ruffec approx. 17 km on N 10. For the Forêt de Boixe go S from Mansle and the dolmen is well signposted after about 3.5 km, *Pierre du Sacrifice.*

Saint-Brice Charente

Sight:

Dolmen de Garde Epée dating from about 2500 B.C. two large, very thick capstones and five large standing stones. Fairly good condition.

Poitou-Charente: Saint-Brice. Dolmen de Garde Epée

Location:

Saint-Brice is just 5 km E of Cognac, which is SW of Poitiers and E of Saintes. Take the D 157 E of Cognac and on the S side of the road, just before km marker #3, lies the dolmen. Signposted.

St.-Cybardeaux
Charentes
Sights:

Les Bouchads. Gallo-Roman rural sanctuary. It was possibly the remains of Germanicomagus, destroyed in 275 during an invasion. Ruined remains of large first-century amphitheatre built into the hillside and said to be the fourth largest in Gaul, 105 m in diameter.

Location:

S of Poitiers and NW of Angoulême. Go to St. Cybardeaux on the D 745, ca. 21 km, then turn right (N) to site 2.3 km. Signposted on D 756.

St.-Fort-sur-Né Charente
Sight:

Located here is the dolmen considered to be the most remarkable in the Charente. One large capstone rests on three very tall standing stones. Composed of sandstone rather than granite.

Location:

Saint-Fort is SW of Poitiers and S of Cognac ca. 14 km on the D 731. The dolmen is well signposted and stands in a vineyard.

Poitou-Charente: St.-Fort-sur-Né. Dolmen

St.-Germain-de-Confolens Charente
Sight:

On an island in the river (private property that can be reached over a walking bridge if permission is requested) stands a unique dolmen altered in the eleventh century to form an oratory. Under the capstone which rests on four columns, was a chapel dedicated to Ste.-Madeleine.

The Menhir du Repaire is on the S side of the D 30 from Confolens toward Lesterps. It is 2.65 m high. Another menhir, La Pierre-Fade, lies 1.5 km N of Availles-Limouzine on the D 8 to the left of the road.

At Confolens there is a dolmen that was moved to the churchyard in town. It has a sarcophagus lying on top of it.

Location:

S of Poitiers and NE of Bordeaux. St.-Germain lies S of Poitiers 58 km on the D 741 then SE 12 km on the D 148/D 948, then N 6.5 km on the D 951. Availles-Limouzine is 6.5 km N of Lessac, which is 1 km W on the D 71. Confolens lies 7 km S of St.-Germain-de-Confolens.

St.-Léomer Vienne

Sights:

The original Celtic sanctuary was replaced by the Gallo-Roman sanctuary of Masamas in the second half of the first century. Rectangular enclosure ca. 75 x 100 m, the site was abandoned in the third or fourth century. Little now to see beyond slight foundations of two temples rising less than 1 m off the ground, and some foundations of other buildings.

Location:

SE of Poitiers, go E of Montmorillon 9 km on the D 727. Turn right (S) toward St.-Léomer and the sanctuary is signposted to 6.5 km beyond.

Ste.-Même Charente-Maritime

Sight:

Gallo-Roman tower (*pile*), ca. 16 m high, shored up at the bottom.

Location:

SW of Poitiers and N of Saintes 15 km on D 150, then E on D 230 toward Ste.-Même. The tower is on the right side of the road in a cornfield. It is 6 km beyond Ecoyeux.

St.-Romain-de-Benet Charente-Maritime

Sights:

To the S of the town, 500 m from the distillery behind the railway line, the square, Gallo-Roman tower, *Pile de Pirelonge*, stands 24 m high. It has a partially-preserved conical top of stones carved into scales. A mound to the right of the main road (N 150) further W was possibly a Roman camp.

Location:

St.-Romain is SW of Poitiers and SW of Saintes 18 km on the N 150.

Saintes Charente-Maritime

Sights:

After conquering the Gauls, Caesar made this town of the Santones a flourishing capital.

On rue St.-Vivien on the N side of town are the ruins of Les Thermes de St.-Saloine. Visible are the walls and substructures of two rectangular and three circular pools, the caldarium being the best-preserved. The eighth-century church of St.-Saloine has wall bases built on top of the baths.

The Arènes constitutes the impressive remains of an amphitheatre, one of the oldest structures of its kind, with seating for over 20,000 spectators. Built in the first century in a natural depression, it originally had seventy-four arches, three of which are still standing. Above the podium some tiers of seats have been restored. On the E side was the main entrance. The gate on the W side was for removal of the vanquished.

The Roman votive Arc de Germanicus consists of two large arches supporting the architrave, erected in honour of Tiberius and Drusius Germanicus in the year 19. It stood on the Roman bridge until it was demolished in 1845 and removed stone by stone to its current location.

Near Les Arènes is the Church of St.-Eutrope. Signs state that it has a Gallo-Roman crypt, but it is actually eleventh century and contains the tomb of the saint.

The Musée Archéologique is built into the fifth-century ramparts.

Location:

SW of Poitiers and N of Bordeaux 90 km on the E 05-A 10. All sites signposted in town. Map available from S.I.

Sanxay Vienne
Sights:

Sanxay, was an important site on the banks of the Vonne. Its Gallo-Roman theatre could seat about 6500 spectators and was built in three tiers with an arena for fights and games. Sections of the lower tiers of seats had stone foundations. The upper sections were probably of wood. There are vestiges of a rectangle which originally had a wooden stage for speech-giving and performances.

There are visible remains of an octagonal temple which served a water cult, but its gods remain unknown. It is in the shape of a cross with a cella in the centre, that contained a statue of the divinity. It was surrounded by a porch where 7-8000 people could gather to attend ceremonies.

Perhaps most spectacular to see here are the remains of the three public baths (under cover) which were reputedly transformed from three rooms of a temple. The section closest to the river dates to the early first century. A sudatorium (hot) as well as tepidarium (tepid) and caldarium (warm) are visible. They were enlarged with additional pools and a palaestra.

An aerial photograph in the museum clearly shows where houses were located, but to date they have not been excavated. Small museum in situ.

Location::

SW of Poitiers on the N 11 ca. 22 km to Augerie, then right (N) 10 km on D 26. Or, leave A 10-E 5 autoroute at exit 31 about 31 km SW of Poitiers. Then take the N 11 E, 3 km. Signposted throughout. See also entry for nearby Bougon.

Thaims Charente-Maritime
Sights:

The church of St.-Pierre de Thaims was built on the site of a Gallo-Roman villa of which there are still some remains visible in the form of sculptures and tombs in the gardens, along with vestiges of walls up to 2.5 m high at the foot of the church tower. Merovingian and Carolingian vestiges are in the church itself, and sarcophagi are in the garden.

Location:

SW of Poitiers and SW of Saintes ca. 20 km on D 114.

Usson-du-Poitou Vienne
Sight:
Roman bridge, one hump and two small arches. Some slight renovations. Here also is the Dolmen de la Plaine.
Location:
SE of Poitiers 41 km on D 741. Take road out of town toward Confolens (D 741) and go ca. 2 km to old château Artron on left (small sign). Turn left by château and go 700 m and thus over the Roman bridge.

Vendeuvre-du-Poitou Vienne
Sight:
Small excavation of a Gallo-Roman villa, Tours Mirandes. Visible are walls, foundations of a basilica with heating system, a reconstructed pool, and commercial and residential quarters. Site has great potential but little reparations done to date. Signposted in town.
Location:
N of Poitiers on the D 757 ca. 12 km.

Other sights in the area include: NEUVILLE-DE-POITOU. Dolmen. Pretty well collapsed with two large capstones. NW of Poitiers 10 km on N 147. Cross the D 62 and a sign (R) points to the dolmen just after the Neuville city limits. Dolmen on left. ST.-MAIXENT-L'ECOLE. The seventh-century crypt of the former church of St.-Léger contains the empty sarcophagi of St.-Maixent and St.-Léger. SW of Poitiers. NE of Niort 24 km on the N 11-E 601. ST.-SAUVANT. Medieval sarcophagi all about the church grounds. SW of Poitiers and E of Saintes ca. 10 km on N 141, then N 1.5 km to St.-Sauvant.

Provence-Alpes-Côte d'Azur (Marseille)

Alpes-de-Haute-Provence (04), Haute-Alpes (05), Alpes-Maritimes (06), Bouches-du-Rhône (13), Var (83), Vaucluse (84)

Extending from the lower Rhône River to the Italian border with a long Mediterranean coastline, Provence is protected by the Alpes to the north, and it embraces a comfortable climate with subtropical vegetation. The capital, Marseille, is one of the oldest cities in France, having been founded by a colony of Greeks about 600 B.C. to exploit the trade possibilities of the Rhône Valley. It was an independent ally of the Romans even before their conquest of southern France at the end of the second century B.C. However, it made the mistake of supporting Pompey in his civil war with Caesar, prompting the latter to capture and conquer it in 49 B.C. In spite of this, Marseille remained an ally rather than a subject city afterwards. Archaeological vestiges of all epochs are found in the region, the most prominent being the many thousands of rupestrian engravings in the Vallée des Merveilles, and Roman architectural structures.

Aix-en-Provence Bouches-du-Rhône

Sights:

Aquae Sextiae. Situated in the central hall of the Etablissement Thermal is a Roman bath, but in fact very little survives here from the period when it was an important Roman city.

To the right of the entrance to the cathedral of Saint-Sauveur is a fourth-fifth century Merovingian baptistry (renovated in the sixteenth century). It is built on the site of a Roman forum using eight Roman columns. Behind the high altar is the fifth-century Chapelle de St-Mitre with the tomb of the saint. There is also a seventh-eighth century cloister.

The Iron age Oppidum d'Entremont, a Celto-Ligurian settlement, was founded around the beginning of the second century B.C., and grew rapidly due to influences from nearby Greek Massalia. Only a few years later, in 124 B.C., the city succumbed to the imperialistic power of Rome. It was conquered, pillaged, abandoned and nearly forgotten while Aquae Sextiae (Aix-en-Provence) flourished. The oppidum is partially excavated. Fragments of pillars indicate the layout of individual buildings and houses, and there are also extensive remains of apartment houses, streets, dwellings, and various industrial establishments. There are about 150 m visible of the northern rampart, which was originally 3 m thick and 380 m long, but the part that survives today is only 1.5 m thick. Rectangular towers with curved corners are along the curtain wall. A mosaic pavement and the remains of what seem to have been charnel houses give evidence of a sanctuary situated on the highest part of the hill. There are some traces of the Ville Haute, including fragments of wall, towers, and houses, and of the Ville Basse, with monoliths, furnaces, oil press, and other vestiges of houses. A platform permits fine viewing of the site and surroundings.

At Le Tholonet part of an aqueduct, Le Mur des Romains, is visible but only some of the 3 m thick, 15 m high walls survive.

See also, entry for Meyrargues.

Location:

Aix-en-Provence is located NE of Marseille 29 km on the A 51. The Oppidum d'Entremont excavations lie 2.5 km to the N of the cathedral on the D 14. It is reached by continuing from the Avenue Pasteur. Park just before a bridge crossed by the N 296, and then walk up a path to the right (signposted). Le Tholonet is reached by going E on the D 17, 6 km. It is signposted on the inner ring road of Aix, by the D 17. To see the aqueduct it is necessary to walk through the property of the *CEMAGREF* organization.

L'Almanarre Var

Sights:

Ruins of Greek and Roman Olbia, later the Roman settlement of Pomponiana. Most of this large site remains to be excavated. Underwater exploration has brought to light an ancient port, part of which can be seen on the beach, across the street from the excavations. To be seen also are street paving, a drainage gully in the centre of the road, a sanctuary of Artemis, a small Roman bath complex, and what is perhaps a small altar stone of a temple to Aphrodite.

Location:

SE of Marseille and E of Toulon 20 km on the D 559. Turn N on the Chemin de Pomponiana (by sign: *Hospital Olbia*), and the excavations are on the right, facing the sea.

Antibes Alpes-Maritimes

Sights:

Vestiges of late Roman walls can be seen on rue Barque-en-Cannes (corner tower), rue de l'Esperon/Cours Massena (gateway), rue des Saleurs (rampart), and in front of the Grimaldi Château, on the coast side, there is a section of wall about 5 m high.

E of the city ca. 4 km on N 7 is the Villeneuve Loubet public park which contains some remnants of the Vaugrenier temple, abandoned in the first century B.C.

Location:

Antibes is E of Marseille and about 5 km N of Cannes.

Apt Vaucluse

Sights:

The former cathedral of Ste.-Anne has an altar resting on a fourth-century Paleo-Christian sarcophagus. It is constructed of marble from the Pyrenees and was taken from a necropolis outside of town. The lower pre-Romanesque crypt contains some sarcophagi.

To the W is the three-arched Roman bridge of Pont-Julien once situated on the Via Domitia. It is considered to be one of the best-preserved ancient bridges in France.

Near Cereste, 6.5 km further E on the N 100, is the Necropolis of Carluc, with several dozen rock-cut, anthropomorphic tombs. The Abbaye de St.-Victor was founded in the fourth-fifth centuries. Abandoned in the ninth and tenth centuries, this was probably a place of pilgrimage.

The Fort de Buoux stands on a rock that was occupied by Ligurians and Romans, among others. Three defensive walls, a Romanesque chapel, houses, silos cut out of the rock, a keep, and a Ligurian sacrificial altar remain.

In the Luberon mountain range are about 3,000 bories or drystone huts, the most numerous being in the area of Gordes. These constructions with drystone walls and corbelled roofs have been inhabited from time to time since the Iron Age, and are traditionally found near the Mediterranean.

Location:

Apt is N of Marseille, E of Avignon and E of Cavaillon 9 km on the D 2 then ca. 20 km on the N 100. The Pont-Julien is on the N 100 8 km W of the town, about 250 m off the road. Cereste is ca. 18.5 km E of Apt, and Carluc lies between Cereste and Reillanne. E of Cereste, take the RN 100 2.5 km to the site. For the Fort de Buoux go S of Apt 9 km on the D 113. To reach the site it is necessary to walk approximately thirty minutes to the gate, after which follow the path to the porter's lodge. Bories can be seen at the Village des Bories on the D 2 going N from the N 100 toward Abbaye du Sénanque, W of Apt some 20 km.

Arles Bouches-du-Rhône

Sights:

Ancient Arelate, settled by Greeks in the sixth century, B.C. and by the Romans in the first century, became an important commercial and naval port. Many ruins and monuments bear witness to centuries of history in this city, which has been a religious centre since the fourth century.

Provence-Alpes-Côte d'Azur: Arles.
Les Arènes

The first-century amphitheatre (Les Arènes) is the largest edifice of its kind north of the Alps, with a seating capacity of about 25,000. Its three towers (originally four) are remnants of its use as a fortress in Medieval times, after which it was taken over by the poor and houses were built on top of it. The site was not cleared until the nineteenth century. There are two storeys, and each has sixty arcades of varying widths.

Less than 100 m S, the late first-century, B.C. theatre has a seating capacity of about 7000. It has been restored, and cultural events take place in it today. Adjoining it was the forum. Two Corinthian columns have been built into the S side of the Place du Forum in the walls of the Hôtel du Nord.

The La Roquette quarter has an extensive mausoleum and a Roman Circus, excavation of which has ceased due to lack of funds. Parts of the seating foundations are visible. An obelisk of Egyptian granite found here was removed to the centre of the Place de la République.

About 300 m N of the obelisk on the Rue Général de Gaulle are situated the Baths of Constantine, constructed in the fourth century. The caldarium and traces of the hypocausts and tepidarium survive.

From the theatre, following the N side of the adjacent public gardens, the most interesting section of the ramparts stands on Roman foundations. Within this corner of the ramparts are the remains of the Abbey of St.-Césaire, and the foundations of the apse of a fourth or fifth century Paleo-Christian church.

The Alyscamps entrance is all that remains of the necropolis of ancient Arles. This avenue, bordered by marble tombs, formed the approach to the city by the Aurelian Way. In the apse of St.-Honorat Church there is a beautiful fourth-century white marble tomb and three Carolingian sarcophagi.

The Cryptoporticus, in a series of underground galleries, can be entered from the Chapelle du Collège. There are varying opinions as to why this was built—perhaps as a base for the forum, perhaps as a place to house public slaves, or maybe as an emergency storage-centre for food.

Near the former church of St.-Genèst, in the suburb of Triquetaille, is part of another fourth-century Christian cemetery, founded on the site of second-century Roman baths, along with a mausoleum. For admission, apply at the S.I.

The Esplanade excavations have revealed a fourth-fifth century Gallo-Roman quarter with baths, houses, and shops. There are Roman mosaics in the

Provence-Alpes-Côte d'Azur:
Arles. Alyscamps

basement of the Crédit Agricole building, just SW of the S.I. on the Boulévard des Lices. Application to see them should be made at the Musée Réattu. In the courtyard of the Museon Arlaten is a Roman exedra.

Along the D 17 toward Fontvieille the road passes near several late-Neolithic tomb chambers, but they are not readily visitable, as they are on private land. Some 2 km S of Fontvieille are the ruins of a Roman aqueduct, and nearby, a fourth-century Gallo-Roman flour mill. See entry for Barbegal.

Location:

Arles is 8 km NW of Marseille, and 30 km SE of Nimes on the A 55.

Barbegal Bouches-du-Rhône

Sights:

Impressive remains of a pair of Gallo-Roman aqueducts and hydraulic flour mills—rare examples of mechanical engineering of this era. The mills once covered the entire hillside, and this is the largest surviving unit of its kind in the old Mediterranean world. They have been dated to the end of the third century.

The main aqueduct from Eygalières, ca. 50 km away, split into two: one part branched to the W to Arles, while the other went E and via a trench in the rock to a basin which supplied water to the flour mills below on the hill. A triangular-shaped cistern fed two channels which then activated eight mills successively on different levels down the slope, the water gushing down the hill and turning the sixteen waterwheels, each of which drove a millstone. From the cistern to the last mill, the fall is more than 20 m. The Pont de la Voie is a small Roman bridge over the stream.

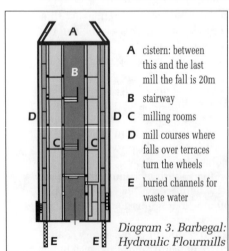

A cistern: between this and the last mill the fall is 20m

B stairway

C milling rooms

D mill courses where falls over terraces turn the wheels

E buried channels for waste water

Diagram 3. Barbegal:
Hydraulic Flourmills

Location:

Barbegal is NW of Marseille and just E of Arles. Take the D 33b NE from nearby the Alyscamps, to Pont de Crau. Then follow the road signposted 7 km to Barbegal. Turn left at sign for Fontvielle, and after bridge (7.4 km from Pont de Crau) is a sign, right, *Meunerie romain* (Roman mill). The ruins are visible against the rocks from here, but do not enter here, as it is private land. Instead continue 700 m further on the road to where the D 82 crosses it, and there is a sign for the

Roman aqueduct indicated to the right. 300 m down that road, park and walk in by the aqueduct and down to the mill.

Carpentras Vaucluse
Sights:

The only remaining vestige of Roman occupation is in the Place d'Inguimbert, in the courtyard of the Palais de Justice, behind the cathedral. It is a much damaged relic of a first-century Roman triumphal arch, with mutilated reliefs of barbarian captives chained to a tree. It once provided the entrance to the Gallo-Roman town and commemorates victories of the beginning of the first century. It was moved to its present site during the Middle Ages.

Seven km E is the town of Mazan, which has a cemetery containing sixty-two Gallo-Roman sarcophagi, forming the wall of a churchyard. They once lined the Roman road from Carpentras to Sault.

Location:

NW of Marseille and SE of Orange 24 km on the N 7/D 950. Carpentras is NE of Avignon 22 km on the N 107/D 942. Mazan is 6.5 km E on the D 942.

Château-Bas Bouches-du-Rhône
Sights:

In the gardens of the Château-Bas are the ruins of a Roman temple, probably dating from the late first century B.C. All that remains are some of the foundations and walls. One 7-m column is still intact. Visible also is a semicircular precinct wall enclosing the temple, that may have formed part of a sanctuary. There are also some vestiges of another temple.

Location:

N of Marseille and SE of Avignon ca. 50 km on N 7. It is some 23 km NW of Aix-en-Provence off the N 7 to the W of Cazan 5 km on the D 22. The site is signposted 1.5 km from the village.

Draguignan Var
Sights:

Gallo-Roman baths opposite the Hermitage of St.-Hermentaire on private property are not at present open to the public.

The Dolmen La Pierre de la Fée, with a capstone 6 m x 4.50 m (weighing 40 tons) rests on three, 2-m-high standing stones.

Location:

E of Marseille. The town is W of Nice some 88 km on the A 8-E 80, then 11 km on the N 555. The dolmen is 1 km from town, on the left, on Avenue de Montferrat. Signposted in town.

Fréjus Var
Sights:

The Forum Julii, founded by Julius Caesar, became a stage on the Aurelian Way. A naval base was constructed here in the reign of Augustus, but it declined in the second century. Saracens destroyed part of the town in the tenth century, but there are still many traces of the Romans throughout the town.

La Lanterne d'Auguste. This tower, topped with a pyramid, reaches a height of 10 m. It was probably a marker for the harbour entrance. It was much restored in the nineteenth century. This lantern has been attributed to the Romans but others have seen it as a later, Medieval construction.

Walls of the Villeneuve twin baths are visible on the Aiguières wine merchants' property. They are well-preserved.

The first-second century heavily restored amphitheatre, les Arènes, seated 10,000 people. It is easily seen from the N 7 coming from Aix-en-Provence, or from the D 37 from the autoroute.

The Roman ramparts are best seen NE of the town on N 7 on either side of the gateway that stood beside the aqueduct that brought waters of the Siagnole, near Mons (50 km N) to the city. Remains of columns, massive pillars 12-13 m high, that supported the aqueduct can be seen along the RN 7 coming into town from Cannes. Some of these are strengthened with buttresses. At the point where the aqueduct reached the city walls, it turned N, making use of the walls as support. On the N side of Avenue du Quinzième Corps stands a lone column decorated with cross marks. It is located where the gateway once stood, and there are traces of the ramparts here, as there are elsewhere about town. The S.I. will provide a map. Beyond the town, more remains of the aqueduct can be seen in the park at Château Aurélien, St.-Brigitte, Combe de Rome, Vert Estérel estate, Gargalon, Le Reyran Valley, and of the l'Esquine arches in l'Apié d'Amic valley.

To the SW, not far N of the cathedral on rue du Théâtre Romain, are a few remains of the Roman theatre. The key may be obtained from the town hall in the cultural section. It is used in summers for performances. The semicircular Roman Porte des Gaules retains one of its two towers.

The Plate-forme on rue des Marsouins is considered to have been an important residence. Built around a central courtyard with a tiled pool, it contains a cistern. The best view of this is from the Villa Marie park but the site is mostly overgrown.

Near Villeneuve school on rue de la Tourrache are the remains of a large, circular mausoleum with four small and one large niche that once held coffins and urns.

The cathedral has a restored fifth-century baptistry that is still used. There is some late-Roman walling, along with part of a mosaic in the church.

Very slight remains of a Roman bridge, Pont des Esclapes, are located ca. 2 km W of Fréjus, about 15 m W of a modern bridge. Take a secondary road S opposite Les Esclapes Industrial Estate, and after about 75 m, just beyond the railway track, the vestiges are to be seen amidst the reeds of the drainage channel.

Location:
E of Marseille and SW of Cannes 30 km on A 8-E 80, 30 km. For the aqueduct remains it is necessary to cover a distance of approximately 10 km between the roundabout on D 437 and the Malpasset dam. Go N out of Fréjus on N 7, and at the crossroads of N 7 and D 437 in Château Aurélien there are vestiges of arches for about 500 m. Continue on N 7 to just after it turns off to La Tour de Mare. Here is a low piece of wall behind the campground. 600 m beyond the Europa campground at La Combe de Rome in the La Pinède housing estate by Avenue du Pont Romain, there are some pillars supporting a channel. Take the D 637 ca. 1 km from where it joins with the N 7 to where the road goes under a large arch,

15 m high. It is one of the last of the fourteen Gargalon arches that crossed the river. Next take the D 37 to the Vert Estérel estate to the Arcs Berenguier, which are on the Avenue de Val des Arches about 200 m from D 37. S.I. will provide maps.

Ganagobie (Prieuré de) Alpes-de-Haute-Provence
Sights:
A grouping of megalithic monuments, a small basilica of the eighth century, and the ramparts of a Carolingian camp occupy the plateau of Ganagobie. A nearby second-third century Roman bridge is found by following the path toward Lurs.
Location:
NE of Marseille and S of Sisteron ca. 20 km on the N 85-E 12/N 96.

Gréoux-les-Bains Alpes-de-Haute-Provence
Sights:
Recent excavations have brought to light remains of a various buildings, including a swimming pool and an inscription at these second-century Roman baths. Today there is also a modern spa on the site.
Location:
NE of Marseille. Cross the river going SE from Manosque, then pick up the D 82 for 8.5 km to the town.

Istres Bouches-du-Rhône
Sights:
During Hellenic times the oppidum of St.-Blaise (its ancient name has not been determined) depended on salt for its commerce and livelihood. Here are some of the best Hellenistic ramparts in the south of France. Interspersed with towers, they were raised between about 175 and 140 B.C. The site appears to have suffered disastrously from a Roman siege in ca. 125 B.C., and subsequently declined. In the

Provence-Alpes-Cote d'Azure:
Istres. St.-Blaise

fifth century it was reoccupied and two churches were constructed of which only the apse of St.-Vincent remains near the main gate. Rock-cut tombs are in the necropolis extending to the south. Abandoned in the ninth century after destruction by the Saracens it was reoccupied for a time and abandoned again. An interesting site. There are remains of ramparts, walls, churches, habitations, streets, some with sidewalks, cellars with urns, graves, and a metal foundry workshop among many other stone ruins.
Location:
W of Marseille and SE of Arles 36 km on the N 568, then left (N) ca. 6 km on the N 568 to Istres. St.-Blaise lies some 4 km S on the D 5.

Marseille Bouches-du-Rhône

Sights:

Ancient remains of the Phocaean Greek colony of Massalia date back to 600 B.C. In the second century B.C. the prosperous and cultured city was surrounded by a defensive wall against the Celtic-Ligurian tribes of the interior. Even Julius Caesar, unable to storm the city, had to starve it into submission, although he did not sack the city. Massalia was a major Greek power in the West, with colonies from Nice to Ampurias in Spain. It remained independent of Merovingian and Carolingian control, and was ruled by bishops and counts, reverting to France only in the fifteenth century.

The Musée des Docks Romains is situated on the eastern half of a warehouse that stood beside the quay in Roman times. One of the most interesting exhibits consists of thirty-three enormous earthenware jars (dolia), 1.75 m wide and more than 2 m in height, that were buried in the floor. There are also remains of ancient boats and of Roman port installations dating from the first century.

In the Jardins des Vestiges behind the Stock Exchange are remains of the ancient port, fortifications, a fourth-century entranceway, and part of a second-century, B.C., 3-m thick Hellenistic wall with towers and bastions.

There are slight remains of a Roman theatre at the base of the hill of St.-Laurent (surrounded by buildings belonging to a school) but they are not impressive. The most interesting feature is that the seats have been carved in such a way as to prevent people's feet sliding into the backs of those sitting in front of them, commonly found in Greek theatres in Sicily.

The abbey church of St.-Victor has an interesting fifth-century lower crypt in the pagan necropolis, built by St.-Cassianus to honour the relics of St. Victor. A passageway in the catacombs links the chapels with the cave where the saint was buried. The crypt contains several sarcophagi of the second-fifth century and the sacristan will show these. In the central chapel is a third-century shrine to the town martyrs.

Location:

Marseille is SE of Paris on the Mediterranean. The S.I. will provide maps.

Meyrargues Bouches-du-Rhône

Provence-Alpes-Côte d'Azur: Meyrargues. Roman Aqueduct

Sight:

Below the castle are remains of a Roman aqueduct that brought water to Aix-en-Provence. It was originally 30 km long but much of it was underground.

Location:

NE of Marseille and N of Aix-en-Provence about 15 km on the N 96. Take the Chemin du Pas de l'Etroit Ligoures off Avenue St.-Pierre going toward the castle. Above the cemetery, the aqueduct may be seen a few hundred metres to the left.

Nice Alpes-Maritime

Sights:

At the Musée Terra Amata, 25 Blvd Carnot, a 400,000 year-old prehistoric site has been excavated, revealing hearths and tools of Homo erectus.

On the Hill of Cimiez, in the Jardin du Monastère, are some rampart blocks, the sole remains of an oppidum of the Vediantii. Here also are extensive remains of the Roman military centre of Cemenelum, founded in the first century B.C. Remains of a fairly small first-third century amphitheatre which held about 5000 persons, are currently used for open air productions. It is thought that the original, even smaller amphitheatre only had between 500 and 600 wooden seats, and that it may have been a military training centre.

About 100 m from the amphitheatre lie the remains of second-third century baths within the walls of the Villa des Arènes. To be seen are two entrances, latrines, reconstructed pool, and frigidarium. Most of the tepidarium and the caldarium are ruined. The baths E of the villa include a caldarium with hypocaust. Those SE include a schola or meeting place for artisans. Between the two is a first-century wall. Decumanus II is a fine piece of road constructed of polygonal paving stones.

The baths to the W, beneath the baptistry and the fifth-century Paleo-Christian basilica, seem to have been constructed for women, as the drains were found replete with hairpins and jewellery. The arches for hot airflow are still visible, but the furnaces were destroyed to put in the six-sided baptismal pool. There is an oval-shaped bath that was used as a sacristy. Museum in situ.

Location:

Nice lies NE of Marseille, on the coast. Cimiez is about 3 km NE of Nice. The archaeological site is in front of the Musée Matisse.

Orange Vaucluse

Sights:

Arausio, a strategic centre of a Gallic confederation, had become a Roman colony by the first century, its name derived from the local god of the spring.

One of the finest surviving Roman theatres anywhere, still used for cultural events, can be found in the centre of the city. The great stage wall, 36 m high with remains of its elaborate decoration, forms the external façade. It dates from the first century (some of it has been partially restored) and has excellent acoustics. It is the only Roman theatre to have preserved a statue (now also much restored) of the Emperor Augustus.

Adjoining the theatre on the W are the remains of a temple, opposite the Municipal Museum where items recovered from the excavations are displayed. In the exterior of the west wall there are vestiges of what may have been a gymnasium or part of the forum.

On rue Pontillac a 16 m-high wall crosses the street and a tall, arched entrance cuts through. On Rote de Roquemaure, opposite the cemetery, is a gate tower.

The great Triumphal Arch on N 7 entering town, was erected to commemorate the founding of the town as a colony for veterans in the first century. It has three arches (the central arch measuring 8 m x 5 m) with two flanking arches, and four façades. It is highly decorated with a relief depicting a

battle between Romans and Gauls, recalling the conquest of Gaul and proclaiming victory on both land and sea. The major themes include the spoils of war, naval and battle scenes, and trophy reliefs. Originally it had statues on the top but these are no longer in evidence. The W face dating from the time of Augustus has been restored. The arch has survived due to the fact that it was used as a fortress to guard the northern entrance to the city in the Middle Ages.

Provence-Alpes-Côte d'Azure: Orange. Theatre

The Musée Lapidaire contains an exhibit unique in that it displays the remains of a first-century Roman property register. In addition there is an exhibit of public records inscribed on marble.

Location:

Orange lies NW of Marseille some 158 km in the Rhône valley.

Riez Alpes-de-Haute-Provence

Provence-Alpes-Côte d'Azur: Riez. Roman Temple

Sights:

There are four, 6 m high Corinthian columns here; the bases and capitals are in white marble. They support an architrave and constitute vestiges of the east side of a first-century temple dedicated to Apollo.

Built over the Roman baths is a restored seventh-century baptistry using Roman materials in the form of eight granite columns. There was a baptismal pool in the middle that was surrounded in the fifth century by a gallery 4 m wide with a corridor that led to the church. Today only the design of the lower portions of the pool are original; the rest has been restored.

Some excavations opposite reveal part of the Gallo-Roman town and foundations of a fifth-century cathedral.

Location:

Riez is NE of Marseille and E of the A 51-E 712 between Aix-en-Provence and Manosque. From Manosque go E 34 km on the D 6. Access to the columns is via the Rue des Cordeliers, which branches off the road to Digne. Sites signposted in town.

St.-Chamas
Bouches-du-Rhône
Sight:
Remains across the Touloubre River of the one-span first-century Roman bridge with a triumphal arch at each end surmounted by lions, only one of which is original (the other three are from the eighteenth century). The small humpbacked bridge probably replaced a wooden bridge. There is an inscription which indicates the bridge was constructed by Flavian.

Location:
Go NW of Marseille on the motorway A 7-E 714 to Coudoux, then take the D 10 W ca. 20 km to St.-Chamas. The bridge is just before the town, near the N shore of the Etang de Berre.

St.-Chamas. Flavian's Bridge

St.-Dalmas-de-Tende Alpes-Maritimes
Sights:
Nearby Vallée des Merveilles, Massif du Bégo is an area of lakes and eroded hills. Thousands (some estimate as many as 100,000) prehistoric carvings and graffiti decorate the rock faces and are said to date from a Ligurian cult that survived from Paleolithic times up into the Iron Age. The pictures are composed of horned rectangles, human figures, chequered patterns, and circles. This is a remarkable series of rupestrian graffiti.

Location:
NE of Marseille and NE of Nice near the Italian frontier. Perhaps the easiest way to approach it is to take the S 20 N from Ventimiglia (in Italy) and follow it 40 km to St.-Dalmas. Special transport and guides can be hired here to go into the Massif du Bégo area. Be prepared to hike.

St.-Rémy-de-Provence
Bouches-du-Rhône
Sights:
One km S of town are the remains of ancient Glanum, situated by a sacred spring. The first phase of building appears to be totally Greek and lasting from the sixth to the second century, B.C. The second phase exhibits Roman influence, and the third, from 46 B.C. to the third century A.D., is Gallo-Roman, a creation of the Augustan period. It

Provence-Alpes-Côte d'Azur: St.-Rémy-de-Provence. Glanum

Provence-Alpes-Côte d'Azur: St.-Rémy-de-Provence. Glanum. Triumphal Arch

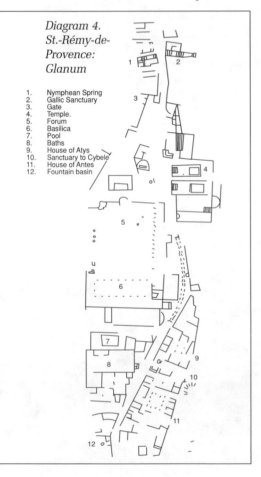

Diagram 4.
St.-Rémy-de-
Provence:
Glanum

1. Nymphean Spring
2. Gallic Sanctuary
3. Gate
4. Temple.
5. Forum
6. Basilica
7. Pool
8. Baths
9. House of Atys
10. Sanctuary to Cybele
11. House of Antes
12. Fountain basin

contains two forums, baths, triumphal arch, twin Imperial temples, and possibly an aqueduct, all built by A.D. 10. Decline set in with the Germanic invasions. The town seems to have been abandoned by the third century.

To visit this site, it is recommended that the visitor begin at the top, S end walking downhill, seeing the earliest remains first.

One of the most outstanding relics of this Greco-Roman town is the Commemorative Arch, with its exceptional carved decorations. The arch has lost its upper parts but the well-preserved sculptures represent chained male-and-female captives.

The first-century Mausoleum is over 19 m high, and stands on a square pedestal. There are two main storeys, topped by six Corinthian columns supporting a cupola under which are two male statues. Bas-reliefs represent scenes of battle and hunting.

The very extensive excavations of the city include baths (dating to the time of Julius Caesar with gymnasium, frigidarium, tepidarium, caldarium, and palaestra), mosaics, Greek houses of the second century B.C., a second-century fountain, a forum (underneath which a Greek *agora* was found), a gate, nymphaeum, Gallic sanctuary, and two, first-century, B.C. temples.

It is recommended that the visitor obtain a plan of the area at the entrance, as there is a great deal to see at this excellent site.

Location:

NW of Marseille, 32 km NE of Arles and ca. 30 km SE of Avignon on the D 571.

Sisteron Alpes-de-Haute-Provence
Sight:
At the far end of the Défile de Pierre-Ecrite, near a small bridge, is a long Roman inscription in honour of the Consul Dardanus, Prefect of the Gauls, and his wife, Nervia, who opened the mountain passage at the beginning of the fifth century.

A small chapel, Notre-Dame de Dromon, clinging to the side of the Rocher de Dromon, contains a crypt that is probably eighth-ninth century.
Location:
Sisteron is NE of Marseille, S of Gap, and W of Digne ca. 41 km on the N 85. The Défile is NE of town on the windy D 3. The chapel is reached by a track ca. 2.5 km from St.-Geniez, which is further E of Sisteron on D 3.

La Turbie Alpes-Maritimes
Sights:
Just above the village stands the enormous Trophée des Alpes or Trophée d'Auguste, a monument erected by the Roman Senate in 6 B.C. to Emperor Augustus. It contains an inscription commemorating the Roman victory over the Alpine tribes. Originally 38 m square, standing 46 m high with twenty-four marble Doric columns, the structure was reconstructed in 1920-33, financed by an American philanthropist. (See Aquitaine, Pays Basque, Urkulu for a note on trophies.)
Location:
NE of Marseille and 18 km E of Nice. At an elevation of 487 m above sea-level, it is ca. 8 km NW of Monaco.

Vaison-la-Romaine Vaucluse
Sights:
This site, according to artifacts discovered here, was once occupied by Neolithic peoples. In the fourth century, B.C., the Ligurians constructed an oppidum. In the first century A.D., Vaison became a Gallo-Roman city, and both Pompey and Caesar granted citizenship to upper-class tribal leaders, and to those who commanded cavalry units. It became an episcopate in the fourth century.

In the Quartier de Puymin the foundations of many buildings have been uncovered, including the House of the Messii containing a family cult room, dining room, courtyard and pool, kitchen, ovens, baths and noble rooms (where the owner's wealth was displayed to visitors). The reception room had marble tiles and views into the garden, and was very grand. Another room has stairs leading to a lavatory. A warehouse is to the E. The Portico of Pompey is a covered walk where some of the (Tuscan) columns have been set upright. There are also some remains of a nymphaeum with a spring.

The Quartier de Thès is perhaps the most important area that is open, and consists of the Peacock Villa, which has mosaic floors, particularly in the central room. The mosaics depict not only a peacock but also many other birds, geometric designs, an octopus, Cupid riding a dolphin, and still lifes. The room containing the largest mosaic with fifteen octagons displays an eagle, lion, and flowers among other motifs. Four shops were destroyed by fire after the third century but were reoccupied late in the sixth. One housed a butcher, and the others sold such items as oil, clothes, and cloth. NE of these is a 15 m-long, 1.8 m-high wall which could have been the base of a temple.

Built into the N side of the Puymin hill, is the carefully-restored first-century theatre with its stage hewn out of the rock, and the nearby river Ouvèze, which is spanned by a Roman bridge with a single 17 m-high arch. On the W side are some buildings and the so-called Praetorium House (the residence of the praetor or magistrate), containing baths, pool, garden, kitchen, latrines, and storerooms. S of this is a wall with alcoves in it, perhaps storerooms of some kind. There are sarcophagi here.

The excavations of the Quartier de la Villasse have revealed most of the principal baths surrounded by drains, a colonnaded street and a street of shops, as well as the Dolphin House, containing an entrance, atrium with pool and columns, reception rooms, service area, and noble rooms to impress the guests. There are vestiges of a late first-century basilica (which was later identified as baths since a caldarium was discovered close by), and a fourth-century apse, as well as another apse of the sixth or seventh century. Notre-Dame-de-Nazareth contains Roman materials, including sections of fluted Roman columns taken from a Roman temple, and the tomb of St.-Quenin, bishop here in the sixth century. There is a street of shops that leads down to the basilica.

The House of the Silver Bust contains a garden with peristyle and swimming pool, kitchen, doorways and a system of dual baths. Two other houses are also found in this quarter.

The in situ museum displays many of the finds. Excellent site.

Location:
N of Marseille and 27 km NE of Orange on the D 975.

Vénasque Vaucluse
Sights:
Notre Dame has a sixth-century baptistry, altered in the eleventh century. The building, built on a Greek cross plan, is in the form of a square with an apse on each side, with either reused ancient, or Merovingian capitals. It is said to be among the oldest religious buildings in France.
Location:
N of Marseille and SE of Orange 24 km to Carpentras. Then take the D 4 11 km to Vénasque.

Other sites in the area include: CADENET. In the church is a baptismal font made from a third-century Roman sarcophagus. It is decorated with reliefs showing the Triumph of Ariadne. N of Marseille and 33 km E of Cavaillon on the D 973. CAVAILLON. The former capital of the Cavares and later the Roman colony of Cabellio has vestiges of a first-century carved Roman double arch, the Arc de Marius. Cavaillon is NW of Marseille and SE of Avignon 23 km on the A 7-E 714. CONSTANTINE. From 1 km NW of Château Calissanne on D 10, the Etang de Berre is overlooked from the N by an oppidum with a 350 m-long wall, and the remains of ten towers. NW of

Marseille on A 7-E 714 ca. 20 km to exit # 28, then W on D 10 about 8 km. **ILES LERINS.** Ile Ste.-Marguerite exhibits traces of Roman baths, cisterns, and a port. E of Marseille, the island is a 15-minute boat ride from Cannes. **LA LAUZET-UBAYE.** Close by, a Roman bridge crosses the river near the modern bridge. NE of Marseille and NE of Sisteron. Take the N 85 from Sisteron 34 km to where the D 942 branches right (E). Follow this ca. 7 km and take right branch again on D 900, 36 km to the town. Bridge signposted. **MARTIGUES.** reconstructed and preserved dwellings in situ from the Iron age. W of Marseille ca. 35 km on A 55, the site is located astride the channel that joins the Etang de Berre with the Mediterranean. **PONT DE ST.-LÉGER.** A Roman bridge can be seen below the road, with part of a Roman road at each end. NE of Marseille and NW of Nice. Go approx. 48 km on N 202, N of Nice to Puget-Théniers, then NW on D 16 ca. 5 km. **ROQUEBRUNE-CAP-MARTIN.** Where the Avenue Paul Dowmer meets Avenue Bedoux is a first-century large, elaborate mausoleum. NE of Marseille and just NE of Monaco, take the Cap-Martin turning off the N 7 below Roquebrune. **VENCE.** To the left of the main door of the cathedral is an inscription honouring the third-century Emperor Gordianus. In the SE chapel is a Gallo-Roman relief. NE of Marseille, NW of Nice and N of Antibes. Take the motorway W of Nice to the airport, then go N 9.5 km on the D 36.

Rhône-Alpes (Lyon)

Ain (01), Ardèche (07), Drôme (26), Isère (38), Loire (42), Rhône (69), Savoie (73), Haute-Savoie (74)

The region of Rhône-Alpes is bounded on the west by the Rhône River and on the east by the Italian frontier. Its capital is Lyon, the old Celtic town of Lugunum which was annexed by the Romans in 43 B.C. The area contains the highest peak in France, the 4807-metre-high Mont Blanc. Celts dominated this land until their defeat by the Romans in 121 B.C. Resistance to Roman rule continued, however, until the time of Augustus in 13 B.C. Barbarian invasions in the fifth century led to Burgundian control, and in 535 the Franks became masters of the Alpine massif. Important in situ remains include fourth millennium B.C. engravings at Boulc, and Roman remains at Lyon, Vienne, and St.-Romain-en-Gal.

Most recently caves with some 300 prehistoric paintings, as well as engravings, have been discovered in the Ardèche at Vallon-Pont-d'Arc. They include a particularly varied group of animals, but these galleries will almost certainly not be opened to the public.

Aix-les-Bains Savoie

Sights:

The Thermes Nationaux display remains of Roman baths, which originally had twenty-four different kinds of marble in their decoration. In a large room in the basement, parts of a caldarium and a circular pool are visible.

The Museum of Archaeology is housed in the so-called Temple to Diana. The third-fourth century Arch of Campanus, 9 m high, was erected by Lucius Pompeius Campanus.

Location:

Aix-les-Bains is E of Lyon ca. 90 km on the E 70-A 43.

Alba-la-Romaine Ardèche

Sights:

Alba Helvorum. Ongoing excavations on both sides of the D 107, 1 km N of the village, have brought to light a second-century theatre, two restored public buildings, a temple-complex with five shops, traces of a forum, villas, some stretches of Roman road, and some necropoli: second-fourth century St.-Pierre and first-second century St.-Martin. But most of the site is rather disappointing. Museum in the village.

There is a well-preserved second-century milestone on the N side of N 102 ca. 6 km from the site toward Le Teil.

Location::

S of Lyon on A 7 to Montélimar, then SW to Le Teil on D 102, 11 km and Alba is just to the S. Maps and tours may be obtained from the Mairie or Centre de Documentation Archéologique in town.

Boulc Drôme

Sight:

The cave, La Tune, in the cliffs of the Varaime, has hundreds of unusual schematic and symbolic engravings of people, flora, fauna, zigzags, and arrows dating from the fourth millennium B.C.

Location:

SE of Lyon and S of Grenoble ca. 80 km on N 75-E 712. From Valence take the D 111, SE 28 km to Crest, then the D 93, E to 6 km S of Die. Take the D 539 E ca. 24 km to Boulc. From here it is on a secondary road. To view the site it is necessary to go on foot with a guide. Ask in village.

Bourg-St.-Andéol Ardèche

Sights:

The church has an early third-century sarcophagus of St.-Nicolai, who was martyred in 208.

Signposted from the main square is the Mithras bas-relief, unique in France, as it has been carved on a rock face. It is very worn and mutilated but there is a sign in front of it showing how it looked originally.

Location:

S of Lyon, NW of Orange and S of Montélimar 23 km on the N 7, then W 8 km on the D 59. The rock is located in a small park reached by leaving the square and going about 200 m toward the railway, but turning right onto a footpath just before reaching the old public wash-house. Cross the little bridge on the left of the path over to the little park, and the bas-relief can be seen on the cliff to the right.

Charavines Isère
Sight:
Archaeological site of Colletière on Lac de Paladru. There are guided visits here in July and August to the Medieval village. It is now under water, but can be viewed from the pier. A museum in the village houses artifacts brought out of the lake.
Location:
SE of Lyon and SW of Chambéry. From Lyon take the autoroute A 43-E 70 SE, switching onto the autoroute A 48-E 711 after Bourgoin-Jallieu. Continue SE, 25 km and exit at Grand-Lemps. From here take the D 520 N going parallel with the autoroute and turn off right (E) on the D 50 E to Charavines.

Col du Petit St.-Bernard Savoie
Sights:
Just beyond the pass going NE is the marble Roman Colonne de Joux (Jupiter's Column) to which a statue of St.-Bernard was added in the nineteenth century. Just below is a large Iron Age stone burial circle, and close to the Italian Customs are the remains of a Roman posting station.

Further below the village of Aime is the church of St.-Martin with two crypts—one is possibly from Roman times, and was used in the fifth century as a church; the other is ninth or tenth century.
Location:
In the extreme eastern part of the country near the Italian frontier, the Col du Petit St.-Bernard is E of Lyon, NW of Val d'Isère and NE of Bourg-St.-Maurice 31 km on the N 90. Aime is S of Bourg-St.-Maurice 13 km on the N 90.

Die Drôme
Sights:
Dea Augusta Vocontiorum. The NE Gallo-Roman ramparts were hastily constructed of stones taken from monuments during an early barbarian invasion. Part of the Roman aqueduct is under the old rampart, and there is also a tower with Roman blocks used for the foundations. A wall over 4 m high, 3 m thick, and about 2000 m long surrounds the Roman-Medieval site.

Near the viaduct is the third-century Porte St.-Marcel, one of the principal gates to the city. On its outer side a fortified Medieval gateway was built into the Gallo-Roman ramparts.

The porch of the cathedral is eleventh century, but two of its columns come from a Roman temple and the wall has Roman stones incorporated in it. To the right of the W door is a Roman inscription which has been inserted upside down.

In the Mairie stands a chapel containing a mosaic pavement representing the four rivers of Paradise, apparently from a seventh-century baptistry.

There is also a fourth-century Christian tomb. In the adjacent outer wall is a Roman taurobolium; others are in the museum. There are also Roman inscriptions on the terrace.

In the vicinity are several other sites:

Take the D 93, W from Die and at Vercheny there are some Roman remains. Crossing on D 739 to the village of Barsac, just E is a fourth-century military stone in front of the church between Pontaix and Vercheny. It has the names of several emperors on it, the last being Valentinien II, Theodosius and Arcadius.

Further west on the left bank of the Drôme, near the monument to the dead, Aouste has a fragment of a large lintel that was part of a tomb of Julius Dionysius.

Location:

SE of Lyon and SE of Valence 65 km on D 111/D 93.

Faverges Haute-Savoie

Sights:

The Gallo-Roman villa of Le Thovey, constructed in the first century, enlarged in the second and destroyed in the year 270 by invading Alemans, has ongoing excavations revealing the hypocaust system with frigidarium, tepidarium, and caldarium. Also to be seen are vestiges of living quarters, but only about one-tenth of the villa has been exposed at time of writing.

Beside the museum is the church of St.-Jean-Baptiste, under which Gallo-Roman walls can be seen. The first church built here was in 600, the second in 800, the third in 1000. Subsequent structures have since been erected.

Location:

NE of Lyon. Take the N 6 90 km to Chambéry and then go N, 40 km on the A 41 to Annecy. For Faverges, follow N 508 26 km SE of Annecy along the lake. To go underground in the church in order to see the walls, an appointment must be made, except in July/August. For Le Thovey, go through town and turn right at l'Arclosan restaurant. Take first right again on rue du Brel. At the end of the road, at T-junction, turn right. Go a further 200 m to fork, and turn right into field. Excavation is within 100 m. Site is fenced but easily visible. For permission to enter, ask at museum.

Grenoble Isère

Sights:

Under the E side of the hill crowned by the Fort de la Bastille is the restored eleventh-century church of St.-Laurent. It is built over an older church. The St.-Oyand Merovingian crypt of the sixth-seventh centuries, built on the site of a pagan burial ground, is extensively excavated.

In the cathedral excavations have revealed foundations of Gallo-Roman walls, and vestiges of Paleo-Christian times. Traces of walls are also visible at Passage de la République and in the gardens of the Hôtel de Ville.

Location:

Grenoble is SE of Lyon in the Alps.

Hières-sur-Amby Isère
Sight:

The archaeological site of Larina has free entry and is permanently open to the public. Its 21 hectares are delimited on one side by cliffs overlooking the Rhône Plain, and by extensive ramparts, 950 m long, on the other.

From 3000 B.C. there is evidence of occupation here. From the eighth century, B.C. to the sixth century, B.C. there were huts, graves, and fortifications. From the first century B.C. there are remains of the settlement with ramparts and "La Chuire", a place

Rhône-Alpes: Hières-sur-Amby. Larina

of worship.

In the first and second centuries, A.D. there was probably a Gallo-Roman settlement plus at least one temple to Mercury (which was destroyed before the fourth century). From the fourth century, there was a settlement consisting of a village of huts built on stone foundations set around a small fourth-fifth century villa with farm buildings, 1500 sq. m. It includes workshops, rooms, and enclosures for animals, and other buildings, remains of which are all well-marked. A necropolis of slate-covered graves was built on the site of an earlier cemetery. More than 125 graves have been excavated to date.

Location:

E of Lyon on the D 517, 28 km to Pont de Chéruy. When the road splits, take the D 65B NE to the archaeological park. Larina is well signposted from Cremieu.

Izernore Ain
Sights:

Three large standing columns, pillars of a temple from Roman Izernodurum and some broken ones on the ground are found here. Constructed during the reign of Augustus, it survived until about 455. One stone has an inscription to Mercury.

Location:

NW of Lyon, go E of Bourg-en-Bresse 35 km on D 979, then N on D 18 ca. 5 km. The excavation is marked in town on road for Thoiry. Well signposted.

Lyon Rhône
Sights:

Ancient Lugdunum, at the confluence of the Saône and the Rhône, was founded in 43 B.C. Above the old town on the hill of Fourvière stand two Roman theatres and a Gallo-Roman museum. The larger of the theatres, one of the oldest in France, built by Augustus in the first century, was doubled in size by Hadrian in the second century to accommodate 10,000 spectators. The smaller, a second-century odéon, seated ca. 3000, and was used for such events as music recitals and poetry readings. Visible also are vestiges of sewers, a small bit of a fresco, and a restored, decorated mosaic. (There are only two odéons in Gaul and the other is situated at Vienne, just S of Lyon, see entry.) There is a small amount of Roman road visible, exhibiting ruts from chariots.

Currently being excavated are the foundations of a large first-century residence which was later replaced by a public edifice, and E of this are remains of a large cistern.

On the way up the hill to the theatres three mausolea are passed, one of which, from the first century B.C., houses Turpio, a Gaul who became Roman.

Although excavations unearthed the huge first-century Trois-Gaules amphitheatre, little or nothing is left to see today.

Ste.-Irénée has a fifth-eighth century crypt built on Roman foundations. In the courtyard are tombs—one with a Latin inscription.

Abutting the N side of the cathedral is the recently excavated Jardin Archéologique. Visible are the relics of a fourth-fifth century Paleo-Christian baptistry remodeled in the eleventh century, Gallo-Roman baths, and foundations of the eleventh-twelfth century Church of St.-Etienne.

Under the choir of the Church of St. Nizier on the rue du Président Herriot, there is a sixth-century crypt decorated with modern mosaics. In Vieux Lyon, no. 21 rue Juiverie has a Gallo-Roman cella in its basement.

On both sides of rue Roger-Radisson are vestiges of one of the four Roman aqueducts that once supplied Lyon. The Arches Champonost consist of about forty arches of an aqueduct, which are visible at the bottom of the Yzeron Valley to the SW of Lyon.

Location:

Lyon is SE of Paris on the E 15-A 7, and due N of Marseille. The S.I. will give maps and directions to all sites.

Soyons Ardèche

Sights:

The fifth-century oppidum of Malpas has ongoing excavations revealing Medieval, Gallo-Roman, Iron Age (Hallstatt), Bronze Age and Neolithic sites including prehistoric caves, sepulchres, tumuli and a Medieval enceinte on top of the hill, with fortified château and walls.

There is a museum in the village that will provide maps and guides.

Location:

S of Lyon and S of Valence 7 km on the N 86.

Vienne Isère

Sights:

Roman Vienna has remains of a large Roman theatre possibly from the first century, built into the flank of the hill of Mont Pipet with a magnificent view out over the Rhône. It had forty-six tiers built over vaulted passageways. The four rows nearest to the front are of white marble, their seats about five cm wider than the others, being reserved for officials and separated by a green balustrade. The theatre is currently used in summer.

To the S is a smaller, second-century odéon. It had a diameter of more than

Rhône-Alpes: Vienne. Saint-Romain-en-Gal

70 m and could seat some 3000 people. Stone bases of the stage are visible, as well as some for the seats. This is one of only two odéons built by the Romans in Gaul, the other one being in Lyon (see entry).

In the centre of the Jardin Archéologique are the Portiques des Thermes Romains, part of the colonnade around the Roman forum (two arcades of which are visible). The decorated double archway may have been connected to the baths. The huge N wall of a third theatre, associated with the cult of the Goddess Cybèle, lies to the right of this.

The temple of Augustus and Livia has had continuous use—as a church before the sixth century, later as a market place, then a museum before its restoration in the mid-nineteenth century. Because of this it has survived as one of the best-preserved in the country. It is thought to have been one of the first temples dedicated to the cult of the emperors.

A small section of a fourth-century Roman road showing ruts from carriage wheels is found in the Jardin Publique. There is also a fourth-century military stone. S of this is the Pyramid, a 20-m high obelisk unearthed and set up in what was thought to be its original place. It has a square stone base with an arch on each side standing over 7 m high, above which is the stone obelisk. It is said to be the only survivor of a massive circus that was here (but not all scholars agree on this interpretation).

On the far bank of the Rhône, well signposted, is the archaeological site of Saint-Romain-en-Gal (under excavation), an extensive Gallo-Roman settlement which formed part of Roman Vienna. Vestiges of the residential and artisanal quarters are visible along with shops, roads, baths, workshops, and warehouses. Remains of water conduits are throughout the site, along with fountains, cisterns, lavatories (which flush), drains, and pools.

Some traces of sumptuously decorated villas with mosaics, works of art, and baths have been found in the old Roman suburb of Saint-Colombe (on the boundary with Saint-Romain-en-Gal).

Ninth-twelfth century St.-André-le-Bas is at time of writing under restoration. There are two Roman columns with Corinthian capitals in the chancel.

St.-Pierre was rebuilt with Roman materials, in the ninth-tenth centuries after being destroyed by the Moors in the eighth century and by the Carolingians in the ninth century. It has fourth-sixth century foundations and was used mostly as a funerary basilica. It now houses the lapidary collection.

Location:

Vienne is S of Lyon 27 km on the N 7.

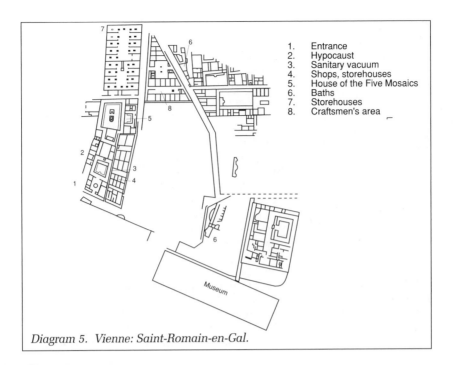

1.	Entrance
2.	Hypocaust
3.	Sanitary vacuum
4.	Shops, storehouses
5.	House of the Five Mosaics
6.	Baths
7.	Storehouses
8.	Craftsmen's area

Diagram 5. Vienne: Saint-Romain-en-Gal.

Viviers Ardèche

Sight:

Roman bridge supported by nine semicircular arches over the river Escoutay.

Location:

S of Lyon on route A-7 to Montélimar. Continue ca. 10 km SW on the D 73. The bridge is found by taking RN 86 NW out of town. Just before a sharp curve in the highway and before the modern bridge, continue straight on an unpaved road. The Roman bridge is on the right.

Other sites in the area include: **CHAMBÉRY**. The crypt of the Eglise St.-Pierre has a Carolingian baptistry. SE of Lyon and S of Aix-les-Bains some 20 km on N 201. **RUOMS**. In the rugged region of the Ardèche are many megaliths, mostly dolmens, but some are in poor condition and others difficult to find. Check with the S.I. in Ruoms, St.-Alban-Auriolles, Barjac, Lussan, and Pont-St.-Esprit for directions and maps. SW of Lyon and SW of Montélimar, Ruoms is located N of Alès. **TAIN-L'HERMITAGE**. In the main square stands a second-century inscribed taurobolium. S of Lyon and just N of Valence 14 km on N 7. **TERNAND**. In the church are Carolingian capitals and in the crypt, murals from the same period. NW of Lyon 11 km then NW of Limonest ca. 20 km on the D 485. **TOURNON**. Several sites near here include a Roman dedicatory inscription to Trajan by the Rhône boatmen at St.-Jean-de-Muzols, fragments from a Gallo-Roman temple in a church at Andance, and an eleventh-century church incorporating Roman capitals and sculptures at Champagne. Tournan is S of Lyon and N of Valence 14 km on N 86. St.-Jean is 2 km beyond on the same road. Andance lies 22 km N of Tournon on N 86 and Champagne is 4 km further N.

GLOSSARY

Abri	Rock shelter or grotto
Acanthus	Plant whose leaves were copied for decoration
Agora	Greek marketplace
Alignment	Row or group of rows of standing stones (menhirs)
Allée couverte	See gallery grave
Angevin dolmen	Typically from the Loire area and usually very large with portico, anteroom, and partitioned chamber
Angled dolmen	A dolmen whose entrance passage is at an angle (see entry for dolmen)
Anthropomorphic	In the shape of a human being
Apodyterium	Changing room in a bath
Architrave	The lower part of the architectural order below the roof and above the columns
Atrium	Main reception room of a Roman villa, with an opening in the roof and usually a small fountain or pool below
Baptistry	A room where baptisms take place
Basilica	Roman public building used as a meeting place. Became the architectural model for Late Roman Christian churches. Church with two or more aisles and a nave whose roof is higher than that of the aisles
Cairn	Stones surrounding a tomb, or several tombs
Caldarium	Hot room of Roman baths
Calvary	Representation of the crucifixion of Christ, usually carved in wood or stone and situated in the open air
Capital	Part on top of a column
Castrum	camp often fortified by a ditch (fossa) and palisades (vallum)
Cavea	Seats in a theatre or amphitheatre
Cella	Sanctuary. Main room of a temple which contained an image of a deity
Corinthian	Decorative style used mainly in capitals with acanthus design at the base. Very popular during Roman times
Cromlech	Circle of stones (menhirs), sometimes around a dolmen
Cryptoporticus	Warehouse, often underground
Curtain wall	Outer wall of a castle
Dolium, -a	Large globular jar with wide mouth, used especially for storage of oil
Dolmen	Neolithic-Bronze age, usually collective tombs consisting of megalithic stone slabs placed in an upright position with a covering capstone. See also Angevine dolmen, Angled dolmen, Gallery grave, Passage grave, Transeptal dolmen, Tumulus, V-dolmen

Dolmen à couloir	See passage grave
Exedra	A room for conversation, furnished with seats
Fanum	A Romano-Celtic temple, usually square, consecrated to a god
Forum	An open square, a market place, surrounded by public buildings
Fossa	a defensive ditch or trench
Frigidarium	Cold room of Roman baths
Gallery grave	Megalithic monument with elongated chamber covered with flat stones. May include partitions
Horreum	Storehouse or granary
Hôtel de Ville	Town hall in large city
Hypocaust	Heating system used by the Romans. Consisted of a space below the floor and/or in the walls, in which the hot steam could circulate
In situ	At the same place, at the site where it was found
Labrum	Basin or tub (bathing place)
Lanterne des Morts	(Lanterne of the Dead.) An oil lamp representing the flame of the divine light watching over the dead. Usually placed in a hollow tower in the cemetery
Lapidary	Concerned with stones
Mairie	Town hall in small town or village
Martyrium	A building or chamber where early Christians were buried, or the relics of martyrs preserved
Mausoleum	A tomb which is often in the form of a small house or temple
Megalith	Large stone monument
Menhir	An upright stone which stands alone or in lines (see alignment). Some engraved. Thought to delimit boundaries or to have had religious or phallic significance in prehistoric times
Monolith	Single, large stone, as a menhir
Motte	Mottes were the precursors of the fortified châteaux, usually built of wood and located on top of a hill
Narthex	Vestibule of a basilica or church
Nave	Central aisle of a church
Necropolis	Burial site
Nymphaeum	Roman house of pleasure, often decorated with statues and fountains; a shrine associated with water nymphs
Odéon	Building or theatre in which music, literary readings, or other artistic performances took place
Oppidum. -a	Ancient, fortified settlement, often found on top of a hill
Palaestra	Public place for training of athletes (i.e., gymnasium)
Paleo-	Early, old (as in Paleo-Christian: Early Christian)
Passage grave	Dolmen with round mound covering the burial

	chamber, and approached by a narrower entrance way
Peribolus	An enclosed court, especially around a temple
Peristyle	Colonnade or covered passageway surrounding a temple; or open courtyard of a Roman villa
Podium	A wall around the arena of an amphitheatre, serving as a base for the tiered seats; also a platform on which Roman temples were constructed
Polissoir	Grooved stone used in the Neolithic for polishing implements
Porch	Covered entrance to a building
Portico	Entry to a megalith, consisting of two upright stones supporting a covering slab (prehistoric); porch supported by columns (Roman)
Proscenium	Stage of a theatre
Rupestrian	Composed of or inscribed on rock
Sarcophagus.	Stone coffin, sometimes decorated
Syndicat d'Initiative (S.I.)	Office of Tourism
Stele	Stone or slab inscribed to commemorate something or someone
Tablinium	Reception room or study in a Roman villa
Taurobolium	Stone altar where bulls were sacrificed and the blood used to baptize worshippers of deities such as Cybèle or Mithras
Tepidarium	Warm room in the Roman baths
Thermae	Warm or hot springs
Tholos	Beehive-shaped burial chamber
Transept	Part of a church that is at right angles to the nave
Transeptal Dolmen.	A dolmen with small rooms on either side of the main chamber
Triclinium	Eating area in a Roman villa, often adjacent to the kitchen
Troglodyte	Cave dweller
Tumulus	Mound covering a tomb or dolmen
Tumulus Carnacéen	An enormous tumulus (larger than ordinary), dating back to the Middle Neolithic
V dolmen	Dolmen with a narrow entry that widens in a V-shape toward the end of the tomb
Vomitorium	Entrance/exit to an (amphi) theatre

1. Alsace: Saverne. Tombs

2. Aquitaine:
Pays Basque.
Urkulu.
(Courtesy
Lucien
Labedade)

3. Bourgogne: Quarré-les-Tombs. Tombs

4. Bretagne. Carnac. Kermario Alignments

5. Bretagne: Lannion. St.-Dusec Menhir

6. Champagne-Ardenne: Trancault (Marcilly). Polissoir

7. Champagne-Ardenne: St.-Quentin-le-Verger. Dolmen

8. Franche Comté: Marigny. Lac de Chelain

9. Languedoc-Roussillon: Loupian. Mosaic

10. Languedoc-Roussillon: Lunel. Bridge at Ambrussum

11.
Languedoc-
Roussillon: Lunel.
Ambrussum.
Roman Road

12. Languedoc-Roussillon: Pont du Gard

13. Lorraine: St.-Dié.
Celtic Camp de Bure

14. Midi-Pyrénées:
Vals. Monolithic
Church

15. *Midi-Pyrénées: Labarthe-Rivière. Gallo-Roman Funerary Monument*

17. *Midi-Pyrénées: Montréal. Séviac. Mosaic*

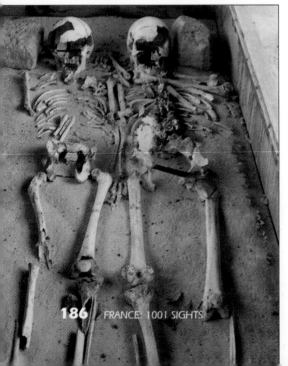

16. *Midi-Pyrénées: Montréal. Séviac. Merovingian Lovers*

18. Nord-Pas-de-Calais: Sailly. Les Bonnettes Cromlech

19. Nord-Pas-de-Calais: Labourse. 9th C St.-Martin

20. Haute-Normandie. Lillebonne. Roman Theatre

21. Pays de la Loire: Dissignac. Tumulus

22. Pays de la Loire: Bagneux. Dolmen. (Courtesy Bryan Pryce)

23. Pays de la Loire: Laval.
7-9th C Notre Dame de Pritz

24. Picardie. Champlieu. Gallo-Roman Baths

25. Poitou-Charentes: Saintes. Arc of Germanicus

26. Poitou-Charentes: Civaux. Merovingian Necropolis

27. Provence-Alpes-Côte d'Azur: St.-Rémy-de-Provence. Glanum. Detail of Mausoleum

28. *Provence-Alpes-Côte d'Azur: Mazan (Carpentras). Tombs*

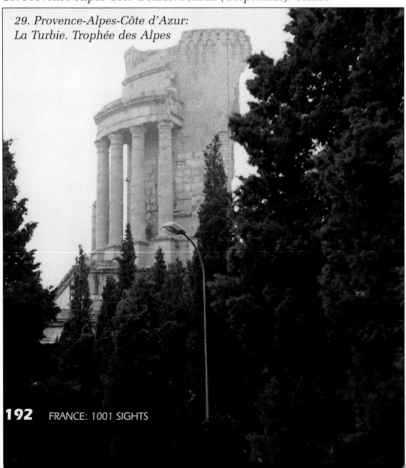

29. *Provence-Alpes-Côte d'Azur:*
La Turbie. Trophée des Alpes

30. Provence-Alpes-Côte d'Azur: Fréjus. Roman Aqueduct

31. Rhône-Alpes: Vienne. Temple of Augustus

32. Rhône-Alpes: Viviers. Roman Bridge
33. Rhône-Alpes: Lyon. Odéon

BIBLIOGRAPHY

Bernet, D. *Guide de la France avant la France*. Paris: Pierre Horay Éditeur (1984).

Blot, Jacques. *Archéologie et Montagne Basque*. Donostia: Elkar, S.L. (1993).

Briard, Jacques. *The Megaliths of Brittany*. Luçon: Ed. Jean-Paul Gisserot (1991).

Bromwich, James. *The Roman Remains of Southern France*. London: Routledge (1996).

Burl, A. *Guide des Dolmens et Menhirs Bretons*. Paris: Editions Errance (1987).

Combier, J. et al. *Archéologie de la France*. Paris: Flammarion (1990).

Cunliffe, B. *Greeks, Romans and Barbarians*. London: B.T. Batsford (1988).

_____, ed. *The Oxford Illustrated Prehistory of Europe*. Oxford University Press (1994).

Delluc, B. et G. A. Roussot, J. Roussot-Larroque. *Discovering Périgord Prehistory*. Trans. by S. L. Olivier. Luçon: Editions Sud-Ouest (1992).

Delpal, Jacques-Louis. *France. A Phaidon Cultural Guide*. English translation (1985). Oxford: Phaidon Press Ltd. (1975).

Durliat, Marcel and Victor Allègre. *Pyrénées Romanes*. Paris: Publications Zodiac (1969).

Duval, Paul-Marie. Dir. *Recueil des Inscriptions Gauloises (R.I.G.)* Vol. I, II par Michel Lejeune, Editions du Centre National de la Recherche Scientifique. Paris (1985).

Einhard. *The Life of Charlemagne*. First published about A.D. 830. Trans. from Monumenta Germaniae. University of Michigan Press (1960).

Fichtenau Heinrich. *The Carolingian Empire*. Trans. from *Das Karolingische Imperium*. Oxford: Basil Blackwell (1957).

Grand P.M. *Prehistoric Art*. London: Studio Vista Ltd. (1967).

Gregory, Bishop of Tours. *History of the Franks*. Trans. by Ernest Brehaut. (Dept. of History, Columbia University). London: W. W. Norton & Co. (1969).

Laule, Bernhard and Ulrike, Wischermann, Heinfried. *Kunstdenkmäler in Südfrankreich*. Darmstadt: Wissenschaftliche Buchgesellschaft (1989).

Lommel, Andreas. *Prehistoric and Primitive Man*. New York: McGraw-Hill (1966).

Michelin *Green Guide* Series.

Mohen, J-P. et. al. *Archéologie de la France.* Paris: Flammarion (1990).

_____, *Narbonne et La Mer de l'Antiquité à nos jours.* Narbonne: Musée Archéologique (1990).

Phillips, Patricia. *The Prehistory of Europe.* London: Allen Lane. (Penguin) (1980).

Pobé, Marcel and Jean Roubier. *Kelten-Römer.* Olten (Switzerland): Walter Verlag AG (1958).

Rigaud, J-P. et al. *Les Hauts Lieux de la Préhistoire en France.* Paris: Bordas S.A. (1989).

Rivet, A.L.F. *Gallia Narbonensis: Southern France in Roman Times.* London: Batsford, Ltd. (1988).

Robertson, Ian. *Blue Guide, France.* London: A. & C. Black (1991).

Scarre, Chris. *Exploring Prehistoric Europe.* Oxford University Press (1998).

Service, A. and J. Bradbery. *A Guide to the Megaliths of Europe.* London: Granada (1981).

Sturzebecker, Russell L. Photo Atlas. *Athletic-Cultural Archaeological Sites in the Greco-Roman World.* Self-published by the author (1985).

Trump, D.H. *The Prehistory of the Mediterranean.* London: Allen Lane (1980).

Werner, K.F. *Histoire de France. Les Origines.* Vol. 1, Paris: Librairie Arthème Fayard (1984).

INDEX OF TOWNS AND VILLAGES*

*(Site names are in italics)